NEIGHBORHOODS IN TRANSITION

THE MAKING OF SAN FRANCISCO'S ETHNIC
AND NONCONFORMIST COMMUNITIES

Neighborhoods in Transition

The Making of San Francisco's Ethnic and Nonconformist Communities

by Brian J. Godfrey

UNIVERSITY OF CALIFORNIA PRESS
Berkeley • Los Angeles • London

UNIVERSITY OF CALIFORNIA PUBLICATIONS IN GEOGRAPHY

Editorial Board: Antony R. Orme, James J. Parsons, Jonathan D. Sauer,
David S. Simonett, Frederick J. Simoons, Waldo Tobler, James E. Vance

Volume 27

UNIVERSITY OF CALIFORNIA PRESS
BERKELEY AND LOS ANGELES, CALIFORNIA

UNIVERSITY OF CALIFORNIA PRESS, LTD.
LONDON, ENGLAND

ISBN 0-520-09718-1
LIBRARY OF CONGRESS CATALOG CARD NUMBER: 88-2461

© 1988 BY THE REGENTS OF THE UNIVERSITY OF CALIFORNIA
PRINTED IN THE UNITED STATES OF AMERICA

Library of Congress Cataloging-in-Publication Data

Godfrey, Brian J.
   Neighborhoods in transition: the making of San Francisco's ethnic
and nonconformist communities / Brian J. Godfrey.
      p.   cm. — (University of California publications in geography;
v. 27)
   Based on thesis (Ph.D.)—University of California, Berkeley,
1984.
   Bibliography: p.
   ISBN 0-520-09718-1 (alk. paper)
   1. San Francisco (Calif.)—Social conditions. 2. Neighborhood—
California—San Francisco. 3. Community organization—California—
San Francisco. 4. San Francisco (Calif.)—Ethnic relations.
5. Subculture.   I. Title. II. Series.
G58.C3 vol. 27
[HN80.S4]
307'.09794'61—dc19   88-2461
                                                                            CIP

To San Francisco, the irresistible city that inspired this study

Contents

List of Maps, ix
List of Figures, x
List of Plates, xi
List of Tables, xiii
Preface, xv

1. INTRODUCTION: SAN FRANCISCO AS A CITY OF SUBCULTURES　　1
　　San Francisco's Social Diversity, 2
　　How "Different" is San Francisco?, 5
　　Contemporary Demographics and Development Trends, 8
　　The City as Cultural Seedbed, 15

2. A SOCIAL THEORY OF COMMUNITY MORPHOGENESIS　　22
　　Concepts of Neighborhood and Community, 24
　　Urbanism and Subcultures, 26
　　Ethnic Identities and Ethnic Enclaves, 29
　　"Deviants" or "Urban Pioneers"?, 31
　　Subcultural Intensification in the City, 34
　　Classic Models of Urban Spatial Structure, 36
　　The New Ethnographies, 39
　　Nonconformist Communities in the City, 43
　　Phases of Neighborhood Evolution, 47

3. FROM INSTANT CITY TO METROPOLIS: URBAN MORPHOGENESIS
　　AND SUBCULTURAL INTENSIFICATION　　54
　　The Making of an Instant City, 55
　　Foreign Immigrants Among the "Forty-Niners", 58
　　Functional Specialization and Social Sorting, 62
　　Racial Minorities

European Immigrant Groups, 72
Bohemian Quarters, 85
Interwar Assimilation, 89

4. POSTWAR SAN FRANCISCO: MORPHOLOGICAL ADAPTATION
   AND SUBCULTURAL SUCCESSION 94
   Japanese-Americans, 95
   Blacks, 98
   Chinese-Americans, 102
   Filipino-Americans, 105
   Smaller Asian and Pacific Groups, 108
   Hispanics, 111
   Postwar Nonconformists: Beats, Hippies, and Gays, 113
   Urban Revitalization and Subcultural Succession, 123

5. THE MISSION DISTRICT: EVOLUTIONARY MORPHOGENESIS
   OF A HISPANIC *BARRIO* 131
   Hispanics as an Ethnic Prototype, 136
   External Connections and Latin American Immigration, 138
   Settlement Inception in the Mission District, 142
   Morphological Adaptation: The Making of a *Barrio*, 148
   Urban Spatial Structure and the Ethnic Community, 161

6. THE HAIGHT-ASHBURY DISTRICT: SUBCULTURAL SUCCESSION
   AND INNER-CITY REVITALIZATION 172
   Bohemianism and the Social Dynamics of Gentrification, 173
   Neighborhood Inception and Growth, 178
   Physical Deterioration and Community Flux, 182
   The Bohemian Influx, 186
   The Middle-Class Transition, 189
   The Bourgeois Consolidation: Neighborhood Image and Reality, 194

7. SUMMARY AND CONCLUSIONS: SUBCULTURAL SUCCESSION
   AND COMMUNITY MORPHOGENESIS 205
   San Francisco as a Study Site, 207
   Conceptual Bases, 208
   The Historical Geography of San Francisco, 210
   The Case Study of an Ethnic Enclave, 212
   The Case Study of a Nonconformist Community, 213
   Evolutionary Community Morphogenesis: Subcultural Identity
      and Spatial Structure, 216

References, 219

List of Maps

1. Selected San Francisco neighborhoods and districts, 4
2. The growth of San Francisco: Patterns of street and property development, 64
3. The founding of Irish-Catholic churches south of Market Street in San Francisco, 78
4. Areas of ethnic concentration in San Francisco before World War II, 84
5. San Francisco's Japanese population, 96
6. San Francisco's Black population, 99
7. San Francisco's Chinese population, 106
8. San Francisco's Filipino population, 109
9. San Francisco's Vietnamese population, 112
10. San Francisco's Hispanic population, 114
11. Gay and lesbian businesses in San Francisco, 118
12. Ethnic areas in San Francisco, 1970, 125
13. Ethnic areas in San Francisco, 1980, 126
14. The Mission District and adjacent neighborhoods, 133
15. Mission District streets, 134
16. Expansion of San Francisco's Hispanic areas, 1950-1980, 152
17. "Los Otros" in San Francisco's Hispanic areas, 1980, 157
18. The Haight-Ashbury District, 180

List of Figures

1. Three Classic Models of Urban Spatial Structure, 38
2. Viviendas—Otro Rompe-Barrios [Housing—another neighborhood-breaker], 160
3. The relationship between the percentage of Hispanics and relative housing prices in the Mission district core, 1950-1980, 163
4. Attention: Entering Haight-Ashbury gentrified zone, 174
5. The battle for Haight Street, 193

List of Plates

1. San Francisco's downtown skyline, as viewed from Twin Peaks, 18
2. San Francisco's downtown skyline, as seen from Telegraph Hill, 19
3-4. Views of the renovation of a house on Sanchez Street in Noe Valley, 1980 and 1985, 20
5. The Haight-Ashbury street fair, May of 1983, 21
6. A "Filipino-Mexican-American" grocery store on Mission Street, beside a Spanish-language pharmacy and bar, 51
7. The Ticonica bar on Mission Street, 52
8. Pedestrians on Castro Street, 53
9. A view of the Mission District, 1860, 91
10. San Francisco Chinatown, turn of the century, 92
11. A view of Mission Street about 1920, showing the small businesses which grew up along this transportation corridor, 93
12. Chinatown's symbolic entrance, the "Dragon Gate," at Grant and Bush Streets, 128
13. The extension of San Francisco's Chinatown into North Beach, 129
14. Mission Dolores, with a Gray Line tour bus in front, 130
15. A view of the deteriorated Mission Dolores in 1856, 165
16. The entrance to Woodward's Gardens, 166
17. The J.D. Spreckles Mansion, located at Howard and 21st streets, 1887, 167
18. A view of the refugee camp set up at "Mission Park," present-day Dolores Park, after the Earthquake and Fire of 1906, 168
19. Banco Comercial Agrícola de El Salvador, Mission at 25th streets, 1987, 169
20. Crowds on 24th Street at the Cinco de Mayo Parade, 1982, 170
21-22. Two examples of neighborhood graffiti in the Inner Mission District, 171

23. The Haight-Ashbury District, looking toward the entrance to Golden Gate Park, 1902, 199
24. Haight Street, circa 1947, 200
25. The corner of Haight and Ashbury streets, 1969, 201
26. Demolition of the Straight Theater, 1979, 202
27. Haight Street, 1987
28. A row of tastefully restored houses, 1987, 204

List of Tables

1. The foreign-born as a percentage of the total population in ten large American cities, 1860-1980, 12
2. The percentage of family and nonfamily households in ten large American cities, 1980, 13
3. The foreign-born and foreign-stock populations of San Francisco, 1860-1980, 61
4. The population of San Francisco by race and ethnicity, 1870-1940, 68
5. San Francisco's foreign-born population, by selected countries of origin, 1860-1970, 74
6. San Francisco's population of foreign parentage, by selected nationalities, 1910-1970, 75
7. The population of San Francisco by race and ethnicity, 1940-1980, 97
8. Gay- and lesbian-identified businesses and social gathering spots in San Francisco, 1969-1988, 119
9. Gay- and lesbian-identified businesses and social gathering spots, by San Francisco neighborhoods, 1984-1988, 120
10. Housing characteristics in the Mission District, 1980, 135
11. Total Hispanic and Mexican-origin populations in the Bay Area, 1980, 143
12. Foreign-born population in San Francisco and the Mission District, 1910-1980, 149
13. Average monthly rents and house sale prices in the Mission District, 1940-1980, 151
14. The Hispanic population in the Mission District, 1950-1980, 154
15. Average monthly rents and house prices in the Haight-Ashbury District, 1940-1980, 184
16. Racial composition of the Haight-Ashbury, 1940-1980, 185

Preface

A city like San Francisco, famous for its social diversity and cultural traditions, presents the researcher with a sense of both peril and opportunity. The peril lies largely in the city's heterogeneity. In such a complex urban center, exceptions to the norm can call into question even well-established city patterns; such irregularities sometimes belie the onlooker's interpretation of common forms and ongoing processes, no matter how carefully conceived. On the other hand, a sense of opportunity also derives from the highly differentiated cityscape, which beckons the observer with all sorts of unanswered questions, arousing curiosity and inviting further study. Although the premonition of peril warns one to focus narrowly upon a sharply delimited topic, the lure of opportunity tempts one to search for larger verities through a more general and comparative approach.

The lure of this opportunity prevailed upon me. In this geographic inquiry I examine the evolving spatial patterns of San Francisco's principal ethnic and nonconformist communities, within the historical context of social and physical changes in the city's neighborhoods. Since an exhaustive historical geography of the city's many minority communities exceeds the scope of a single volume, I have concentrated on the major ones in this work. Even so, I cannot cover them all equally well. The most reasonable goal is to achieve a fair balance between breadth and depth of coverage. In this spirit, I discuss herein the historical and contemporary geographies of a variety of groups before focusing in greater detail on two selected case studies of communities.

The single-minded academic specialist, requiring extreme precision and ample documentation of data, might avoid the study of such a broad and occasionally elusive subject. But comparative community analysis raises important issues that a narrower focus would ignore. Rarely have ethnic and nonconformist districts been treated as interlocking parts of the social-geographic fabric, despite their common juxtaposition in the inner city. Although San Francisco may be unusual in the range and size of its minority communities, the processes through which those communities came into being appear to apply to other central cities as well. In this sense, San Francisco's experience may serve as a microcosm of broader cultural currents and socioeconomic forces operating in American metropolitan cores.

This monograph is based on my doctoral dissertation in geography, filed in 1984 at the University of California, Berkeley. I would like to thank the Series Manager at the University of California Press, Rose Anne White, for her continual assistance and gentle prodding in my revision of the dissertation and preparation of this final manuscript. The copy editor, Marjorie Hughes, acted as both an exacting arbiter on matters of style and an enthusiastic commentator on San Francisco neighborhoods. Also deserving of thanks are the many people who helped me earlier in carrying out this study; I consulted too many to acknowledge all individually, but a few merit special mention for their repeated assistance. Although none of the following persons should be held responsible for any shortcomings that remain in my work, I appreciate their efforts to improve it.

My doctoral committee at Berkeley was always courteous and thoroughly professional. Its chairman, Professor James E. Vance, Jr., enthusiastically welcomed me into the field of urban geography and proved to be a sensitive and thoughtful adviser, unfailingly supportive and encouraging without ever being overly directive. My intellectual debt to him is apparent in the number of references to his work in the text of this study. Professor Vance's culinary expertise, which I also savored on occasion, provided an enjoyable fringe benefit to my graduate work. Professor James J. Parsons, the second reader of my dissertation, previously served as chairman of my Ph.D. oral examination committee. Professor Parsons has impressed me with his keen geographic curiosity and ready helping hand ever since I first met him in South America, before I began graduate work at Berkeley; subsequently, his office door was always open for consultation. Professor Claude S. Fischer, the extra-departmental member of my dissertation committee, took the time to provide frank and thoughtful comments on my work at various stages. His solid grounding in classical and contemporary theories of urban sociology, as well as his work in subcultural theory, proved particularly useful to me.

At San Francisco State University, where I frequently taught urban geography, several delightful colleagues helped me with this study. Professor Jean Vance, the departmental chair, served on my "orals" committee at Berkeley and was always accessible, supportive, and helpful. Associate Professor Max Kirkeberg freely shared his encyclopedic knowledge of San Francisco with me, both informally and during his neighborhood walking tours; Max's skills at field observation and analysis were a true inspiration. With the friendship of Assistant Professor Nancy Wilkenson came an unflagging encouragement in both my teaching and research.

Other friends and colleagues, besides helping in substantive ways, provided comradery to break the isolation and tedium that occasionally enveloped me while writing and revising this manuscript. William J. Ketteringham, now retired from the Department of Geography at the California State University, Fullerton, originally stimulated my interest in the geography of urban communities. Assistant Professor Paul Groth, a cultural geographer teaching in Berkeley's departments of Architecture and Landscape Architecture, provided an occasional ear and sound counsel regarding the plight of being a doctoral candidate. Several discussions with Bonnie Loyd, the editor of *Landscape*, contributed to the evolution of my thought on nontraditional communities. Cherie Semans at Berkeley and Robert Winter at California State University, Hayward, assisted me with my cartography. Harvey K. Flad, Associate Professor of Geography at Vassar College, proved to be a thoroughly congenial colleague and an unfailing source of support in establishing myself at a new institution.

My friends and family contributed to this work in ways less academic, but certainly just as important. If they questioned whether I would ever finish this study, at least they never let me know their doubts! In San Francisco, I particularly enjoyed the companionship of Paul Rose, Patricia Mau, James Chappell, Dennis Hopkins, Galen Workman, Louise Queenville, and Kim Storch; Eileen Donahue offered welcome company, frequently on informal neighborhood walks; and my good friend Richard Juhl endured this work, patiently for the most part, almost as long as I did. At Vassar, a new group of friends and colleagues welcomed me to the East Coast: James Montoya, Sidney Plotkin, Marjorie Gluck, Karen Stolley, David Littlefield, Patricia Kenworthy, Robert Pounder, Iva Deutchman, Dennis Anderson, Carol Jones, and Mary Flad. Both my mother, Thies G. Murphy, and my father, John H. Godfrey, also deserve many thanks for their encouragement and trust through my many years of higher education. My parents, both educators themselves, showed me that teaching can make an important difference in people's lives; I hope that the publication of this study vindicates their belief in me.

Brian J. Godfrey
Department of Geography
Vassar College
Poughkeepsie, New York

1

INTRODUCTION
San Francisco as a City of Subcultures

> It is an odd thing, but everyone who disappears is said to be seen in San Francisco. It must be a delightful city, and possess all the attractions of the next world.[1]
>
> Oscar Wilde, 1891

Ever since the city's rapid rise to worldwide notice during the California Gold Rush, San Francisco has continually attracted fortune-seekers of the most diverse origins. The ongoing population flux of "Baghdad-by-the-Bay" has involved every conceivable type of foreign immigrant and domestic in-migrant. In this sense, Oscar Wilde's nineteenth-century quip that "everyone who disappears is said to be seen in San Francisco" still rings true in the twentieth century. During 1967's "Summer of Love," for example, a popular song written by John Phillips exhorted youthful seekers: "If you're going to San Francisco, be sure to wear some flowers in your hair."[2] By the mid-1980s, gay supervisor Harry Britt could justifiably call San Francisco "a city of refugees," referring to both foreign immigrants and life-style groups.[3] As a consequence of a history of selective migrations, the city has witnessed a long parade of distinctive social groups, or subcultures, marching through its residential districts.

Amid all the human diversity of this cosmopolitan city, two kinds of subcultures stand out: ethnic and nonconformist groups. Both have created highly visible neighborhoods. Areas such as Chinatown, North Beach, Haight-Ashbury, and the

---

[1] Oscar Wilde, *The Picture of Dorian Gray* (first edition 1891; Baltimore: Penguin Books, 1982), p. 234.

[2] John Phillips, "If you're going to San Francisco, be sure to wear some flowers in your hair," 1967 song.

[3] Tim Schreiner, "The Bay Area exception," *San Francisco Chronicle,* December 14, 1986, "This World" Supplement, p. 15.

Castro District have gained worldwide notoriety as focal points for the respective group identities of the Chinese, Italian and bohemian, counter-cultural, and homosexual communities. So San Francisco serves as an attractive study site in which to evaluate the factors contributing to the emergence of such special-identity neighborhoods in the American inner city. As long-time local newspaper columnist Herb Caen observes: "A new minority arrives every minute and takes over a neighborhood."[4]

Residents and visitors alike tend to regard San Francisco as a unique city. In the sense that every city has its own particular characteristics, it is. But while San Francisco has probably attracted more than its share of ethnic and nonconformist elements, the city is not alone in collecting large minority communities; San Francisco shares that quality with other American urban centers, particularly those that serve as ports of entry for foreign immigrants and cosmopolitan centers of tolerance for life-style experimenters. To put San Francisco's experience in broader perspective, this chapter examines the city's social diversity, compares it with other metropolitan cores in the United States, and explores the nature of subcultural cohesion and intergroup conflict.

SAN FRANCISCO'S SOCIAL DIVERSITY

Ethnics and nonconformists by no means constitute the only social formations of note in San Francisco. Several other types of communities have also greatly influenced the city's cultural evolution. The social cachet of neighborhoods such as Nob Hill, Pacific Heights, and St. Francis Wood—whose very names have become synonymous with wealth and status—indicates the importance of the city's upper classes. Unlike the situation in many American urban cores, San Francisco's elite quarters have remained fashionable and seldom suffer the ill effects of urban flight, in effect "preserving the view that to live in the central city is a desirable thing."[5]

Although less well known to outsiders than the city's posh quarters, more proletarian districts also have long been identifiable in San Francisco, particularly south of the traditional socioeconomic divide, Market Street. Still home for many of San Francisco's blue-collar union headquarters, "South of the Slot" historically was the bastion of aspiring white working classes, largely of Old World immigrant stock. Irish, Germans, Italians, Scandinavians, diverse Eastern European groups, and others settled

---

[4]Herb Caen, "Everybody's favorite city," *San Francisco Chronicle,* "Sunday Punch" Section, June 6, 1982, p. 1.

[5]James E. Vance, Jr., *Geography and Urban Evolution in the San Francisco Bay Area* (Berkeley: University of California, Institute of Governmental Studies, 1964), p. 77.

here in the late nineteenth and early twentieth centuries, gradually moving out as they became more successful and acculturated. New settlers, largely Latin American, black, and Asian, occupied many of the worker cottages and flats after World War II. A more affluent clientele—mainly youngish professionals and white-collar workers—has in recent years "gentrified" neighborhoods with superior location and special charm in this part of town, including such areas as Eureka and Noe valleys, the western Mission District, Potrero Hill, Glen Park, and Bernal Heights.

American nativist culture has flourished in the predominantly middle-class districts on the city's western side, most notably in the Sunset, West of Twin Peaks, and Richmond districts. Developed as early twentieth-century "automobile neighborhoods," these western areas of San Francisco became somewhat suburban in character, consisting largely of lower-density, single-family detached homes, relative to the inner-city zones to the east. Many of the city's longer-resident ethnic groups—such as the Irish, Italians, and Chinese—have moved from the eastern to the western parts of San Francisco as a sign of upward mobility. In the Richmond District, for example, Clement Street's Chinese restaurants now rival those of Chinatown itself in both number and quality (see Map 1).

San Francisco's ethnic and racial minorities now collectively make up about half of the city's population. Unlike the situation in many American central cities, however, San Francisco does not have just one or even two clearly predominant ethnic groups. The 1980 U.S. Census showed San Francisco's black, Hispanic, and Chinese populations to be roughly equal in size, each accounting for just over 12 percent of the city's population of 678,974. In addition, the rapidly growing Filipino population reached 5.6 percent of the city's total; one of the country's largest Filipino communities is scattered through San Francisco's southerly Mission District and adjacent Daly City, a working-class suburb. Community activists of these different ethnic groups often charge that because of undercounting, particularly among undocumented immigrants, census figures of their respective populations should be even higher. This contention may be justified by the fact that over half of the city's public school students now speak a language other than English at home.[6]

In addition to the city's ethnic groups, San Francisco also has a long association with what are now often deemed "alternative life-styles." San Francisco historically has fostered a variety of nontraditional communities, beginning with the restless "forty-

---

[6]Charles C. Hardy, "Faces changing in San Francisco's schools," *San Francisco Examiner,* May 5, 1980, pp. 1, 9.

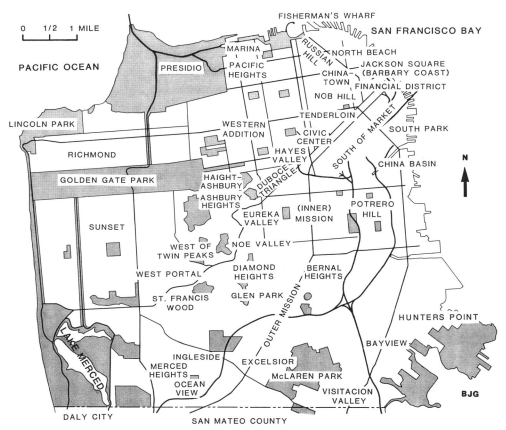

MAP 1. SELECTED SAN FRANCISCO NEIGHBORHOODS AND DISTRICTS.

niners" who flocked to the city during the Gold Rush. This tradition of nontradition continued with the turn-of-the-century literary and artistic bohemians and culminated with the beats and beatniks, hippies, and gay men and lesbians that have attracted such widespread attention since World War II. San Francisco has stayed at the cutting edge of American culture. The long-term presence of such nonconformity in the city raises an important question: How representative is San Francisco of broader trends in American cities?

HOW "DIFFERENT" IS SAN FRANCISCO?

Along with Marin County and the city of Berkeley, San Francisco has come to be widely viewed as idiosyncratic because of its highly publicized "deviant" life-styles. National journalists have long exploited the Bay Area's colorful side to file sensationalistic reports, contributing to popular perceptions of San Francisco as both an exotic immigrant enclave and "sin city," a modern-day Sodom and Gomorrah. Syndicated columnist Mike Royko of the *Chicago Sun-Times,* for example, railed against San Francisco's bid for the 1984 Democratic National Convention (he was naturally in favor of Chicago) in the following terms:

> San Francisco isn't exactly your typical brawling, two-fisted city of big shoulders. It's more a city of slender, swiveling hips.
>
> Don't misunderstand me. It's a nice little town. Kind of cute and quaint with hills and fog. You can see seals swimming, if that's what thrills you, and get a good bowl of won ton soup.
>
> But is San Francisco really the kind of city where the Democratic Party should hold its national convention? Do the Democrats want to be thought of as the party of quiche-eaters and wine-sippers?[7]

Such caustic stereotypes might be written off as satire when perpetrated by a normally polemical political columnist like Royko. But even supposedly "serious" journalism, such as that of CBS News, has engaged in extensive media hyperbole about San Francisco in recent years. For example, a lurid 1980 CBS documentary, "Gay Power, Gay Politics," portrayed the "gay vote" as a dominant, even corrupting factor in San Francisco politics, somehow ignoring the importance of a variety of other power-brokers. The documentary's excesses merited an investigation and eventual censure by the prestigious National News Council.

---

[7]Mike Royko, "Why S.F. shouldn't get the Demo convention," *San Francisco Examiner,* April 19, 1983, pp. 1, 4.

Another illustrative case of media myopia occurred in a CBS "60 Minutes" segment by Morley Safer, purportedly on the ill-fated 1983 campaign to recall Mayor Dianne Feinstein, in which he saw fit to call San Francisco a "non-stop theater of the absurd" and an example of "democracy gone haywire." Rather than presenting a balanced view of the various groups on both sides of the recall campaign, the "60 Minutes" crew focused mainly upon the attitudes of selected leaders in the gay community, which Safer matter-of-factly put at 200,000 voters (about half the city's electorate!); this figure was probably exaggerated by a factor of at least three or four. Forty-five seconds into the segment Safer cut to an interview with a notorious male transvestite in nun drag, "Sister Boom Boom," who had nothing to do with the mayoral recall campaign and who later remarked that Safer seemed more interested in his/her legs than in his/her politics anyway.[8]

Such "news" accounts imply that San Francisco is simply too avant-garde to be taken as representative of American culture. Even Herb Caen, that staunch defender of the city, sniffs that "San Francisco is 'different,' and most San Franciscans are pleased that it is."[9] Such sentiments are certainly widespread in the city. Haight-Ashbury neighborhood activist Calvin Welch, for example, observes:

> If California is the lunatic fringe of the United States, and San Francisco is the lunatic fringe of California, then the Haight is the lunatic fringe of San Francisco—the heart of the heart. And I say this with all the due bias of a San Franciscan who loves his neighborhood.[10]

But how "different" really is San Francisco? Although the city tends to be relatively liberal in terms of its voting record and its stance on social issues, some objective measures suggest in this regard that San Francisco's situation as a central city in a larger region is not entirely atypical. Sociologist Claude Fischer contends:

---

[8] A good examination of the numerous factual and interpretive errors in this "60 Minutes" segment, "Marching to a different drummer," was presented by Spencer Michels in KQED's televised rejoinder, "30 minutes on '60 Minutes'."

[9] Herb Caen, "Sunday punchdrink," *San Francisco Chronicle,* "Sunday Punch" section, May 1, 1983, p. 1.

[10] Burr Snider, "CALVIN: *Nothing* comes between him and his City," *San Francisco Examiner*, January 25, 1987, p. E-3.

Even if San Francisco were somewhat more "deviant" than other major cities, the question remains whether it is more deviant compared with its hinterland than are other major cities compared with theirs. That is more difficult to answer, but there is reason to believe not. At least San Francisco's contrast to its hinterland on this dimension is much the same as Los Angeles'.[11]

While San Francisco does indeed exhibit a striking subcultural diversity, this may be regarded as an accentuation of general tendencies in U.S. metropolitan cores. Urban geographers have observed that many American central cities have become well known for their ethnic and nonconformist communities. Brian Berry notes that cosmopolitan centers have long existed in some American cities and "seem to be sprouting up in other cities as they grow and are able to provide a critical mass of local grown talent and misfits, to create their own symbolic milieus of tolerance."[12] James Vance argues that it is in the central-city "zone of narrow-community identity" that "those groups consciously opposing inclusion in the broad 'national' culture have sought to create their own 'turfs' with an accompanying narrowly circumscribed life-style."[13]

In this sense, San Francisco's abundance of ethnic and nonconformist communities makes the city especially expressive of certain features of American urban life. A *New York Times* feature article acknowledges that San Francisco might be the most unconventional city in America, but concludes that San Francisco's role is far from parochial:

> San Francisco has a far more driving pertinence for the country as a whole than most people, booster or critic, resident or merely observer, might imagine, for in the variety and complexity of its ethnic, social, and economic issues, it seems to speak to the country as a whole.[14]

The natural beauty and liberal ethos of San Francisco, while giving the city a distinctive flavor, should not be allowed to hinder a comparative analysis of urban

---

[11]Claude S. Fischer, *To Dwell Among Friends: Personal Networks in Town and City* (Chicago: University of Chicago Press, 1982), p. 270.

[12]Brian J. L. Berry, *The Human Consequences of Urbanization: Divergent Paths in the Urban Experience of the Twentieth Century* (New York: St. Martin's Press, 1973), p. 65.

[13]James E. Vance, Jr., *This Scene of Man: The Role and Structure of the City in the Geography of Western Civilization* (New York: Harper and Row, 1977), pp. 400, 402.

[14]Lacey Fosburgh, "San Francisco: Unconventional city for the Democratic convention," *New York Times Magazine,* July 1, 1984.

evolution. Rather than being seen as an aberration from urban norms, San Francisco may serve to illustrate a number of significant trends among North America's central cities, as indicated by an examination of the city's contemporary demographics and development.

CONTEMPORARY DEMOGRAPHICS AND DEVELOPMENT TRENDS

San Francisco's social diversification has been accompanied by a polarization of the population into rival classes and groups: rich and poor, small white households and large ethnic families, major corporations and small businesses. As white middle-class families have left the city, their places have been taken largely by young urban professionals and immigrants, creating a variegated urban mosaic held together by the politics of pluralism, despite constant internal tension. The pressures of gentrification and displacement have exacerbated these subcultural tensions in recent years, but a remarkable civic ethos of tolerance serves generally to reduce intergroup acrimony to levels required to maintain a functioning urban society and economy.

San Francisco's total population has declined in the last three decennial census counts, but that generally has been the case among already built-up cities in the United States. In San Francisco's case, this population decline has not been due to housing abandonment, but rather to a decrease in average household size—resulting from smaller families, postponed parenthood, and higher divorce rates—that is most notable in American central cities. San Francisco's shrinking average household size is reflected in the fact that, while the city's population declined by 5.1 percent during the 1970s, the number of housing units actually increased by 2 percent. In 1980, the average San Francisco household was composed of 2.17 persons, compared to 2.65 persons statewide and 2.75 nationally.[15]

In a related demographic development, the number of single persons in San Francisco has been on the increase in recent years. "Nonfamily households" made up 53 percent of San Francisco's 1980 population, compared with 44 percent a decade earlier; Oakland, across the Bay, had 44 percent in such nontraditional household arrangements in 1980, while the national figure stood at 27 percent. No less an authority than the Director of the U.S. Census Bureau has claimed that San Francisco is not an isolated case, however, but rather in the forefront of a national trend: "The decline in marriages and the decrease in families with children portend a vastly different society as we move through the '80's."[16]

---

[15] U.S. Census, 1980.

[16] Michael Harris, "S.F. is 'singles city'," *San Francisco Chronicle*, Sept. 10, 1982, pp. 1, 5.

San Francisco's nontraditional households therefore can be viewed more as precursor than idiosyncrasy. Smaller households of what are often deemed young urban professionals or "Yuppies" tend to be the in-movers in gentrifying inner-city neighborhoods all across the United States. Many of San Francisco's older neighborhoods, which historically have witnessed a "filtering" process as the aging housing stock has trickled down to lower-income groups, have recently experienced widespread physical renovation, largely because of an influx of these smaller household units with larger disposable incomes.

As in other regional office centers, an expansion of San Francisco's white-collar economy, which in recent years has created thousands of new jobs in the additional skyscrapers of a burgeoning downtown, has fueled this reverse cycle of urban revitalization. Downtown San Francisco currently employs more than 400,000 people, about half of them city residents; the employment level for the year 2000 is projected to grow by about a third to some 600,000 jobs in the city's central district.[17] Although the number of blue-collar jobs in the manufacturing and wholesale trades has steadily declined, this loss has been countered by an even greater employment increase in retail, finance, insurance, real estate, transportation and utilities, and tourism.[18] As gateway to the rapidly growing countries of the "Pacific Rim," San Francisco has maintained its position as an important center of international banking and commerce, now second only to New York among American cities.[19]

The evolution of San Francisco's economic base from blue- to white-collar, which has had such a profound influence on the city's residential neighborhoods, is also reflected in the physical growth of high-rise buildings downtown. The San Francisco business district now contains more than 60 million square feet of office space, as well as about 40 million square feet of space for retail activities, hotels, housing, industries, government and cultural institutions. The amount of office space in the city more than doubled between 1965 and 1983, prompting protests from historic preservationists and

---

[17]For an assessment of the dilemmas posed by this office development in the central district, see San Francisco Planning and Urban Research Association (SPUR), "Thinking about growth," report no. 180, December 1981.

[18]Chester Hartman, *The Transformation of San Francisco* (Rowman and Allanheld, 1984), pp. 1-14.

[19]R. B. Cohen, "The new international division of labor, multinational corporations and urban hierarchy," in Michael Dear and Allen J. Scott (eds.), *Urbanization and Urban Planning in Capitalist Society* (New York: Methuen, 1981), p. 303.

neighborhood activists about the disruptive effects of the "Manhattanization" of San Francisco: escalating rents and property values displaced many of the poor and even the middle class, traffic congestion worsened, new high-rises blocked prized views, and commercial office development squeezed out the industrial and service sectors.

In 1985 the San Francisco Planning Department attempted to moderate high-rise building with the implementation of the much-touted "Downtown Plan," which emphasized historic preservation and in effect shifted the focus of new development to the South-of-Market area.[20] Critics of unbridled development were not appeased, however, for the Downtown Plan permitted new construction to continue at a rapid pace. Concerned that "Manhattanization" was reducing San Francisco's social diversity and physical beauty, local voters narrowly approved in 1986 a ballot proposition requiring strict growth controls. "Proposition M" limited construction of new office space to an annual total of 950,000 square feet—equivalent to about one big high-rise—and stressed: "That existing housing and neighborhood character be conserved and protected in order to preserve the cultural and economic diversity of our neighborhoods."[21]

In addition to gentrification and displacement, another demographic trend in revitalizing San Francisco, this one ironically related to the city's ethnic communities, also reflects broader national patterns. Despite a long-term decrease in the number of San Francisco residents since the 1950s, in recent years an influx of Asian and Latin American immigrants has pushed the city's population back up to over 700,000—a yearly increase of about 10,000 people since 1980—often entailing shared housing, due to the high rents and low residential vacancy rate.[22] According to conservative estimates, there were more than 28,000 refugees (three-fourths of them from Southeast Asia) in San Francisco in 1982—a figure which would not have included undocumented immigrants, such as Central Americans, who did not qualify for official refugee status.[23]

---

[20]San Francisco Department of City Planning, *The Downtown Plan,* 1983.

[21]*Voter Information Pamphlet,* November 4, 1986 General Election, City and County of San Francisco, p. 77-78.

[22]"Newcomers boost S.F. population," *San Francisco Examiner,* April 22, 1982, p. B-1; Malcolm Glover, "Burgeoning population in S.F., California bucks U.S. trend," *San Francisco Examiner,* April 1, 1983, p. B-6.

[23]Ken Thorland, Senior Supervisor of the Refugee Resettlement Program, presentation at SPUR meeting, Oct. 27, 1983.

In fact, since about 1950 San Francisco's foreign-born population has been on the rise, along with that of several other American "ports of entry": New York, Los Angeles, and Chicago. When compared with other large cities in the United States, San Francisco historically has tended to have a high proportion of foreign immigrants: since 1860, San Francisco has always placed in the top five, and frequently in the top two or three, among ten selected cities (see Table 1). This indicates that San Francisco has long had a high degree of ethnic concentration, although not out of line with some other ports of entry. At last count, San Francisco was about on a par with New York and Boston among major U.S. cities in terms of the percentage of its population composed of foreign immigrants and their American-born offspring—about 45 percent in 1970.[24]

San Francisco also has been a place of nonconformist concentration, although this is harder to demonstrate with official statistics. A comparison of the 1980 U.S. Census data on nonfamily households, however, provides one index of the degree of San Francisco's nonconformity. Table 2 indicates that in terms of such nontraditional household arrangements, San Francisco (53 percent) ranks highest in a comparison of ten large American cities. But the city is lower than the New York City borough of Manhattan (58 percent), a not unlikely counterpart for a dense, compact central city like San Francisco; and Boston (47 percent) is close to San Francisco in the proportion of nonfamily households.

Although these data indicate that San Francisco is indeed an "atypical" American city, they also show that it is not a total anomaly. The city best represents cosmopolitan urban centers: San Francisco is a regional financial center and headquarters city, as well as being a mecca for minorities. Although San Francisco differs from a hypothetical norm in the size and diversity of its ethnic and nontraditional communities, given the city's modest scale, it is not as unusual as both the news media and popular opinion often maintain. In any case, it is precisely San Francisco's long-standing role as a socially diverse central city that has made the Bay Area, again like metropolitan New York and Boston, a cultural hearth area for far-reaching developments in American life:

---

[24]In 1980 the U.S. Census Bureau unfortunately discontinued use of this "foreign stock" category, employed since the late 1800s to measure the number of foreign-born and their native-born children, substituting in its stead a more general and ambiguous "ancestry" count.

TABLE 1

The Foreign-born as a Percentage of the Total Population
in Ten Large American Cities, 1860-1980

City	1860	1890	1920	1950	1980
Baltimore	24.7%	15.9%	11.6%	5.4%	3.1%
Boston	35.9	35.3	32.4	17.9	15.4
Chicago	50.0	41.0	29.9	12.5	14.4
Cleveland	44.8	37.2	30.1	14.5	5.8
Detroit	46.8	39.7	29.3	14.9	5.7
Los Angeles	--	25.3	21.2	12.5	27.1
New York	45.5	38.8	36.1	22.6	23.6
Philadelphia	30.0	25.7	22.0	11.2	6.4
San Francisco	50.1	42.4	29.4	15.5	28.3
St. Louis	59.8	25.4	13.4	4.8	2.6
San Francisco's place among the ten cities	#2	#1	#5	#3	#1

Source: U.S. Census, various years.

TABLE 2

The Percentage of Family and Nonfamily Households
in Ten Large American Cities, 1980

City	Total Population	Family Households	Nonfamily Households
Baltimore	786,775	66.7%	33.3%
Boston	562,994	53.3	46.7
Chicago	3,005,072	64.6	35.4
Cleveland	573,822	65.2	34.8
Detroit	1,203,339	66.8	33.2
Los Angeles	2,966,850	61.1	38.9
New York	7,071,639	63.0	37.0
(Manhattan)	1,428,285	41.9	58.1
Philadelphia	1,688,210	66.7	33.3
San Francisco	678,974	47.0	53.0
St. Louis	453,085	60.0	40.0

Note: The U.S. Census defines a household as all individuals occupying a housing unit (separate living quarters). Family households consist of at least two people, living together, who are related by birth, marriage, or adoption; conversely, nonfamily households consist of individuals living alone or with people not related to them by family ties.

Source: U.S. Census, 1980.

Cultural pluralism is generally considered to be a pronounced trait of American society as as whole. But it is more salient in some areas than others. Cities such as New York and Boston, for example, which are composed of highly diverse ethnic groups and which serve as cosmopolitan centers of trade and communication, illustrate higher levels of cultural pluralism than average. The Bay Area is also one of the areas that manifests a high degree of pluralism, much of which must be attributed to its unique history.[25]

San Francisco thus is a particularly apt site in which to study the emergence of ethnic and nonconformist communities. The city has a rich array of such communities within a topographically varied and relatively small urban area of less than 50 square miles, making for a strong sense of neighborhood identities. The city's neighborhoods, often identified with hills and valleys, are commonly likened to a series of urban villages, serving to humanize life in a larger metropolis. There are many popular guides to the city's neighborhoods, inspired by San Francisco's highly differentiated cultural landscape.[26] The city's high population density makes community interactions and boundaries highly visible. San Francisco's current residential density is about 15,000 people (and more than 6,000 automobiles) per square mile, one of the highest among U.S. cities.[27] Including out-of-town visitors and commuters, the total daily population density increases to at least 20,000 persons per square mile.

An enormous amount has been written about San Francisco, but all too often groups in the city have been examined in relative isolation from both each other and the evolution of urban structure. Given its scenic physical setting and its rich social history, San Francisco has been the subject of innumerable accounts of pure local color; while frequently entertaining, popular books on the city's past and present all too often have begged for interpretation and analysis. A notable gap in the literature on San Francisco is the lack of comparative analysis of the city's ethnic and nontraditional neighborhoods.

---

[25]Robert Wuthnow, *The Consciousness Reformation* (Berkeley: University of California Press, 1976), p. 217.

[26]For example, see Randolph Delehanty, *San Francisco: Walks and Tours in the Golden Gate City* (New York: Dial Press, 1980); Margot Patterson Doss, *San Francisco at Your Feet* (New York: Grove Press, 1974); and Susan Shepard, *In the Neighborhoods: A Guide to the Joys and Discoveries of San Francisco's Neighborhoods* (San Francisco: Chronicle Books, 1981).

[27]"S.F. now ranks 4th in density of population," *San Francisco Examiner*, Nov. 1, 1982, p. A-6.

THE CITY AS A CULTURAL SEEDBED

How has civic order been maintained in the face of San Francisco's assertive minorities and the high degree of nonconformity to established norms? Two theories have been advanced to account for this seeming paradox. Frederick Wirt contends that San Francisco's ethnic conflict has been effectively played out in the "politics of deference," an ongoing process whereby successively arriving minorities struggle ". . . to achieve recognition of a group's worth in the urban and national scheme of values. That struggle runs through all the city's social institutions, past and present."[28] So just as already "arrived" European immigrant groups—like the Irish, Germans, and Italians—long ago achieved material success and institutional recognition in an earlier city, the newly "arriving" Asian, black, and Latin American minorities now grapple for power in contemporary San Francisco within a long-standing framework of coalition politics. Whether all of the latter "new" groups are as successful as the former ones, however, remains to be seen.

In addition to Wirt's concept of the "politics of deference," sociologists Howard Becker and Irving Horowitz claim that a "culture of civility" has developed in San Francisco: residents have come to regard unconventional behavior as a civic resource rather than as a dangerous threat.[29] The concept of a "culture of civility" does have merit: San Francisco's remarkable subcultural diversity seems to have engendered an ethos of relative tolerance. Yet there has been abundant intergroup conflict throughout San Francisco's history, sometimes resulting in such notable episodes as the anti-Chinese labor demonstrations of the late nineteenth century, the general strikes of the 1930s, and the uproar surrounding the assassinations of Mayor George Moscone and Supervisor Harvey Milk in 1979. Rather than attributing San Francisco's famous social tolerance merely to widespread altruism, then, enlightened self-interest on the part of elites is probably a better explanation: the city's "culture of civility" results largely from a calculated acquiescence to the hard-won gains of sizable minority communities. Manuel Castells notes the continual tension between the forces of urban cohesion and social discord:

---

[28]Frederick M. Wirt, *Power in the City: Decision Making in San Francisco* (Berkeley: The University of California Press, 1974), p. 15.

[29]Howard S. Becker and Irving Louis Horowitz, "The culture of civility," in *Culture and Civility in San Francisco* (Transaction Books, 1971).

> So the city lights shine brighter than ever. The sun still plays on the ornately painted facades of the Victorian buildings. Chinatown still feeds tourists and weaves garments. The Mission in 1980 still welcomes Salvadorans and low riders. Gays still discover themselves and enjoy their free city. Yet there is a feeling of uncertainty, as if the city was more a delicate pattern of coloured laser beams than a solid patchwork sewn by a patient woman's hands. Behind the urban decor preserved by the neighborhood movements, San Francisco seems to await a social earthquake.[30]

Despite the frequent social tremors, however, the social earthquakes have been relatively few. At least the extremes of ethnic conflict and religious intolerance that have plagued some eastern cities have spared San Francisco. The liberal reputation for tolerating diverse ethnic and nonconformist minorities has even been successfully marketed to attract tourism (now one of the largest local industries) to "everybody's favorite city."

To better understand the development of San Francisco's complex social geography, such theories as the "politics of deference" and the "culture of civility" need to be put into a geographic or spatial context. This study examines the cultural significance of place for San Francisco's ethnic and nonconformist communities, which have found symbolic and substantive focal points in the city's neighborhoods. Class differences are, needless to say, fundamental to the city's social geography: working-class, middle-class, and upper-class districts formed early in the city's history and, despite some fluidity in their demarcation, have remained important forces in ordering urban space. But a geographic analysis of class divergences can explain only the broad contours of the urban landscape. The subcultural fragmentation of social classes—based on differences of race, language, religion, customs and life-styles—also must be factored into an examination of the development of the city's distinctive neighborhoods. Thus the emergence of urban social areas is studied here in terms of the intersection of class and culture in the city's minority communities.

This work focuses on the roles of different types of social groups in the evolution of *urban spatial structure,* which is considered to be the geographic arrangement and interrelation of the city's human activities and physical forms. Social groups in San Francisco, as elsewhere, have used urban space to foster subcultural identities within the dominant, mainstream society. Yet most groups have not been free to develop territorial bastions of subcultural identity under conditions of their own choosing:

---

[30]Manuel Castells, *The City and the Grassroots* (Berkeley: University of California Press, 1983), p. 172.

common forces of both urban decay and renovation have conditioned the formation of ethnic and nonconformist communities. In this study, therefore, the evolving locational patterns of San Francisco communities are related to the broader social, political, and economic forces affecting them and the city as a whole. Of particular concern is the interrelation of subcultural identification and spatial structuring in the emergence of distinctive inner-city neighborhoods.

Plate 1. San Francisco's downtown skyline, as viewed from Twin Peaks. The steady expansion of the financial district, and its encroachment on adjacent areas, such as the South-of-Market District, has transformed the cityscape since the late 1950s. Critics of this "Manhattanization" of San Francisco have stressed the need to preserve the special charms of the city's diverse neighborhoods. (Photograph by Brian J. Godfrey.)

Plate 2. San Francisco's downtown skyline, as seen from Telegraph Hill. A wall of skyscrapers looms over North Beach and Chinatown. Housing built as part of the Golden Gateway redevelopment project, along with the stalled Embarcadero Freeway, can be seen in the foreground, next to San Francisco Bay. (Photograph by Brian J. Godfrey.)

Plates 3 and 4. Views of the renovation of a house on Sanchez Street in Noe Valley, 1980 and 1985. As downtown development created tens of thousands of new white-collar jobs in the city, pressures mounted to renovate abandoned and deteriorated housing. Such renovated housing generally is expensive. In this case, the renovated apartment flats in the building rented in 1985 for $1,100 and $1,800 a month. (Photograph by Brian J. Godfrey.)

Plate 5. The Haight-Ashbury Street Fair, May of 1983. During the 1970s many San Francisco neighborhoods initiated annual street fairs, featuring exhibits by merchants, artisans, and community organizations. Such communal celebrations both reflect and reinforce neighborhood social identities. (Photograph by Brian J. Godfrey.)

2

A SOCIAL THEORY OF COMMUNITY MORPHOGENESIS

> The social dynamic must be given an increasingly important place in urban morphogenesis, particularly in its expression as cultural attachment and detachment.[1]
>
> James E. Vance, Jr., 1975

This study examines the making of San Francisco's principal ethnic and nonconformist communities in terms of long-term processes of neighborhood change. It takes a historical-geographic perspective on the transformation of urban residential areas, focusing on the connections between the evolving forms and functions, spatial structures, social classes, and subcultural identities of inner-city neighborhoods in transition. The central concern is, in short, the relation of people to place that has given rise to such distinctive social districts in the city. San Francisco's specialized urban communities clearly have adapted the built environment to their own uses and perceptions as an expression of cultural detachment.

Studies of urban morphogenesis concentrate essentially on what geographer James Vance calls "the creation and subsequent transformation of city form."[2] The evolution of urban form or morphology is in turn inextricably related to a broad range of social, political, economic, and cultural developments. After all, the city's spatial structure is not merely a result of official urban planning or conscious physical design: it represents the end-product of a society's changing land uses, collective behaviors, and popular

---

[1] James E. Vance, Jr., "Man and super-city: The origin and nature of the intricate social geography of the Bay Area," in Michael E. Eliot Hurst (ed.), *I Came to the City: Essays and Comments on the Urban Scene* (Boston: Houghton Mifflin, 1975), p. 28.

[2] James E. Vance, Jr., *This Scene of Man: The Role and Structure of the City in the Geography of Western Civilization* (New York: Harper and Row, 1977), p. 37.

tastes. The concept of urban morphogenesis generally has been applied to specific building types in the city, stressing the origins of the physical form of a place. In this sense, the city has been viewed as a collection of morphological subareas, based on physical components of urban spatial structure.[3] Seldom has urban morphology been studied explicitly in terms of the shaping of social districts in the city.[4] This study does precisely that: it uses the concept of urban morphogenesis as a conceptual base from which to study the processes of community formation. Specific building types inevitably are involved in such urban processes, but the central concern here is the geographic structuring of subcultural districts, the emergence of spatial form in internally cohesive social areas.

Every urban community exhibits a certain locational distribution and therefore can be studied in terms of its spatial relationships. The understanding of such geographic patterns provides insights into the cultural history of a community: the evolving morphology of a social district in the city reflects a people's ways of life, yet all too frequently this geographic reality is ignored in studies of urban society and culture. It is often implicitly assumed that people somehow operate without much regard for the varieties of their environments, moving like billiard balls across a clear spatial field. The fallacy of such an ungeographic notion becomes apparent in examining the clustering tendencies of urban subcultures, distinctive social worlds that gather not merely in abstract spaces, but more concretely in specific places.

Traditional academic models of urban spatial structure, such as concentric zones and radiating sectors, have relied mainly on rent theory. This body of literature suggests that urban space is allocated by the ability to pay: in a competitive capitalist marketplace, payment for land eventually matches the potential value or bid rent of property. Sociocultural analysts have criticized rent theory, arguing that the intangibles of human environments cannot be adequately captured by economic measures. Studies in this vein maintain that places are imbued with cultural meanings, creating social ties among residents that inhibit the changes predicted by rent theory.[5]

---

[3] See Risa Palm's critique of urban morphogenetic studies, "Reconsidering contemporary neighborhoods," *Landscape*, 26, 2 (1982): 17-20. On morphological subareas, see David Herbert, *Urban Geography: A Social Perspective* (New York: Praeger, 1972), pp. 124-127.

[4] In my literature review, only a study of Detroit's black ghetto was found to apply the concept of morphogenesis to the creation of an urban social district: Donald R. Deskins, Jr., "Morphogenesis of a black ghetto," *Urban Geography*, 2 (April-June 1981): 95-114.

[5] For a review of rent theory and sociocultural approaches, see Mark La Gory and John Pipkin, *Urban Social Space* (Belmont, Calif.: Wadsworth, 1981), pp. 175-182.

Both of these perspectives add something important to the understanding of neighborhood evolution, but each ignores other variables. Economic accounts of urban land values shed light on neighborhood change, but certainly social sorting is also an important dynamic at work in the cultural differentiation of residential districts within the city; rent theory focuses solely on economic sorting in community formation. Sociocultural analyses provide more insights into the making of subcultural identities and their role in forming distinctive urban enclaves: the formation of distinctive urban communities involves social relations and cultural processes, not simply the "laws of land rent." But neither rent theory nor the sociocultural perspective adequately recognizes the importance of physical form and spatial relationships in community life. Yet the city is actually a dynamic combination of such interrelated elements.

This study advances the notion of *urban community morphogenesis* to analyze the interwoven human and physical fabrics of urban districts, analytically extending the traditional concept of morphogenesis to include the emergence of social areas. Whether it dominates a place or merely demonstrates a discernible presence there, a distinctive social group somehow expresses itself in physical terms. The relative locational patterns of residential districts may be construed as socio-spatial morphology; the emergence and evolution of specialized communities represents *evolutionary urban morphogenesis,* a continuous process of initiation and adaptation of the built environment, which can be examined on a small scale to indicate local geographic patterns. As a means of integrating the diverse variables involved in the historical geography of community formation, a social theory of neighborhood change is proposed in this study.

CONCEPTS OF NEIGHBORHOOD AND COMMUNITY

Neighborhoods experienced a resurgence in American public awareness during the 1970s, becoming a rallying point for those interested in local access to political power and government largesse, historic preservation, and urban renovation. Unlike the related concept of community, which may be spatially dispersed, a neighborhood is fundamentally bound by a sense of place. It is best regarded as an urban residential area, consisting of continuous territory, which is commonly recognized as an identifiable unit by both inhabitants and outsiders; the basis for this recognition varies widely, however. Urban neighborhoods base their identities upon any of a wide variety of characteristics, as the following report notes:

Defining just exactly what a neighborhood is has long vexed students of city planning. It can be a geographic area, recognized by boundaries like a street, freeway, or railroad tracks. It can be distinguished by a conspicuous physical feature—like a park or a hill or a building (a school, a church, a library, a factory). It can be defined by a certain type of housing (perhaps row houses, perhaps all built at the same time or by the same developer) that is different enough from the surrounding housing types to stand out clearly. The neighborhood can also be defined socially—by political groups, religious affiliations, or ethnic similarities. In addition, since most areas do not have widely varying prices for housing, and since income largely (but not exclusively) determines buying power, neighborhoods can be defined by income groupings, or as "housing sub-markets."[6]

The essence of the concept of neighborhood is the common recognition of an area's identity by residents and knowledgeable outsiders, on the basis of any number of distinguishing traits. The perception of neighborhood identities, boundaries, and even designations may vary among people and over time, of course, but that reflects the changing social geography of urban areas. Free-standing criteria for neighborhood identification seem best suited to the vagaries of local conditions.

The local residential area traditionally has been used as the typical basis of "community." In recent years, however, there has been much comment on the spatially dispersed "community without propinquity." Although communities may be based upon residence in the same locality, they essentially center on the shared attitudes and behaviors that bind together the people themselves. Shared urban territory may foster community bonds, but so may any number of other shared traits: a common occupation, social class, race, religion, national origin, alternative life-style, politics, and so on. These bases for group cohesion may be spatially clustered or dispersed, creating a largely unresolved conceptual dichotomy between "community-as-locality" and "community-as-society."[7]

Communities thus may be organized in two basic ways: around a common outlook, such as the "academic community"; or around a common locality, such as the "Berkeley community." A community of outlook may be spatially dispersed, while a community of place is based on functional interaction within a certain spatial range.

---

[6]James Mitchell, *The Dynamics of Neighborhood Change* (Washington, D.C.: U.S. Department of Housing and Urban Development, 1975), p. 7.

[7]Risa Palm, "Factorial ecology and the community of outlook," *Annals of the Association of American Geographers,* 63 (September 1973): 341-346.

Neighborhoods are therefore synonymous with communities of place. This conceptual distinction between neighborhood and community is far from clear-cut, but it is nonetheless important to recognize: making the concepts coterminous would serve to disguise the diversity of urban areas. An "ethnic neighborhood" is seldom exclusively ethnic, for instance, though ethnicity may predominate. Some amount of diversity is almost invariably evident in both communities of place and communities of outlook: neither is necessarily homogeneous in internal composition, nor absolutely defined in external boundaries.

Although modern technology does allow for more spatially dispersed communities, it would be a mistake to think that increased mobility in American society has now caused neighborhoods to be completely supplanted by what are sometimes now called "communities of taste." The "placelessness" of contemporary American society should not be overemphasized: the maintenance of community identities still is often dependent on institutional and residential clustering in certain areas, as witnessed by the continued existence of neighborhoods with special identities.

URBANISM AND SUBCULTURES

Historically, the urban environment has tended to serve as an incubator for subcultures or distinctive social worlds. Such specialized communities have arisen and proliferated in the city, given its function as the container of a large and differentiated population. Most definitions of the city, in fact, stress that some measure of social diversity goes hand in hand with urbanism. Louis Wirth's classic criterion for the city, for instance, is "a relatively large, dense, and permanent settlement of socially heterogeneous individuals."[8]

It is not surprising that both ethnic and unconventional groups, along with others, should find in the city a haven from the social constraints of a more traditional countryside. The medieval adage that "city air makes men free" has generally been true in the West since the days when a serf could win his freedom by proving residence in a city for a year and a day; subsequently, western cities have been associated with personal freedom, dissent, and social conflict. Subcultural expression has been more constrained in the urban centers of traditional civilizations with tightly bound "moral orders," but cross-cultural comparisons uphold the view of the modernizing city as a force for social change.

---

[8]Louis Wirth, "Urbanism as a way of life," (1938), reprinted in Richard Sennett (ed.), *Classic Essays on the Culture of Cities* (Englewood Cliffs, N. J.: Prentice-Hall, 1969), pp. 143-164.

Anthropologists Robert Redfield and Milton Singer have called the western-type city "heterogenetic" in that it has been a place of cultural variety, social strain, and economic rather than moral primacy; such a pluralistic city is clearly more favorable for the emergence of ethnic and nonconformist subcultures than its polar opposite, the "orthogenetic" city, in which elites allow change only within the context of traditional indigenous cultures.[9] Similarly, in sociologist Gideon Sjoberg's "preindustrial city"—where a ruling class maintains its position by appeals to absolutes and tradition, supplemented by the sanctions of priests and astrologers—distinctive social worlds would hardly be encouraged.[10] Even in tradition-bound orthogenetic and preindustrial cities, however, some degree of social differentiation would be inevitable because of class stratification, and ethnic cleavages could not be entirely avoided.

In any case, such traditional cities have become increasingly rare in the face of modernization. In both the East and West, therefore, urbanism has been alternately praised and damned for promoting changes and unorthodox ways. Innovations have tended to emerge first in cities and then diffuse out to the countryside in time-honored spatial patterns of cultural change. The strong anti-urban bias of American moral reformers, for example, stems largely from the roles of U.S. cities as seedbeds for exotic "foreign" and unconventional subcultures.

The notion that subcultural "deviance" in the city causes social disorganization and moral breakdown is strongly ingrained in the West. It can be traced back at least to classical European modernization theories, forwarded by such diverse thinkers as Karl Marx, Max Weber, Emile Durkheim, and others. Despite their obvious differences in viewpoint, such theorists were all concerned with the transition from a traditional rural-based order to a modern industrial urban-based society. In the late nineteenth century it was commonly assumed that structural changes resulting from industrialization—the increasing scale of production, technological innovation, and social differentiation—led to a breakdown of community and to an increase in deviance. Claude Fischer notes that "the essence of this classic sociological analysis is the connection of the structural characteristics of a society, particularly its scale, to the quality of its 'moral order'."[11]

This view of the modern city causing the disintegration of "natural" communities found its most articulate academic expression in the United States in the work of the

---

[9]Robert Redfield and Milton B. Singer, "The cultural role of cities," *Economic Development and Cultural Change,* 3 (October 1954): 53-73.

[10]Gideon Sjoberg, *The Preindustrial City, Past and Present* (New York: Free Press, 1960).

[11]Claude S. Fischer, *The Urban Experience* (New York: Harcourt Brace Jovanovich, 1976), p. 28.

early Chicago School of urban ecology. Flourishing in the early part of this century under the initial influence of Robert Park, the Chicago School was greatly preoccupied with the processes of social disorganization and individual maladjustment resulting from rapid urbanization. Chicago certainly was a prime study site: the city was in the throes of massive growth, its population increasing by about a half-million people per decade, largely through the receipt of large streams of foreign immigrants; the teeming midwestern metropolis became the scene of an urban turmoil and despair chronicled in both Upton Sinclair's novel *The Jungle* and the social work of Jane Addams in her Hull House. It was in this setting that Louis Wirth framed his widely influential article, "Urbanism as a Way of Life," in which he held that demographic characteristics of the modern city—size, density, and heterogeneity of the population—led to a breakdown of social cohesion, cultural disruption, *anomie*, and a loss of the sense of community.[12]

A series of ethnographic studies of Chicago's diverse social worlds described the ways of life of a variety of urban subcultures: the Jewish ghetto, Polish-Americans, hobos, youth gangs, taxi-dance halls, ethnic slums, rooming-house districts, and elite quarters.[13] Though generally clearly conceived and well written, such studies were seldom comparative or highly analytical; except in the cases of wealthier groups, which tended to be viewed as stable and orderly in composition, the Chicago ethnographies generally stressed the disintegration rather than the maintenance or creation of communities in the city. For example, Harvey Zorbaugh's classic Chicago study, *The Gold Coast and the Slum,* repeatedly stressed the disorganization inherent in the modern metropolis:

> The community, represented by the town or peasant village where everyone knows everyone else clear down to the ground, is gone. Over large areas of the city "community" is little more than a geographical expression. Yet the old tradition of control persists despite changed conditions of life. The inevitable result is cultural disorganization.[14]

Although the premises of the Chicago School have since been widely criticized, the idea that urbanism disrupted naturally stable and enduring communities has proved

---

[12]Wirth, "Urbanism."

[13]For a succinct review and critique of the Chicago School's urban ethnographies, see Ulf Hannerz, *Exploring the City: Inquiries Toward an Urban Anthropology* (New York: Columbia University Press, 1980).

[14]Harvey W. Zorbaugh, *The Gold Coast and the Slum: A Sociological Study of Chicago's Near North Side* (University of Chicago Press, 1929), p. 16.

surprisingly resilient. And until recently, scholars have often regarded both ethnic and nonconformist subcultures as too "disorganized" to constitute true communities. It is true that highly visible enclaves—like Greenwich Village or Harlem—have been studied as separate communities for generations, but even so the emphasis has generally been on the undesirable and bizarre features that made such areas different from mainstream society.

ETHNIC IDENTITIES AND ETHNIC ENCLAVES

The influx of immigrants and the consequent creation of ethnic enclaves in American cities have long been contentious issues. In the nineteenth and early twentieth centuries, immigrants were often blamed for problems of overcrowding, moral decay, and wage depreciation. On the other hand, immigrants were sought as sources of cheap labor in a labor-scarce economy. As urban transportation systems improved in the latter part of the nineteenth century, the middle and upper classes tended to leave central-city residential locations and move to the suburbs; their places were often taken by immigrants, who settled close to their employment in the inner city, creating sizable ethnic neighborhoods.[15]

The term "ghetto" began to be widely applied to these ethnic enclaves in the inner city around the turn of the century. Although initially restricted in use to the growing clusters of East European Jews, the term soon lost its exclusive Jewish connotations and was popularly applied to other immigrant areas. The Chicago School gave academic legitimacy to this view by conceptualizing the ghetto as a socially isolated ethnic area in the city. In the context of growing preoccupation with the impacts of massive foreign immigration upon American life, the ghetto developed a highly negative image. It was viewed as a segregated, crowded, and impoverished area that promoted social pathologies and cultural disruption.[16]

Revisionist studies have found that ethnic areas actually possess much internal social cohesion and cultural coherence, though the basis of that order has been vigorously debated. Anthropologist Oscar Lewis, for example, suggested that ethnic slums are organized around a "culture of poverty," a self-perpetuating series of traits

---

[15]See David Ward, *Immigrants and Cities* (New York: Oxford University Press, 1971).

[16]David Ward, "The ethnic ghetto in the United States: past and present," *Transactions of the Institute of British Geographers,* 7 (1982): 258-259.

that maintains the internal order of poor societies.[17] Critics claim that this theory in effect blamed the victims for their situation, but still it had the positive aspect of stressing the order and stability of the poor's lives.[18]

Sociologist Herbert Gans, who studied the ethnic area as an "urban village," also saw social networks and cultural traditions maintained intact in the city. Where the Chicago School tended to view inner-city communities as transitory and disorganized, Gans thought intimate ties between residents created personalized enclaves in the impersonal modern metropolis: the ethnic neighborhood is where "European immigrants—and more recently Negro and Puerto Rican ones—try to adapt their nonurban institutions and cultures to the urban milieu."[19] Gans may have overemphasized the homogeneity of his case study, a predominantly Italian-American district of Boston, but his research did conclusively show that such neighborhoods were not without organization and therefore did constitute communities.

Though it has tended to be viewed with suspicion, the ethnic enclave in urban America has served many positive functions for immigrants and their offspring. It has been a place of social and economic support for those in a new regional setting, a place of refuge in an alien culture, and a place structuring political participation in the broader society. Involuntary segregation due to exclusionary nativist forces has contributed to the formation of ethnic enclaves, but voluntary congregation for mutual support among recent immigrants has also been an important and underestimated factor.[20] Although many observers now justifiably dispute the notion that place need serve as the basis for community in a mobile society, immigrant neighborhoods do tend to show strong local ties among residents. After all, recent immigrants often do not have the necessary resources or language skills that would allow them great mobility in American society. Sociologist Suzanne Keller notes that "small town, rural, and ethnic or immigrant enclaves in urban areas [place] greater reliance on neighbors than the larger, more heterogeneous, more urbanized settlements."[21]

---

[17]See Oscar Lewis, *The Children of Sanchez: Autobiography of a Mexican Family* (New York: Random House, 1961); and *La Vida: A Puerto Rican Family in the Culture of Poverty—San Juan and New York* (New York: Random House, 1965).

[18]For a critique of Lewis, see Charles A. Valentine, *Culture and Poverty* (University of Chicago Press, 1968).

[19]Herbert Gans, *The Urban Villagers: Group and Class in the Life of Italian-Americans* (New York: Free Press, 1962), p. 4.

[20]James E. Vance, Jr., "The American city: Workshop for a national culture," in John S. Adams (ed.), *Contemporary Metropolitan America,* vol. 1 (Cambridge, Mass.: Ballinger, 1976), pp. 1-49.

[21]Suzanne Keller, *The Urban Neighborhood: A Sociological Perspective* (New York: Random House, 1968), p. 86.

The continuance of ethnic neighborhoods in American cities depends on the persistence of ethnic identities. Ethnicity is largely based on cultural rather than strictly racial differences between groups: conceptions of "race" stem from perceived differences in physical appearance that are often culturally derived.[22] In this study, an ethnic group is conceived as one basing its identity primarily on shared conceptions of racial, religious, or national origin, therefore possessing a sense of common ancestry and cultural tradition. Ethnic identities need not, indeed cannot, be fixed or immutable, however, particularly in complex modern metropolises. As geographer David Sopher remarks: "Although the culture of ethnic groups cannot be but changing, ethnic identity at a given time and place is signalled by the use of selected symbolic traits."[23]

Ethnicity should be viewed not merely in terms of cultural content, the specific traits that characterize a group, but also within a more general cultural context. The sense of being separate in a plural society, detached as a distinct minority, is essential to the maintenance of an ethnic identity. Because the use of cultural traits by an ethnic group may change forms or emphases over time, one scholar prefers to speak of "ethnic *identification,* a process which entails the constant redefinition of cultural boundaries," rather than "ethnic *identity,* a term which implies a discernible state."[24] This difference may be academic, but it does point out that the maintenance of ethnicity entails a dynamic, changing process of adaptation, one reflected in the role and structure of the ethnic enclave in the city.

"DEVIANTS" OR "URBAN PIONEERS"?

Early research on nonconformist communities, like that on ethnic communities, tended to associate them with the "social disorganization" perceived to occur in large cities. Zorbaugh found Chicago's rooming-house district to be populated largely by young, rootless, single adults, deemed "spiritual nomads," acting "in strange and incalculable ways":

---

[22]Joe R. Feagin, *Racial and Ethnic Relations* (Englewood Cliffs, N. J.: Prentice-Hall, 1978), p. 9.

[23]David Sopher, "Place and location: Notes on the spatial patterning of culture," in Louis Schneider and Charles M. Bonjean (eds.), *The Idea of Culture in the Social Sciences* (Cambridge University Press, 1973), pp. 101-107.

[24]Hans C. Buechler, "Comments," in Brian M. Du Toit and Helen I. Safa (eds.), *Migration and Urbanization: Models and Adaptive Strategies* (The Hague: Mouton, 1975), pp. 285-288.

> Such is the world of furnished rooms—a mobile, anonymous, individual world, a world of thwarted wishes, of unsatisfied longings, of constant restlessness; a world in which people, in the effort to live, are building up a body of ideas that free them from a conventional tradition that has become fixed, hard, and oppressive; a world in which individuation, so typical of the life in the city, is carried to the extreme of personal and social disorganization. People behave in strange and incalculable ways; quick and intimate relationships spring up in the most casual way, and dissolve as quickly and casually. Behavior is impulsive rather than social. It is a world of atomized individuals, of spiritual nomads.[25]

This part of the central city generally was thought to epitomize the urban disintegration of long-established social controls, leaving isolated, lonely, and maladjusted individuals: "individuation, so typical of life in the city, is carried to the extreme of personal and social disorganization." Such urban areas encouraged "the bizarre and eccentric divergences of behavior which are the color of bohemia," featuring artists, literati, radicals, homosexuals, "free-love" advocates, hobos, and criminals.[26] Even Gans, who characterized the ethnic enclave as an "urban village" with intimate ties among the residents, called the nontraditional district an "urban jungle":

> [It is] populated largely by single men, pathological families, people in hiding from themselves or society, and individuals who provide the more disreputable of illegal-but-demanded services to the rest of the community. In such an area, life is comparatively more transient, depressed if not brutal, and it might be called an *urban jungle*. It is usually described as Skid Row, Tenderloin, the red-light district, or even the Jungle.[27]

Nontraditional communities did emerge initially in or near vice districts, where social controls were more relaxed, and early studies of such areas therefore suffered from a highly moralistic tone. Only in recent years have revisionist studies found that many nonconformist groups—such as the counter-culture, feminists, homosexuals, political radicals, student and artistic movements, and so on—have attained the requisite

---

[25]Zorbaugh, *Gold Coast and Slum*, p. 86.

[26]*Ibid.*, pp. 86-87.

[27]Gans, *The Urban Villagers*, p. 4.

sense of solidarity, social cohesion, and structured relationships underlying most concepts of community.

Unconventional groups may form viable communities through the development of communications channels in dispersed places that "offer security, services, and group identity."[28] Such "dispersed communities" may also spatially coalesce to the point of forming distinctive residential districts. In recent years, American cities have witnessed the evolutionary morphogenesis of a variety of unconventional communities, reflected in the development of counter-cultural, artistic, gay and lesbian, self-consciously diverse, fashionably chic, and other kinds of nontraditionally inclined neighborhoods. Christopher Winters claims that these "new types of neighborhoods" result from an increasingly divergent social-sorting process:

> In cities where several neighborhoods are being rejuvenated, each tends to acquire a *different* reputation. These reputations are self-fulfilling, because new people move into the neighborhood that appears likely to be the most congenial. Thus, different neighborhoods end up with distinct populations and increasingly divergent social characters. The result of this sorting process is the development of new types of neighborhoods in several large cities.[29]

So besides being cohesive in their internal organization, nontraditional communities have come to be widely regarded as "urban pioneers" in run-down inner cities—something of a revitalizing force, stemming the tide of urban deterioration. Unconventional groups are the prime movers behind the contemporary rejuvenation of many inner-city neighborhoods. A recent study in Chicago, for example, found that "singles" were the "major middle class group still attracted by the bustle of city life" and that there was "no evidence of a substantial return of families from the suburbs to Chicago."[30] Three principal social types stood out in the areas where single people lived: 1) marriage-shy nomads and loners; 2) spouse-seeking and root-seeking singles; and 3) unmarried couples in relationships of varying durability, conventionality, and sexual orientation. These singles constituted the only groups of whites, other than the

---

[28]Bonnie Loyd and Lester Rowntree, "Radical feminists and gay men in San Francisco: Social space in dispersed communities," in David A. Lanegran and Risa Palm (eds.), *An Invitation to Geography* (New York: McGraw-Hill, 1977), p. 8.

[29]Christopher Winters, "The social identity of evolving neighborhoods," *Landscape,* 23, no. 1, (1979), p. 8.

[30]Pierre De Vise, "The Expanding singles housing market in Chicago: Implications for reviving city neighborhoods," *Urbanism Past and Present* 9 (Winter 1979-Spring 1980): 30-39.

elderly, preferring the central city to the suburbs. Constituting the main middle-class agent in the inner-city housing market, singles could pick the more desirable areas. Having minimal contacts with the minority poor in schools, parks, and other neighborhood facilities, middle-class singles could expand into run-down areas where white families would not tread, thereby sparking a process of urban revitalization.[31]

Although recent years have witnessed an expansion of unconventional areas, such subcultural enclaves are not new. Large American cities have long had bohemian quarters: New York City's Greenwich Village, Chicago's Near North Side, and San Francisco's North Beach are only a few of the more famous cases. Greenwich Village, for example, was transformed during the early twentieth century from what had become a working-class immigrant neighborhood—predominantly Italian and Irish—into a mecca for bohemians in search of free love, socialism, avant-garde literature and art, low rents, and the Village's urban atmosphere. Since World War II, the Village has been the focal point for a succession of nontraditional groups—such as beatniks, hippies, students, gays, and artists—all of whom have resisted attempts at public redevelopment and freeway construction. The Village subsequently has seen a steady rise in rents and the displacement of some of the groups that originally made the area avant-garde. Clearly nontraditional neighborhoods undergo successional processes, just as do ethnic neighborhoods, and can benefit from an analysis of evolutionary community morphogenesis.

SUBCULTURAL INTENSIFICATION IN THE CITY

The development of specialized subcultural enclaves in big cities provides insights into the nature of urbanism. Sociologist Claude Fischer, who has advanced the most comprehensive analysis of the relationship between urbanism and subcultures, maintains:

> Among those subcultures spawned or intensified by urbanism are those which are considered to be downright deviant by the larger society—such as delinquents, professional criminals, and homosexuals; or to be at least "odd"—such as artists, missionaries of new religious sects, and intellectuals; or to be breakers of tradition—such as life-style experimenters, radicals, and scientists. These flourishing subcultures, together with the conflict that arises among them and with mainstream subcultures, are both effects of urbanism, and they both produce what the Chicago School thought of as social "disorganization." According to subcultural theory, these phenomena occur

---

[31]*Ibid.*

not because social worlds break down, and people break down with them, but quite the reverse—because social worlds are formed and nurtured.[32]

Urban subcultural theory applies to nontraditional ("deviant," "odd," "breakers of tradition") groups, as well as to "mainstream" communities based upon ethnicity, occupation, religion, and so forth. The proliferation of such distinctive social worlds in the modern city makes subcultural intensification a more accurate theory of urbanism than earlier notions of the breakdown of a supposedly unified "moral order." Contrary to the thrust of the Chicago School, the city does not destroy social ties and cultural cohesion: a large, dense, and differentiated urban population actually multiplies social worlds and provides the basis for a strengthening of attitudes and bonds among new and old groups in the city. This theory of subcultural intensification holds that the demographic qualities of urbanism encourage the emergence of distinctive social worlds in the city and make urban centers the focal points for cultural innovation.

Subcultures proliferate in cities for a variety of reasons. Urban centers attract large numbers of migrants, who bring with them different cultural backgrounds; and large population concentrations produce structural differentiation, reflected in the occupational specialization, specialized institutions, and special-interest groups with which subcultures are usually associated. In addition, a large population permits the "critical mass" that allows "what would otherwise be only a small group of individuals to become a vital, active subculture." Contacts between subcultures, while sometimes promoting positive exchanges, also tend to intensify the sense of separate social worlds in the city.[33]

Fischer has empirically tested the effects of urbanism on social ties at various points along the American "rural-urban continuum": semi-rural, small town, suburban, and inner-city. The results of his large-scale survey in Northern California tended to replicate the findings of other studies. Although both rural and urban residents had an equal number and quality of social ties, the types of relationships did tend to differ. Big-city dwellers were clearly less traditional than small-town people, and a more urban residence did help to "encapsulate respondents in specific subcultures," particularly when the subcultural involvement would be a "problem" in mainstream American culture. Large and omnipresent subcultures, such as white Protestants, had equal

---

[32]Fischer, *The Urban Experience,* p. 38.

[33]*Ibid.,* pp. 35-39; and Claude S. Fischer, "Toward a subcultural theory of urbanism," *American Journal of Sociology,* 80, no. 6 (1975): 1319-1341.

cohesiveness in both rural and urban settings, but subcultures based upon "atypical traits" such as ethnicity and alternative life-styles definitely were stronger in the inner city:

> Urbanism clearly reduced respondents' involvements with people drawn from the "traditional" complex of kin, neighborhood, and church, and slightly increased their involvements with people drawn from more modern and more voluntary contexts of work, secular associations, and footloose friendships. . . . Whatever causal force urbanism had could be attributed to population concentration itself.[34]

The main limitation of Fischer's theory is that the degree of population concentration alone does not shed much light on the spatial structure of subcultures within metropolitan areas. There is the implication that the critical factor is access of people to one another, which would help explain why most minority subcultures locate in central cities: a central location enjoys maximum access from all points in the metropolis. Still, even within central cities, unconventional and ethnic communities surely form more readily in certain settings than in others.

Subcultural theory can help to explain why distinctive social worlds best find in the city the "critical mass" that permits "what would otherwise be only a small group of individuals to become a vital, active subculture."[35] But it is not merely demographic size that makes the city the scene for subcultural intensification: urban spatial structure also plays an essential role. After all, subcultures do not form just "in the city," but rather in certain *parts* of the city. One principal means by which ethnic and nonconformist communities develop is through clustering in selected urban areas. The sociological notion of subcultural intensification needs to be put in a more geographic context to account for the evolutionary morphogenesis of minority areas in the American city.

CLASSIC MODELS OF URBAN SPATIAL STRUCTURE

Early models of urban spatial structure stressed the homogeneity of metropolitan subareas. During the early twentieth century, the influential Chicago School of urban ecology divided cities into subareas with distinct boundaries, determined mainly by

---

[34]Claude S. Fischer, *To Dwell Among Friends: Personal Networks in Town and City* (University of Chicago Press, 1982), p. 258.

[35]Fischer, *The Urban Experience,* p. 37.

economic forces, and respectively inhabited by people of similar social and cultural characteristics; the city was a collection of such "natural areas," each with a distinct population. The Chicago School emphasized the assimilation of immigrant groups into the larger society through social and spatial mobility. Park and Burgess suggested in the 1920s that groups migrated from the central city to the urban periphery in a series of concentric rings, as they moved up the social ladder; new migrants replaced the old in the inner city and the process repeated itself (see Figure 1).

This concentric-zone theory held that expansion of the central business district produced around it an undesirable "zone of transition," a deteriorated low-class area where speculators and absentee landlords tended not to maintain existing structures, since they foresaw greater profits in later onverting the sites to other uses. The Chicago School was most interested precisely in this "zone of transition," an area inhabited by a highly mobile population of both first-generation immigrants and nonconformist groups:

> In the zone of deterioration encircling the central business section are always to be found the so-called "slums" and "bad lands," with their submerged regions of poverty, degradation and disease, and their underworlds of crime and vice. Within a deteriorating area are rooming-house districts, the purgatory of "lost souls." Nearby is the Latin Quarter, where creative and rebellious spirits resort. The slums are also crowded to overflowing with immigrant colonies—the Ghetto, Little Sicily, Greektown, Chinatown—fascinatingly combining old world heritages and American adaptations. Wedging out from here is the Black Belt, with its free and disorderly life. The area of deterioration, while essentially one of decay, of stationary or declining population, is also one of regeneration, as witness the mission, the settlement, the artists' colony, radical centers—all obsessed with the vision of a new and better world.[36]

The concept of "ecological succession" arose to explain the process of population turnover in such inner-city areas. Derived from the biological concept, in which an ecosystem changed through the replacement of one species by another, the human ecologists suggested that the city changed through a similar process of urban ecological succession, although based more on social than environmental causes. Park and Burgess called the replacement of one human community by another "invasion and

---

[36]Ernest W. Burgess, "The growth of the city: An introduction to a research project," in Robert E. Park, Ernest W. Burgess, and Roderick D. McKenzie (eds.), *The City* (University of Chicago Press, 1925, reprinted in 1967), pp. 54-56.

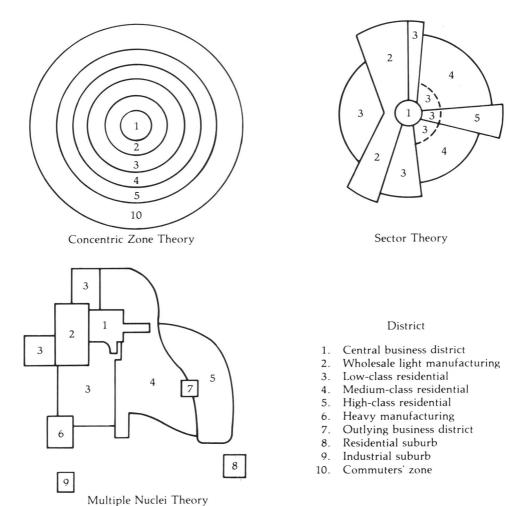

Figure 1. Three classic models of urban spatial structure. Source: Mark La Gory and John Pipkin, *Urban Social Space* (Belmont, Calif.: Wadsworth, 1981), p. 91.

succession," a concept that has most often been applied to racial transition in the inner city. Ecological succession has become the most common way of describing neighborhood change, but certain shortcomings of the concept need to be noted. Since succession focuses on population turnover, the concept deals mainly with the social aspects of neighborhood change, downplaying concomitant physical changes in residential areas. Inner-city neighborhoods tend to go through predictable life-cycles: the physical structures age and deteriorate with time, leaving the housing stock to "filter down" to lower socioeconomic groups. This process is far from universal, as certain neighborhoods have managed to maintain a higher-class appeal, but generally neighborhood succession has accompanied the *downward filtering* of aging physical structures. Thus Vance prefers to speak of "abandonment and replacement," rather than "invasion and succession."[37]

The primarily descriptive ethnographic emphases of the classic Chicago School waned by the late 1930s, by which point ethnicity appeared to be on the decline, largely as a result of the restrictive immigration laws limiting the influx of foreign immigrants. The new conceptions of urban spatial structure were based on functional economic models. Homer Hoyt, a land economist at Chicago, proposed a sector model in 1939, basing residential differentiation on rent-paying ability and downplaying social and cultural factors in the development of urban communities. Hoyt posited that residential areas tended to extend outward from the city center in wedges; the higher-class sectors were located the farthest from industry (see Figure 1).

Another classic model of urban spatial structure corrects some of the deficiencies of the concentric-zone and sectoral conceptions, both of which assume single-centered cities. Chauncy Harris and Edward Ullman proposed a multiple-nuclei theory in 1945, suggesting that many functionally specialized districts grew up in the modern city, so that a single-centered geometry was inappropriate. The precise size, variety, and arrangement of districts varied among cities, depending on such variables as urban history, population, and economic activity, but a generalized model is shown in Figure 1. This model takes into account the growing independence of distinct urban realms in the contemporary dispersed metropolis of the United States, but still is too simplistic to account fully for the complex social geography of urban areas.

The development of more sophisticated statistical analyses of urban social areas followed the expansion of the official data base. Census tracts were first used on an experimental basis in New York City in 1910, and were implemented in a few other

---

[37]James Vance, *This Scene of Man*, p. 369.

large cities in the 1920 and 1930 censuses. The use of census tracts to gather official statistics became standard in U.S. cities in 1940, encouraging the development of new quantitative approaches to the study of urban structure after World War II, such as social-area analysis and factorial ecology, which were adopted by many sociologists and geographers in the 1950s. Such work has provided insight into urban social geography, but like the earlier Chicago School has tended to assume too much homogeneity in metropolitan subareas. Even the most sophisticated statistical endeavors have not been able to overcome the basic deficiencies of data collection in complex urban centers: the geographer Risa Palm concludes that "factorial ecology cannot replicate the complex patterns of human interactions."[38]

THE NEW ETHNOGRAPHIES

Recent recognition of the failure of quantitative approaches to capture fully the nuances of community life has brought about a renewed interest in more traditional ethnographic approaches to urban studies. Work by sociologists has returned to community analysis, now with a greater recognition of urban diversity and the subtleties of group interactions; "natural areas" are a thing of the past.[39] In geography, a "new humanism" attempts to integrate qualitative and perceptual elements into landscape analysis.[40] This renewed concern with urban ethnography has paralleled (but not been confined to) the rediscovery of ethnicity in America in recent decades. Nathan Glazer and Daniel P. Moynihan proclaimed in *Beyond the Melting Pot* that a "resurgence of ethnicity" was occurring in the American city. Their study found that the blacks, Puerto Ricans, Jews, Italians, and Irish of New York City maintained their separate group identities over time, using ethnicity as a basis for becoming established as political interest groups. The melting pot simply "did not happen."[41]

One critic claims that this position ignores the important changes that have occurred to ethnic groups within the "melting pot," a much-abused symbol of group interaction that was initially popularized through the presentation of Israel Zangwill's

---

[38]Palm, "Factorial Ecology."

[39]See Gerald D. Suttles, *The Social Order of the Slum: Ethnicity and Territory in the Inner City* (University of Chicago Press, 1968); and William Kornblum, *Blue Collar Community* (University of Chicago Press, 1974).

[40]For example, see D. W. Meinig (ed.), *The Interpretation of Ordinary Landscapes: Geographical Essays* (Oxford University Press, 1979).

[41]Nathan Glazer and Daniel P. Moynihan, *Beyond the Melting Pot,* 2nd ed., (Cambridge, Mass.: M.I.T. Press, 1970).

play by the same name in 1908. Both liberals and conservatives have scorned the melting-pot notion since then, for either forcing a homogenized Americanization or permitting too much ethnic diversity in the first place. Certainly use of the melting-pot image has been ambiguous, tending either to overstate or to understate immigrant acculturation in the United States.[42]

Recent research has tended to follow the lead of Glazer and Moynihan in discounting the assimilation of ethnic groups in America. According to Michael Novak, for example, the "new ethnicity" is essentially a rise in self-awareness among third- and fourth-generation offspring of immigrants to the U.S., particularly those of southern and eastern European stock, but it does *not* involve speaking a foreign language, living in a subculture, residing in a tightly knit ethnic neighborhood, answering to "ethnic" appeals, or even exalting an ethnic heritage.[43] Yet Novak takes the idea of ethnic persistence to an absurd extreme. Third- or fourth-generation descendents of immigrants, who Novak admits do not even constitute a subculture, can hardly be considered part of an ethnic community. Surely ethnicity requires some functional basis, not merely a vague nostalgia about distant "roots." The principal sources of America's "new ethnicity" are recent immigrants from Latin America and Asia, who have raised anew long-standing issues of assimilation, pluralism, and separatism in the United States.

The massive influx of immigrants from Latin America and Asia has been the subject of a series of sensational stories in the American news media in recent years. Whether it be Central Americans abandoned in the Arizona desert, the arrival of the Cuban "Mariel" boatlift, the plight of Haitian refugees, or the flight of the Indochinese "boat people," the immigrant sagas share a common motif: a group of people suffering from political, social, or economic hardship flees to the U.S., where the newcomers get a mixed reception and cluster initially in culturally distinctive communities.

This contemporary immigrant scenario reflects the most recent in a series of great immigrant waves to hit America. The first, in the mid-1800s, emanated mainly from western and northern Europe. The next, called the "new immigration" in its time, peaked around the turn of the century and came chiefly from southern and eastern Europe; the restrictive-entry legislation of the early 1920s, which ended America's long-standing official "open door" policy, curbed this movement. In 1965 U.S.

---

[42]Philip Gleason, "Confusion compounded: The melting pot in the 1960s and 1970s," *Ethnicity*, 6 (1979): 10-20.

[43]Michael Novak, "The new ethnicity," in David R. Colburn and George E. Pozzetta (eds.), *America and the New Ethnicity* (Port Washington, N.Y.: Kennikat Press, 1979), pp. 15-28.

immigration laws were thoroughly revamped for the first time since 1924, which was to have profound implications for minority populations. The former national immigrant quotas, preferential to northern and western European countries, were eliminated as discriminatory. The new system permitted an annual immigration of 170,000 from the Old World, with a 20,000 maximum per country, and preference was given to unite families, promote special skills, and accommodate refugees; New World countries were allowed 120,000 yearly immigrants to the United States. The main sources of American immigration shifted from Europe to Latin America and Asia.

The result of this contemporary immigration has been the emergence of a new array of ethnic groups since World War II, after the older European immigrant stock was essentially assimilated into the American cultural mainstream. Along with the postwar rise in consciousness among domestic minority groups—particularly blacks, who experienced widespread regional migration themselves within the U.S.—the new foreign immigrants have contributed to a renewed ethnic awareness in America. These "new ethnics" are the fastest-growing segment of the U.S. population, and their impact on the cultural landscape is clearly on the rise. Official census figures indicate that the foreign-born population of the U.S. rose from about 8 million in 1970 (just over 4 percent of the U.S. total) to some 14 million in 1980 (over 6 percent); including uncounted "illegal aliens," the numbers are undoubtedly much higher. The American population of Spanish origin, both native and foreign-born, officially constituted 6.4 percent of the U.S. population in 1980, making it now second in numbers only to blacks (11.7 percent) among the nation's ethnic minorities. By 1990 blacks and Hispanics are predicted to jointly constitute one-fifth of the U.S. population, and by the year 2000 Hispanics are bound to be America's largest minority group.[44]

The role of contemporary immigration from Asia and Latin America in the resurgence of ethnicity in America has received surprisingly little attention from geographers, despite the important geographic implications. Recent immigrants have transformed significant portions of the American urban landscape. In consequence, ethnic enclaves—districts inhabited largely by people of a particular national, racial, or cultural origin—have sprung up anew in many central cities, and increasingly in suburbs as well.

The volume and nature of recent immigration has given rise to fears among broad sectors of the U.S. population that the new immigrants will prove more resistant to

---

[44]Cary Davis, Carl Haub, and JoAnne Willette, "U.S. Hispanics: Changing the face of America," *Population Bulletin,* 38 (June 1983): 1-44; John Crewdson, *The Tarnished Door: The New Immigrants and the Transformation of America* (New York: Times Books, 1983).

assimilation than did previous Old World immigrants, who voluntarily crossed formidable ocean barriers to come to this country, and were more willing to leave behind their cultural baggage. The global context is now different: America has grown out of nineteenth-century isolationism to assume inextricable, far-flung political and economic interests, as well as widespread cultural influences, which have created immigrant streams more widely scattered than before. In addition, modern communications and transportation technologies help immigrants both to maintain better contact with their homelands and to retain a stronger "historical memory" than in the past.[45] There is special concern that growing numbers of Spanish-speaking residents may permanently maintain ethnic enclaves in American cities, a preoccupation at the root of controversies surrounding bilingual education and services. A great diversity exists within the Hispanic population, however, making generalizations about acculturation hazardous: recent immigrants are divided by country of origin, social class, ethnicity, and other cleavages. These issues of cultural persistence and change among recent immigrants to the U.S. are of fundamental importance to the future of American cities, and merit further research.

This study focuses on the social dynamics of neighborhood ethnic succession, on the assumption that the morphogenesis of an ethnic community occurs in a predictable life-cycle or series of successional stages. Given the general downward filtration of inner-city housing stock, it would indeed appear logical for the entry of new social groups to be prepared, at least in part, by departure of the established population of a neighborhood. The *invasion,* therefore, generally is preceded by an initial *penetration* of a few upwardly mobile in-migrants. The *invasion* occurs when large numbers of the new group replace the departing former population, followed by a *consolidation* stage in which the new group clearly predominates.

NONCONFORMIST COMMUNITIES IN THE CITY

Both ethnic and nonconformist groups have tended to cluster in American inner cities, though for somewhat different reasons. Vance maintains that ethnic quarters typically occupy the central city "of necessity," largely excluded from the suburbs; nonconformist communities, on the other hand, develop "by choice" through their disagreement with nativist suburban culture.[46] This touches on important differences between ethnic and unconventional communities. Nonconformist communities base

---

[45]Frank Viviano, "The new immigrants," *Mother Jones* (January 1983): pp. 26-46.

[46]Vance, *This Scene of Man,* pp. 400-402, 416-417.

their group identities on unconventional attitudes and alternative life-styles. This nonconformity does not derive from long-standing family traditions, as with ethnicity, but is consciously and independently chosen at some point in the lives of different individuals; the basis for association in nonconformist communities is therefore essentially voluntaristic, and so is often relatively less stable over time.

Consideration of the degree of choice among different communities raises thorny issues that cannot be entirely resolved here. But recognition of the mobility and fluid composition typical of nonconformist subcultures helps to explain spatial patterns: communities based on opposition to mainstream culture are often somewhat fleeting, and their urban impacts transitory, when compared with ethnic enclaves. The counter-cultural communes of the late 1960s, for example, often came and went quickly in inner-city neighborhoods. Nonconformist communities may be cohesive and enjoy surprising longevity, however, just as some ethnic communities may be short-lived. Ethnic identities surge and fade, just as do nontraditional identities. Although questions of cultural continuity and change must ultimately be specific to the group in question, it is interesting to compare the nature of ethnic and nonconformist communities. Both types of communities base their identities on traits somewhat out of the mainstream, providing a sense of belonging to minority subcultures.

Whether nontraditional communities can be considered to be legitimate minority groups is a subject of controversy. The standard criteria for minority-group status in the U.S. have typically involved racial, linguistic, and religious (which all have been categorized in this study as *ethnic*) differences vis-a-vis society's majority.[47] But the traditional ethnic connotations of minority groups no longer suffice in contemporary metropolitan America, where unconventional subcultures act somewhat like immigrant groups in creating distinctive urban enclaves. In recent years, therefore, it has become common to regard some nonconformist groups as minorities, alongside ethnic groups.

A striking example of this trend can be found in the emergence of the gay and lesbian communities, based upon public social identities rather than merely private homosexual activity. Some scholars have viewed these subcultures as emerging minority groups in America's plural society.[48] A comparative study of ethnic and gay groups in Toronto found the latter to amply fulfill the sociological notion of community,

---

[47]Eric Fischer, *Minorities and Minority Problems* (New York: Vantage, 1980).

[48]See Toby Marotta, *The Politics of Homosexuality* (Boston: Houghton Mifflin, 1981); and Dennis Altman, *The Homosexualization of America, the Americanization of the Homosexual* (New York: St. Martin's Press, 1982).

even to the extent of constituting a "quasi-ethnic community."[49] The quasi-ethnic status of the gay community has been stressed in other comparative studies as well. Sociologist Martin Levine, for example, examined gay areas in five large American cities in terms of the Chicago School's conception of the ghetto as a socially segregated cultural community. Based on the classic four-pronged criteria of the ghetto set forth by Robert Park and Louis Wirth—institutional concentration, culture area, social isolation, and residential concentration—Levine found neighborhoods in New York, Los Angeles, and San Francisco to qualify as full-fledged "gay ghettos"; twelve areas in the five cities studied were deemed "partially developed ghettos;" and twelve other areas were "probably not ghettos," despite a significant homosexual presence.[50]

Though the application of the ghetto concept to homosexuals is in some ways problematic, since gay men in particular often appear to have greater residential and social mobility than members of lower-income minority groups, "gay ghettos" do serve to illustrate a few basic similarities between ethnic and nontraditional communities in the inner city. Both types of communities result, at least in part, from external non-acceptance that inhibits full integration into the larger society, as well as from the internal cohesion that helps to bind the group through self-preference. The latter element of congregation by choice is probably more important for nonconformists than for ethnics, but still some elements of discrimination and prejudice face both types of groups.

The basis for minority status, then, rests upon group exception to certain important elements of the dominant culture. In this sense, a wide range of groups could be considered minorities, in addition to homosexuals. The question of which groups deserve minority status remains largely philosophical and polemical, though, and in that sense it cannot be resolved here. But in this study an attempt is made to raise the debate to a higher level of analysis by testing the assertion of both ethnic and nonconformist minority identities against a tangible yardstick: urban form and spatial structure. To the extent that such groups have identifiable neighborhoods, the morphological evidence would suggest that they can indeed be considered to be minority communities; their districts serve as both the symbols and substance of subcultural expression, providing concrete evidence of minority status within mainstream society. Neighborhood residences, businesses, and social gathering spots provide a subcultural

---

[49]Stephen O. Murray, "The institutional elaboration of a quasi-ethnic community," *International Review of Modern Sociology,* 9 (July-December 1979): 165-177.

[50]Martin P. Levine, "Gay ghetto," in *Gay Men: The Sociology of Male Homosexuality* (New York: Harper and Row, 1979): 182-205.

refuge for both ethnic and unconventional groups in the city. These places create, maintain, and reinforce group identities.

Each ethnic and nonconformist community is distinct in terms of specific cultural content, but there are insights to be gained in comparing and contrasting the ways in which different groups carve out territory for themselves in central cities. Unconventional quarters in contemporary American cities have come to resemble in some ways the immigrant neighborhoods that have long played an important role in the U.S. urban landscape. Both types of neighborhoods are peopled largely by migrants, foreign or domestic, who have found some degree of autonomy within mainstream culture by clustering in residential areas with special identities. Although the specific neighborhood forms and functions may vary greatly, both ethnic and nonconformist areas in the inner city serve as bastions of subcultural expression.

One of the most striking differences between ethnic and nonconformist communities is their relationship to gentrification, the conversion of working-class neighborhoods to middle-class neighborhoods through a physical restoration of the buildings. Ethnic neighborhoods tend to maintain a working-class status, at least insofar as they remain truly ethnic, whereas nonconformist enclaves in the inner city are prone to gentrify in time, despite their working-class and bohemian beginnings. In-migrants to gentrifying neighborhoods are often pictured as a rather undifferentiated group of young urban professionals or "yuppies". This may be accurate in a general sense, but it plays down the often initially divergent social identities of gentrifying neighborhoods. Usually there are some distinctive qualities about such neighborhoods that initially attract an avant-garde fringe. The gentrifying neighborhood may become much more homogeneous in time, but it usually retains a characteristic social reputation.

The social dynamics of gentrification may be understood in terms of a successional sequence. The typical life-cycle begins with a *bohemian influx*, in which nontraditional, "footloose" social elements are favored—single people, counter-culturals, homosexuals, artists, feminist households. They discover a neighborhood's special charms, such as social diversity, subcultural identification, architectural heritage, or historical distinction. These "urban pioneers" make a run-down or even dangerous area livable and attractive to others who would not normally venture there. A *middle-class transition* subsequently occurs. At this point, the word gets out about the neighborhood. We see the rise of a local entrepreneurial class on the local shopping strip and a residential middle-class within the community; housing speculation begins. This stage is followed by a *bourgeois consolidation,* when many outside firms enter the local shopping area, catering to a wealthier clientele; the residential population becomes increasingly homogeneous, as rents and property values rise, displacing lower-income residents. The original bohemians often move on to new areas, and the life-cycle is complete.

PHASES OF NEIGHBORHOOD EVOLUTION

Studies of urban communities and neighborhoods present certain conceptual and empirical ambiguities. For one thing, there is no universally accepted definition of either neighborhood or community. In addition, the modern metropolis is such a complex entity that exceptions usually abound to even the most widely recognized patterns. Christopher Winters has observed along these lines:

> For most people self-identification is complicated and constantly changing. This explains why neighborhood character is often short-lived as well as difficult to define. It also prevents government statistics from being helpful in eliciting neighborhood character. What residents believe their neighborhood is becoming may be more significant than what it is. Such trends affect images of neighborhood identity held by inhabitants, by other residents of the city, and by people thinking of moving into the neighborhood. . . In fact, a clear definition of even neighborhood location seldom exists. Historically, neighborhoods in American cities have changed locations and even names. Most have imprecise boundaries. For studies using objective data, neighborhoods make poor subjects. The spatial vagueness of neighborhoods probably reflects the vagueness of the social characters attributed to them, but *precisely* at the neighborhood scale the phenomenon of neighborhood character is significant.[51]

This passage may overemphasize the subjective aspects of neighborhood change: after all, government statistics can be helpful in identifying certain trends, though they may be woefully lacking in many regards. Yet there are real difficulties of definition, boundaries, and data collection in neighborhood research. Some patterns can be verified using official statistics, but certain aspects of community development are completely ignored. The reality of parts of the urban experience difficult to quantify should not be discounted by an unswerving dedication to statistical endeavors. A methodology admitting only the use of "hard data" therefore would be inappropriate here. Rather, the approach in this study is an interpretive one, which emphasizes comparative historical and structural analysis of what geographer Risa Palm calls "the

---

[51] Christopher Winters, "Social identity," pp. 8-9.

whys behind urban form—the processes imbedded in society and economy that account for the evolution of neighborhoods."[52]

A structural framework is needed to integrate the geographical study of urban community formation and neighborhood change. This study examines ethnic and nonconformist communities in terms of an urban morphogenetic sequence of neighborhood change, based on a revised filtering model of the relationship between inner-city physical structure and population flux. Since patterns of initial settlement strongly influence the subsequent evolution of urban areas, the first structural phase involves *neighborhood inception and growth*. In the next phase, *neighborhood decay*, the inner-city area starts to suffer, showing signs of physical deterioration and departure of the sorts of inhabitants that lived there in an earlier heyday, which helps prepare the way for a process of downward filtration and community succession. Then comes the phase of *neighborhood transformation* in which "invasion" by the new minority group and the abandonment by earlier inhabitants fundamentally change the character of the area, giving it a new social identity reflected in the adapted forms and functions of local businesses, gathering spots, and residences. On the heels of this turnaround come the beginnings of *neighborhood revitalization,* an adaptive phase of upward filtering, which brings with it varying degrees of both physical renovation and social resistance to the displacement of local residents.

It is during the general phase of neighborhood transformation that the differences between ethnic and nonconformist communities become apparent in alternate successional sequences. As discussed earlier in this chapter, ethnic neighborhoods experience an initial *migrant penetration* of a few upwardly mobile settlers, followed by a *minority invasion,* in which large numbers of the new group replace the departing population. As the neighborhood undergoes *ethnic consolidation,* the new group comes to predominate in the neighborhood, sometimes reaching high population densities through a crowding of the housing stock. The ethnic subculture in the neighborhood intensifies during these historical stages, after which the area may either repeat a new process of ethnic succession, undergo the gentrification so often associated with initial inroads by nontraditional elements, or simply evolve into a less ethnic but still working-class area.

The nonconformist community life-cycle contrasts sharply with the typical ethnic-neighborhood successional sequence. As also previously discussed, the nontraditional community commonly starts with a *bohemian influx,* in which a run-down

---

[52]Palm, "Reconsidering contemporary neighborhoods," p. 20.

neighborhood is "discovered" by such social elements as counter-cultural devotees, homosexuals, artists, and others. These groups constitute the "urban pioneers" who draw attention to a district and inadvertently encourage an incipient neighborhood gentrification. The *middle-class transition* occurs in the wake of speculation in local housing and businesses, as middle-class groups of homeowners and entrepreneurs arise in the neighborhood. The terminal phase involves a *bourgeois consolidation,* when many outside firms enter the area and rents rise to a level that only a wealthier clientele can afford. Although the neighborhood may not lose its social identity, it certainly becomes more homogeneous in terms of class.

These admittedly variable and overlapping phases of neighborhood evolution merely provide a general comparative framework within which to examine the formation of ethnic and nonconformist communities. This social theory is not intended deductively to determine data selection, but rather to relate case studies to broader processes of urban change. And these urban morphogenetic phases are not regarded here as necessarily universal patterns, but as specific to American central cities, where strong centrifugal forces have tended historically to downgrade inner-city residence under conditions of rapid urbanization, favoring the development of more affluent suburbs on the urban periphery. The American metropolis typically has been left with a situation of urban decay and downward filtering of the housing stock in the more centrally located residential areas, though the inner-city rejuvenation of recent years has somewhat altered this pattern.

Not all central-city neighborhoods have been subject to urban revitalization, of course, because not all of the inner city has experienced a downward filtration of the housing stock and the associated socioeconomic flux. Despite widespread "white flight" from the inner city with massive suburban expansion in the United States, some central-city areas have retained a stable upper-class status. Beacon Hill, for example, has remained an elite neighborhood in central Boston for over a century and a half, a persistence of social esteem that according to Walter Firey shows the importance of symbolism, rather than economics, in inner-city land use.[53]

But most central-city neighborhoods have not proved to be so stable. Present-day slums often were once respectable areas, but experienced a physical deterioration and minority-group "invasion." A classic example is New York City's Harlem, which was transformed from an upper-middle-class white neighborhood in the late 1800s to a crowded black ghetto by the 1920s, largely as a result of speculative overbuilding of the

---

[53]Walter Firey, "Symbolism, space, and the upper class," reprinted in Hurst, *I Came to the City,* pp. 147-150.

housing stock that caused a glut on the local real-estate market around the turn of the century.[54] In the 1980s Harlem began to experience the early stages of gentrification, which could ultimately lead to the displacement of lower-income blacks by more affluent whites.[55] That even Harlem—a national symbol of black inner-city poverty—is undergoing renovation reveals that a significant restructuring of American urban space is underway. The frequency and scale of such contemporary inner-city revitalization indicate that neighborhood change is no longer predominantly a unidirectional process of downward filtration of the housing stock. Many centrally located neighborhoods, particularly those of distinctive architecture and historic interest, have been "recaptured" by upper classes after long periods of socioeconomic decline. A 1976 survey by the Urban Land Institute found that half of all U.S. cities with populations of over 50,000 were experiencing some significant rehabilitation of central-city neighborhoods; probably all such cities could point to widespread inner-city revitalization by the 1980s.

This study examines the roles of ethnic and nonconformist communities in both urban decay and revitalization. Given the dearth of official statistics on such communities, quantitative data cannot be solely relied upon to sustain all the arguments herein. Some ethnic groups, such as Hispanics, presumably are subject to undercounting in U.S. Census figures, while nonconformist communities are not even recognized as categories. Rather than adopting a restrictive quantitative methodology, then, this study takes a broader perspective on the diverse structural factors involved in the shaping of subcultural areas in the city. This historical geography of selected ethnic and nonconformist communities is compiled largely from local histories, journalistic reports, personal interviews, and oral histories. Where available, demographic data is charted over time and analyzed spatially. In addition, field surveys of residential areas and commercial strips will provide morphological evidence of inner-city neighborhoods in transition.

The aim of this study is to illuminate the relation of subcultural identification to physical change in inner-city neighborhoods, as illustrated by case studies of evolutionary community morphogenesis in San Francisco. The study's theoretical basis lies in the social dynamics of neighborhood evolution, and its central hypothesis is that the alternate successional sequences of ethnic and nonconformist communities can provide insights into the social geography of American inner cities.

---

[54]Gilbert Osofsky, *Harlem: The Making of a Ghetto* (New York: Harper and Row, 1964.)

[55]Richard Schaffer and Neil Smith, "The gentrification of Harlem?" *Annals of the Association of American Geographers* 76, no. 3: 347-365.

Plate 6. A "Filipino-Mexican-American" grocery store on Mission Street, beside a Spanish-language pharmacy and bar. The proximity and occasional intermixing of distinct Hispanic and Filipino elements in San Francisco's Mission District attests to a tendency toward ethnic syncretism among immigrant groups in the American inner city. (Photograph by Brian J. Godfrey.)

Plate 7. The Ticonica Bar on Mission Street. This bar, which combines Costa Rican ("Tico") and Nicaraguan ("Nica") national nicknames, has served as a pan-Hispanic gathering spot since its opening in the late 1950s. The syncretism of distinct Hispanic national groups in San Francisco points to the importance of viewing ethnic identities as contextual and relational in nature, rather than as fixed and immutable. (Photograph by Brian J. Godfrey.)

Plate 8. Pedestrians on Castro Street. The upscale commercial strip in the vicinity of Castro Street, between Market and 19th streets, along with the surrounding neighborhood, became a showcase of the fashionable gay life-style during the 1970s. The visible emergence of the gay community in the United States during this period was closely linked to the public identification of such neighborhoods as "The Castro." (Photograph by Brian J. Godfrey.)

3

FROM INSTANT CITY TO METROPOLIS
Urban Morphogenesis and Subcultural Intensification

> This has been a loony bin from the beginning. . . The rugged and ragged individuals survive, conforming only to the idea that San Franciscans will not conform.[1]
>
> Herb Caen, 1983

To understand contemporary San Francisco, it is necessary to look at the city's past. A highly differentiated cultural mosaic had emerged in San Francisco by the outbreak of World War II, the basic contours of which greatly affected the postwar history of the city. The combined effects of progressive acculturation, increased sociospatial mobility, and the entry of new groups transformed the city's cultural landscape after the war, but only within an established urban framework of community location.

A series of relatively stable communities developed in San Francisco during the late nineteenth and early twentieth centuries. Ethnic differentiation of the population—based on diverse national, racial, and religious origins—intensified as waves of immigrant labor flowed into the city, locating principally in working-class districts. San Francisco became a mecca for the unconventionally inclined as well, giving rise to bohemian quarters, situated in close proximity to ethnic groups in the central working-class areas. Although the size, placement, and character of the city's ethnic and nonconformist subcultures were far from static during this period, certain consistent spatial patterns emerged as the "instant city" of the Gold Rush evolved into a Pacific Coast metropolis.

Early subcultural patterns in San Francisco, in many ways foretelling later developments, reflected the city's social geography during the initial periods of urbanization. Before turning to the emergence of contemporary minority areas, it is

---

[1] Herb Caen, *San Francisco Chronicle,* "Sunday Punch" Section, May 1, 1983, p. 1.

important first to analyze the ways in which San Francisco became socially and spatially subdivided before the onset of World War II. This chapter examines the historical dialectic of *urban morphogenesis* (the initiation and adaptation of urban form) and *subcultural intensification* (the formation and proliferation of distinctive social worlds) in the city. It begins with the impact of the Gold Rush, a pivotal event in the city's evolution, and then discusses the morphogenesis of a variety of culturally distinctive communities in San Francisco during the late nineteenth and early twentieth centuries.

THE MAKING OF AN INSTANT CITY

Before the 1840s, only a few small settlements had been established at the site of present-day San Francisco, none of which fundamentally altered the primitive landscape. Earliest, of course, were the native Indians. Although Central California had one of the densest Indian populations north of Mexico before the Spanish arrived in the late eighteenth century, it was concentrated in areas ecologically more favorable for a hunting and gathering existence than San Francisco. Grouped in some 40 different tribelets of about 250 people each between Point Sur and San Francisco Bay, the local Indians did not inhabit in any great numbers the relatively barren, windswept, and chilly site of the future city, which lacked abundant fresh water, timber, plants, and wildlife. Instead, these Costanoan (from the Spanish *costeño*, for "coastal people") or Ohlone Indians preferred to live in the more bountiful inland areas and southerly coasts.[2]

The first European settlers did appreciate some measure of the potential importance of the site of present-day San Francisco, but never found sufficient cause to develop it greatly. The Spanish only discovered the great bay hidden behind the narrow and often fog-enshrouded strait in 1769, centuries after their conquest of Mexico, when an overland party looking for Monterey Bay accidentally came upon this inland sea to the north. Fear of Russian incursions from the north prompted Spain to establish a series of California missions under the Franciscan fathers in these years, centuries after the principal Spanish conquests in the New World. In 1776 a mission was dedicated to Saint Francis of Assisi (although it became known as Mission Dolores, after the name of a nearby stream), along with a ramshackle, sparsely manned Spanish *presidio*, or fort, at the entrance to San Francisco Bay. But the indigenous population of hunter-gatherers lacked a highly developed material culture, so there was not much of value to take possession of locally; settlement efforts languished after an initial spurt of activity

---

[2]Malcolm Margolin, *The Ohlone Way: Indian Life in the San Francisco-Monterey Bay Area* (Berkeley: Heyday Books, 1978).

in pacifying the Indians and setting up an agricultural colony, which supplied the mission and the small presidio nearby with foodstuffs. The site of the present-day metropolis remained a forlorn outpost on the far corner of the crumbling Spanish New World empire during the late eighteenth and early nineteenth centuries.[3]

The Mexican tenure in the Bay Area, lasting from the country's independence from Spain in 1821 until the American takeover in 1846, provided some basis for the further development of San Francisco's site. The Catholic ecclesiastical establishment had sided with Spain during the Latin American wars of independence, so Mexico secularized the Church's holdings in the early 1830s; in California, the Mexican authorities divided up the mission holdings into land grants that were distributed among soldiers and settlers, the *Californios*. This brought about an increase in the local cattle herds, the hides and tallow from which provided the basis for a growing trade with foreign sailors visiting the Bay, especially the Yankee traders from Boston.

In 1835 Englishman W. A. Richardson established a trading-post at the sheltered Yerba Buena Cove, a convenient anchorage for incoming ocean vessels, around which gradually arose a small village, inhabited largely by a small but growing contingent of Americans and other foreigners. A local Swiss resident, Jean Jacques Vioget, surveyed the site of Yerba Buena in 1839 and platted a 12-block grid of streets and building lots, centered on the *plaza* (later Portsmouth Square). Although this early grid was not to be filled up for some time, the village did proceed gradually to expand during the early 1840s. A Hudson's Bay Company trading-post prospered, despite occasional restrictions against foreign commerce imposed by the Mexican authorities. The population of Yerba Buena village increased steadily to several hundred by the mid-1840s, less than half of it Mexican, already dominated by Anglo-Saxon men of commerce.[4]

Increasing conflicts between the Mexican government and the growing population of American settlers in Northern California, which outnumbered the Californios by the mid-1840s, led to open rebellion in the "Bear Flag Revolt" of 1846. The village of Yerba Buena, left virtually undefended, was quickly taken by American forces. Local authorities changed the name of Yerba Buena to San Francisco in early 1847; by taking advantage of the widely known San Francisco Bay, the town leaders intended to gain

---

[3]See Oscar Lewis, *San Francisco: Mission to Metropolis* (Berkeley: Howell-North Books, 1966), pp. 1-19.

[4]Jean Vance, "The Cities by San Francisco Bay," in John S. Adams (ed.), *Contemporary Metropolitan America*, vol. 1 (Cambridge, Mass.: Ballinger, 1976), pp. 222-224.

name recognition and supersede such rivals as Francesca (later Benicia) on the Carquinez Straits, at the northeastern edge of the Bay.[5]

Another enduring legacy of this period of settlement initiation came in 1847 through the appointment of a town surveyor, Jasper O'Farrell, who revised and extended the Vioget survey of 1839. O'Farrell pushed the original street grid westward, added a new grid to the south along the lines of the trail to the mission, and marked off hundreds of "water lots" of land exposed at low tide on Yerba Buena Cove; in all, O'Farrell increased the town plan by some 800 acres. Although this area was not all occupied at first, it provided an essential physical framework within which to expand during the period of rapid growth accompanying the California Gold Rush. The "water lots" were soon filled in as the town expanded through landfill into Yerba Buena Cove, and Market Street became an uneasy junction of two oblique street-grid systems.[6]

The early settlers of newly christened San Francisco clearly had great expectations for the site, despite its obvious shortcomings. The incipient settlement occupied the tip of a peninsula isolated topographically from ready land transport, surrounded by hills and sand dunes, limited by little level ground near the harbor, lacking in supplies of fresh water and timber, and chastened by a harsher climate than that of other parts of the Bay Area. The Carquinez Straits area of the North Bay and the "Contra Costa" shore of the East Bay had milder weather, more level land, and timber resources. But San Francisco had gained an initial advantage in town development which became self-reinforcing: in addition to the added recognition gained by the name change, there was already a history of commerce at Yerba Buena, prompting U.S. government patronage in the location of the customs house, the quartermaster's store, and troops quarters at the site.

Most important of all, there turned out to be a functional logic to the development of San Francisco's during the Gold Rush. In an era of water transportation, Yerba Buena Cove was the most logical intersection of ocean and river traffic in the Bay Area. The Sacramento and San Joaquin rivers, both emptying into the Bay, served as the best routes of access to the "diggings" in both the northern and southern mines; since these inland waterways were navigable only by boats of relatively shallow draft, ocean-going ships at some point had to reload their cargoes onto smaller vessels like river steamers. Rather than attempt to navigate across the occasionally shallow San Francisco Bay, in

---

[5]*Ibid.*, p. 224.

[6]*Ibid.*

which specialized local knowledge was necessary, clipper-ship captains preferred to drop anchor at the first sheltered port.[7] San Francisco thus grew up as the principal point of transshipment for the massive influx of people and goods sparked by the discovery of gold in 1848. As both a labor depot and a supply center for the mining fields, San Francisco experienced a rate of growth that amazed observers. The sleepy village of about 1,000 people in 1848, when gold was discovered, grew to encompass a teeming polyglot population of between 20,000 and 25,000 by 1850, the year San Francisco was incorporated as an American city.[8]

FOREIGN IMMIGRANTS AMONG THE "FORTY-NINERS"

The port provided the lifeblood of this boom town. Yerba Buena Cove took on the appearance of a forest of masts as ships crowded the shore, many simply abandoned as their crews took off for the goldfields. Before the opening of the transcontinental railroad in 1869, over three-fourths of the people arriving in San Francisco came by sea, often via the Central American isthmus of Panama.[9] Initially cut off from the American East Coast by a treacherous overland journey, and tied to the outside world by Pacific Ocean maritime routes, it is not surprising that San Francisco attracted large numbers of foreign immigrants among the original "forty-niners." Early on in the Gold Rush, immigrants poured into the city from countries around the Pacific Basin, especially from China, Latin America, and Australia.

The Chinese came with much the same motivation as other fortune-seekers: to make enough money to return home wealthy. These early Chinese immigrants tended to be male Cantonese peasants from Kwantung Province in southern China, where the ravages of civil strife, population pressure, and overfarming had created an untenable situation in the rural villages. America was called *gum shan*, the "golden mountain," while the Chinese called themselves *gum shan hok*, "guests of the golden mountain."[10] Once in California, most of the Chinese went to the goldfields, but San Francisco

---

[7]James E. Vance, Jr., *Geography and Urban Evolution in the San Francisco Bay Area* (Berkeley: University of California Institute of Governmental Studies, 1964), p. 10.

[8]Charles Lockwood, *Suddenly San Francisco: The Early Years of an Instant City* (San Francisco: A California Living Book, 1978), p. 164.

[9]R. A. Burchell, *The San Francisco Irish, 1848-1880* (Manchester University Press, 1979), pp. 35-36; and J. S. Holliday *The World Rushed In: The California Gold Rush Experience* (New York: Simon and Schuster, 1981), p. 51.

[10]Willard T. Chow, *The Re-emergence of an Inner City: The Pivot of Chinese Settlement in the East Bay Region of the San Francisco Bay Area* (San Francisco: R and E Research Associates, 1977), p. 20.

remained the most important center for supply, transport, and services. In 1851, some 3,000 Chinese could already be found in the city.[11]

Thousands of Latin Americans also descended upon San Francisco, largely from Chile and Peru, as well as from Sonora and northern Mexico, bringing with them relatively advanced mining techniques to use in the "diggings." Because of the shortage of women among the early immigrants, women were recruited in South America to serve in brothels, and early in the Gold Rush the ramshackle "Little Chile" (*Chilecito*), or "Chile Town," at the base of Telegraph Hill near the waterfront, had a virtual monopoly on prostitution, although harlots from Europe, especially France, and the East Coast soon made their presence known. The state census of 1852 found about 1100 Chileans living in San Francisco, not including the probably even larger number residing in the ships anchored in Yerba Buena Cove.[12]

Chile Town was a favorite target for the violent outbursts of roving bands of Australian thugs known as the "Sydney Ducks," rough-and-tumble characters from the British penal colony who tended to congregate nearby on the waterfront in what was known as "Sydney Town." The destructive excesses of the Sydney Ducks ultimately inspired San Francisco's famous vigilante mob justice. But the development of the city's notorious vice district in this part of town could not be restrained, for the influx of male fortune-seekers during the gold rush had generated a severe gender imbalance. In 1853, men outnumbered women by about five to one in San Francisco.[13]

In-migrants of whatever nationality during the Gold Rush—that is, roughly between 1848 and the mid-1850s—were mostly young men. Usually they intended to make a quick fortune and return home to their families as soon as possible.[14] This naturally encouraged the development of vice operations catering to transient males—prostitution, gambling, saloons, dance halls, and so forth—whence came San Francisco's enduring reputation as "sin city." From the 1860s up to World War I, these

---

[11]Lockwood, *Suddenly San Francisco*, p. 164.

[12]Carlos U. Lopez, "Chilenos in California: A study of the 1850, 1852, and 1860 censuses" (San Francisco: R and E Research Associates, 1973), p. xii.

[13]Lockwood, *Suddenly San Francisco*, p. 165.

[14]See the case of William Swain, used as the prototype in Holliday's *The World Rushed In* (New York: Simon and Schuster, 1981.)

vice activities proliferated in the "Barbary Coast," the area around Pacific Street (south of Telegraph Hill) near the waterfront.[15]

In addition to the Chinese, Latin American, and Australian immigrants from around the Pacific rim, Europeans also entered San Francisco in force, especially since the discovery of gold in 1848 coincided with general European political upheaval and economic depression. The French government actively encouraged emigration, and by 1853 nearly 30,000 immigrants from France could be found in California.[16] The crop failures of 1846 and the Revolution of 1848 caused many Germans to emigrate to California. The potato famine of the late 1840s in Ireland sparked a massive diaspora from the Emerald Isle; by 1852, there were already 4,200 Irish in San Francisco.[17]

Some idea of the heterogeneity of San Francisco's resident population during the Gold Rush may be obtained by breaking down the school enrollment figures by nativity. Of the 5,273 students enrolled in San Francisco in 1858, only about 1,000 (19 percent) claimed California as their birthplace. Approximately 3,000 (56.9 percent) emanated from 26 other U.S. states and territories. Of the 1,273 foreign-born pupils (24.1 percent), 517 (9.8 percent of the total enrollment) came from some part of either the British Isles or the British Empire, 273 (5.1 percent) from continental Europe, and 134 (2.5 percent) from Latin America.[18]

San Francisco's Gold Rush origins help to account for the city's long-standing role as a port of entry for immigrants to California. In 1860, a full 50 percent of the city's population was foreign-born; although figures tended to decline thereafter, since the middle of the twentieth century the foreign-born proportion of the city's population has been on the rebound, rising steadily from less than 20 percent in 1950 to more than 28 percent in 1980. The foreign-born population, of course, is only part of the immigrant story: the American-born offspring, while generally somewhat more acculturated, still have tended to maintain an ethnic identity within American society. San Francisco's combined first- and second-generation total fell from a whopping 75 percent of the city's population in 1900 to about 57 percent in 1930—still a majority—well into the twentieth century. In 1970, 44.3 percent of San Francisco's population were still either foreign-born or immigrant offspring (see Table 3).

---

[15]See Herbert Asbury's classic, *The Barbary Coast: An Informal History of the San Francisco Underworld* (Garden City, N.Y.: Garden City Pub. Co., 1933), pp. 49-50.

[16]John A. Lawrence, *Behind the Palaces: The Working Class and the Labor Movement in San Francisco, 1877-1901* (Ph.D. diss., Dept. of History, University of California, Berkeley, 1979), pp. 7-8.

[17]Burchell, *The S.F. Irish*, pp. 3-4.

[18]From figures found in William Laird MacGregor's *San Francisco in 1876* (Edinburgh: Thomas Laurie, 1876), p. 26.

TABLE 3

The Foreign-born and Foreign-stock Populations of San Francisco, 1860-1980

Year	Total S.F. Population	Percentage Foreign-Born	Percentage Foreign-Stock
1860	56,802	50.1%	--
1870	149,473	49.3	--
1880	233,959	44.6	--
1890	298,997	42.4	69.8%
1900	342,782	34.1	70.5
1910	416,912	34.1*	68.3*
1920	506,676	29.4*	63.7*
1930	634,394	27.1	56.7*
1940	634,536	22.1	49.8*
1950	775,357	15.5*	40.3*
1960	740,316	19.2	43.5
1970	715,674	21.6	44.3
1980	678,974	28.3	--

*Whites only.

Source: U.S. Census, various years.

FUNCTIONAL SPECIALIZATION AND SOCIAL SORTING

In addition to the city's role as a port of entry for immigrants to the United States, a number of other enduring characteristics of San Francisco life can be traced to the California Gold Rush. San Francisco's American population tended to be from New England and the mid-Atlantic states—especially the merchants, about half of whom came from either Boston or New York.[19] These men of commerce soon founded a Merchants' Exchange, a Marine Exchange, and a Stock Exchange, along with numerous banks and other financial institutions. By the mid-1860s a true financial district had emerged in San Francisco around Montgomery and California streets, heavily involved in the mining enterprises, particularly hydraulic gold mining in the Mother Lode and silver strikes in Nevada's Comstock Lode.

As the principal urban center on the rapidly developing Pacific Coast, San Francisco benefited from economic activities throughout the far-flung region: mining, agricultural, fishing, and timber interests operated out of San Francisco, adding commercial functions, people, and physical structures to the "headquarters city." By 1880, San Francisco handled 99 percent of all imported merchandise and 83 percent of all exports from the three Pacific Coast states; the city even produced 60 percent of all the manufactured goods in the region. The 1880 U.S. Census described San Francisco as "the commercial metropolis of the Pacific Coast."[20]

In addition to the financial district, wholesale and retail districts quickly came into being. Perishable wholesale goods initially tended to be stored close to the wharves that stuck out into the shrinking Yerba Buena Cove, where a produce market was set up on landfill. Wholesale merchants selling imperishable goods gravitated south of Market Street by the 1870s, where the city's diverse industries also grew up, especially metal works and agricultural refineries. A retail district also developed in San Francisco early on: originally focused on the area around Portsmouth Square, the retail trade tended to move gradually southwestward through the areas north of Market Street until it became fixed near Union Square. By the late 1800s San Francisco's central business district had already been subdivided into distinct financial, wholesaling, and retailing areas.[21] In

---

[19]Peter Decker, *Fortunes and Failures: White-Collar Mobility in Nineteenth Century San Francisco* (Cambridge, Mass.: Harvard University Press, 1978).

[20]U.S. Census Bureau, *Social Statistics of Cities,* Part 2 (Washington, D.C.: Government Printing Office, 1887), p. 803.

[21]See Martyn J. Bowden, *The Dynamics of City Growth: An Historical Geography of the San Francisco Central District, 1850-1931* (Ph.D. diss., Dept. of Geography, University of California, Berkeley, 1967).

short, the period of rapid growth prompted by the Gold Rush provided San Francisco, virtually overnight, with the functional diversification of a cosmopolitan urban center. Different areas of the city became associated with distinctive land uses, some of which have endured since the late nineteenth century.

Along with the economic specialization in distinct functional districts, the city gradually became internally differentiated in social terms. The diverse communities of the Gold Rush city had been somewhat fluid and not yet clearly demarcated spatially; for the most part, early San Francisco lacked exclusive ethnic areas or ghettos. It is true that the Chinese were quickly relegated to their own sections, and a "Latin Quarter" for diverse Catholic groups developed in North Beach. But ethnic groups tended to be quite interspersed with one another early on. The Mexican imprint had been quickly eclipsed, and the growing settlement was raw and fresh. It repeatedly burned down in the early years, being quickly rebuilt each time. There were no long-established neighborhoods to take over, few long-standing ethnic turfs for new groups to contend with. The speed with which urban growth occurred permitted no time for definitive subcultural sorting, especially since the general shortage of women and the lack of family life created a temporary, transient air in the Gold Rush town.

The development of San Francisco's intricate social geography was tied to the increased sorting of residential areas by class and ethnicity during the late nineteenth century. As the instant city of the Gold Rush evolved into a true metropolis, housing was built outside of the central business district to accommodate the city's burgeoning population. In 1870 San Francisco's population reached nearly 150,000 and the city was growing westward past Van Ness Avenue into the Western Addition and southwestward into the Mission District. The population passed a quarter of a million by 1880, when San Francisco became the ninth largest city in the country—and the only one located in the West among the top 50 U.S. cities. At the turn of the century San Francisco's population reached 342,782 and housing development on the urban periphery reached the western and southern extremes of the city, though still leaving significant gaps to be filled in during the twentieth century (see Map 2).

Residential development began to scale San Francisco's famous hills with the invention of the cable car by Andrew Hallidie in 1873. The importance of terrain as a basis for differentiating areas of the city should not be underestimated: the sheer physical landscape created the basis for distinct neighborhood identities. Coupled with settlement by highly diverse groups of people and the functional specialization of an urban economy, a quite variegated cultural landscape emerged in San Francisco by the late nineteenth century. Just as economic activities quickly became centered on certain functional districts downtown, residential areas tended to become specialized in social

MAP 2.
THE GROWTH OF SAN FRANCISCO
Patterns of Street and Property Development

1853

1870

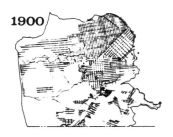

1900

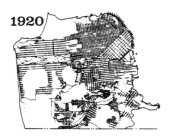

1920

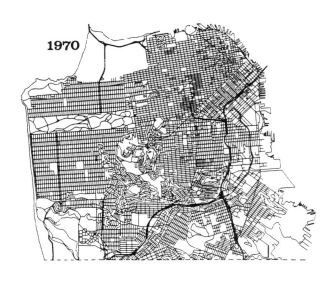

1970

Prepared by the San Francisco Department of City Planning
73-871P

terms. In other words, neighborhoods were socially sorted. Most people had lived near their place of employment in the Yerba Buena village environment, but with urban expansion businesses increasingly displaced housing in the central districts, and the development of early forms of public transportation allowed for greater separation of workplace and residence, especially for the middle and upper classes.

The first elite areas developed south of Market Street, around South Park and on Rincon Hill, where high-class residences were built from the early 1850s. Before long the surrounding area was given over to industry and warehouses, however, and the district lost its residential appeal; the development of cable-car lines permitted the rich to scale Nob Hill, and by the 1870s South Park was being abandoned by the well-to-do. The ostentatious mansions of Nob Hill were destroyed in the 1906 earthquake and fire and were replaced by luxury hotels and Edwardian apartments. As the city expanded in the late nineteenth century, the upper classes consistently tended to occupy the higher grounds on the northern shores, such as Russian Hill and Pacific Heights, where terrain provided relatively inaccessible sites and scenic views of the Bay. Only Telegraph Hill, closest to the docks, remained a working-class hill in this sector of San Francisco.

The middle classes also gravitated away from the city center as San Francisco grew, especially into the areas west of the central business district, surrounding the exclusive hills.[22] Served by horse-drawn omnibuses, streetcars, and cable cars, the middle classes expanded steadily westward in the late nineteenth century, into such areas as lower Russian Hill, Polk Gulch, the Western Addition, and the Haight-Ashbury. The twentieth century witnessed a continuation of the same basic trajectory: the middle classes moved into such areas as the Richmond, West-of-Twin-Peaks, and Sunset districts.

The working-class population clustered closer to the central business district, particularly in the area south of Market Street. San Francisco's first major industrial plant, the Union Iron Works, was established there in the 1850s; originally largely swampland along Mission Bay, the South-of-Market area was filled and reclaimed as foundries, rice and flour mills, refineries, tanneries, sawmills, and railroad yards located there. By the 1870s, it had become a major working-class district, housing a large part of the city's common laborers in both small worker cottages and residential hotels. After the earthquake and fire, which devastated the area, it was rebuilt with fewer detached worker cottages and more blue-collar workshops, high-density flats, and cheap

---

[22]Roger W. Lotchin, *San Francisco, 1846-1856: From Hamlet to City* (New York: Oxford University Press, 1974), pp. 23-24.

hotels. Although somewhat different in residential character, the rebuilt South-of-Market District persisted as a point of entry for newly-arrived immigrants in San Francisco, particularly for unattached male workers. Many of the city's ethnic groups began there, tending to move on to other neighborhoods in time.[23]

Ethnic identities tended to correspond with working-class status, while social mobility meant increased integration into the Anglo-American cultural mainstream. The upper classes at first were largely of English descent, as attested by the long-standing social prestige of the Episcopal Church; thus English immigrants tended to assimilate rapidly and, despite their numbers, never developed characteristic ethnic neighborhoods. As selected Germans, Irish, and others moved up in social status, they very often left their ethnic neighborhoods behind with the cultural trappings of their ethnicity. In a city whose population consisted largely of foreign immigrants and their offspring, class stratification and ethnic identification were coupled as twin forces behind the process of neighborhood differentiation. Ethnic neighborhoods thus tended to be located in working-class districts. Not surprisingly, groups with the most persistent ethnic identities, such as the Chinese, were also the most oppressed and segregated; when ethnic groups were able to improve their lot, they tended to be more mobile in both social and spatial terms.

As San Francisco expanded during the late nineteenth and early twentieth centuries, European immigrant stock tended to move in several directions: first northward, into North Beach and onto Telegraph Hill; then both into the Western Addition, west of Van Ness Avenue, and in a southwesterly direction from the South-of-Market area into the Mission District and adjacent valleys (Noe and Eureka) and hills (Potrero and Bernal), and later southwestward into the Outer Mission and Excelsior districts. This southerly migration of more acculturated white ethnics continued into Daly City (named after John Daly, owner of a dairy farm in that area), which was subdivided and developed into a working-class suburb on San Francisco's southwestern fringe after the earthquake and fire.

Between roughly the 1860s and World War I, the relatively fluid and mobile communities of the instant city were replaced by an orderly series of socially sorted neighborhoods in San Francisco. During the relatively short time-span of half a century, an amorphous frontier settlement had been replaced by an internally

---

[23]See Alvin Averbach, "San Francisco's South of Market District, 1858-1958: The emergence of a skid row," *California Historical Quarterly* Vol. 52 (Fall 1973): 196-223.

differentiated metropolis. Ethnic and nonconformist communities tended to develop in specific working-class districts of the city, reflecting the close relationship between urban morphogenesis and subcultural intensification.

RACIAL MINORITIES

Isolated as cultural outsiders in Chinatown, the Chinese probably constituted the most distinctive of San Francisco's major ethnic communities. Despite their segregation, the Chinese served as an important source of cheap labor in local manufacturing and services. In fact, the Chinese were widely employed throughout the American West in railroad construction, mining, and agriculture until the increasingly open hostility and even violence against them forced a retreat from the countryside and an increasing concentration in big cities during the late 1800s.[24]

The rise in popular agitation against the Chinese during the 1870s, fed by resentful white workers who regarded them as unfair competition (especially during the not infrequent periods of economic depression), intensified the urbanization of California's Chinese population. Passage of the Chinese Exclusion Act in 1882 prohibited the further entry of "laborers" from China, in effect halting the massive immigration of Cantonese peasants. A federal court ruling in 1884 forbade wives of Chinese laborers from entering the U.S., while anti-miscegenation laws prevented the Chinese from intermarrying with whites. Thus, a "bachelor society" was perpetuated during the late nineteenth century, concentrated in a few large Chinatowns.[25]

By 1890, San Francisco had 25,833 Chinese residents, more than a third of all those in the state and making up almost 9 percent of the city's total population (see Table 4). For nearly a century, the bulk of San Francisco's Chinese were confined to Chinatown, an area roughly bounded by California Street on the south, Powell Street on the west, Pacific Street on the north, and Kearny Street on the east. A number of French brothels could be found here early in the Gold Rush, but the area quickly gave way to the incoming Chinese settlers; by the mid-1850s Chinese had established themselves in the Chinatown core, along Dupont Street (later Grant Avenue), which was close to the wharves on Yerba Buena Cove and centrally located within the city. Not speaking

---

[24] Chow, *Re-emergence*, p. 37.

[25] Victor G. Nee and Brett de Bary Nee, *Longtime Californ': A Documentary Study of an American Chinatown* (New York: Pantheon Books, 1972), pp. 30-57.

TABLE 4

The Population of San Francisco by Race and Ethnicity, 1870-1940

Year	White		Chinese		Japanese		Black		Other	
1870	136,059	91.0%	11,728	7.8%	302	0.2%	1,330	0.8%	54	0.0%
1880	210,496	90.0	21,213	9.1	65	0.0	1,628	0.7	557	0.3
1890	270,696	90.5	25,833	8.6	590	0.2	1,847	0.6	31	0.0
1900	325,378	94.9	13,954	4.1	1,781	0.5	1,654	0.4	15	0.0
1910	400,014	95.9	10,582	2.5	4,518	1.1	1,642	0.4	156	0.0
1920	490,022	96.7	7,744	1.5	5,358	1.0	2,414	0.4	1,138	0.2
1930	620,891	95.0	16,303	2.6	6,250	1.0	3,803	0.6	5,147	0.8
1940	602,701	95.0	17,782	2.8	5,280	0.8	4,846	0.8	3,927	0.6

Source: U.S. Census, various years.

English or understanding American ways, the Chinese had good reason to congregate in Chinatown, particularly as hostility toward them rose.[26]

By the 1880s, Chinatown had emerged as a tightly bound, insular, ethnic community, in which men outnumbered women by about 20 to 1. A segregated school was established in Chinatown in 1885, but family life was comparatively rare in the quarter, given that Chinese men continued to outnumber women by such a large margin—in 1910, still nearly 7 to 1.[27] This gender imbalance encouraged the proliferation of vice operations catering to single men, as in the adjacent Barbary Coast, featuring prostitution, gambling, and opium dens instead of saloons.

Life in Chinatown was structured around a complicated series of associations, based upon surname, region of origin, and linguistic dialect; a confederation of the more important organizations, known as the Six Companies, dominated the community politically. With its own distinctive customs, institutions, and social-control mechanisms, Chinatown came to be a ghetto in almost the true medieval sense of the word: it was virtually a city within a city, an exotic district for the most part immune from outside authority.

The Chinese were unable to live outside of Chinatown, and whites were wary of the area, widely regarding it as dangerous and dirty. This popular perception was reinforced by episodic reports of bubonic plague in Chinatown, which became a basis for factional disputes in city politics; some initially feared that open investigation of the problem would lead to a quarantine and hurt the city's business interests.[28] In March of 1900 Mayor James D. Phelan did declare a quarantine on Chinatown because of a disputed case of bubonic plague: "Police were instructed to keep the Chinese in Chinatown, and to bar out the whites."[29] Although Phelan later advised the public that "our Chinatown has been thoroughly inspected and disinfected," the *Chronicle* accused the mayor and "his paltry politicians in the Board of Health" of inventing the scare in "further efforts to break into the treasury."[30]

---

[26]Connie Young Yu, "A history of San Francisco Chinatown housing," *Amerasia Journal*, 8 (Spring/Summer 1981): 95.

[27]U.S. Census Bureau, *Thirteenth Census of the United States, 1910. Statistics for California* (Washington D.C.: Government Printing Office, 1914), p. 593.

[28]See Oscar Lewis, *San Francisco*, pp. 203-206.

[29]"Put a blockade on the Chinese quarter," *San Francisco Chronicle*, March 7, 1900, p. 1.

[30]"Phelan fears his specter: Seeks to offset plague scare with a telegram," *San Francisco Chronicle*, March 27, 1900, p. 1.

Chinatown was leveled in 1906, along with most of the city's core, and serious plans were advanced by local reconstruction committees to relocate the Chinese community away from San Francisco's central district; but in the end Chinatown was too lucrative to be abandoned.[31] The boundaries of Chinatown remained stable, except for a southerly expansion along Grant Avenue to Bush Street, where a steady tourist trade was developing. The Chinese population of San Francisco decreased to less than 10,000 after World War I, albeit with a more equalized male-female ratio. Immigration restrictions remained in place, but an increasing birthrate gradually raised the Chinese population during the 1920s and 1930s (see Table 4).

The Japanese began to immigrate to California in significant numbers in the late 1880s. This was due both to the legalization in Japan of worker emigration in 1885, and to the continuing demand in California for Asian labor—considered to be industrious, uncomplaining, and cheap—after Chinese immigration had been effectively halted.[32] Since San Francisco was the port of entry for most Japanese immigrants to California, the city naturally developed one of the state's larger communities. Compared with the Chinese, however, the Japanese were never very numerous in San Francisco. In 1910, Japanese residents amounted to just over 1 percent of the city's population, as shown in Table 4. The mere presence of this relatively small Japanese population nevertheless provoked an outburst of racism in the early 1900s reminiscent of the anti-Chinese agitation of the late 1870s. The city's union leaders helped form the Asiatic Exclusion League in 1905 to lobby against Japanese immigration and press for school segregation. Giving in to League pressure, the San Francisco school board announced in 1906 that Japanese children henceforth would have to attend the segregated school in Chinatown. This local action prompted an international crisis with Japan, then emerging on the world scene as the recent victor in a war with Russia. President Theodore Roosevelt convened the school board in Washington, D.C., where he persuaded it to rescind the segregation order in return for initiating bilateral negotiations aimed at limiting Japanese immigration to the U.S.—ultimately obtained through the "Gentlemen's Agreement" of 1907-08. After the Japanese school-segregation order was rescinded in San Francisco, Asian groups began to experience a gradual relaxation of segregative pressures.[33]

---

[31]Yu, "Chinatown housing," p. 100.

[32]Harry H. L. Kitano, *Japanese Americans: The Evolution of a Subculture* (Englewood Cliffs, N. J.: Prentice-Hall, 1969).

[33]Robert W. Cherny and William Issel, *San Francisco: Presidio, Port and Metropolis* (San Francisco: Boyd and Fraser, 1981), pp. 43-44.

From Instant City to Metropolis 71

During the late nineteenth century San Francisco's Japanese had clustered on Rincon Hill, near South Park in the South-of-Market area, in mansions abandoned by the upper classes after the 1870s, as well as alongside the Chinese in Chinatown.[34] After the conflagration of 1906, the Japanese began moving out to the northeastern corner of the Western Addition, around the intersection of Post and Laguna streets, where they established Japan Town, or *Nihon Machi*, also known as Little Osaka, which thereafter became the city's principal Japanese neighborhood.

Other races remained relatively small in numbers before World War II. Blacks were the most notable of the non-Asian minorities, having constituted a small group in San Francisco since the Gold Rush: the 1860 census showed 1,176 "free colored" (503 black and 673 mulatto) residents in San Francisco, just 2 percent of the total population. The numbers remained fairly constant, but the percentages dipped in succeeding decades (see Table 4). As with Asian groups, racial barriers confronting blacks were strong in San Francisco. Blacks were allowed to join trade unions only after the turn of the century, and even then the unions were not pressed to permit them entry. Blacks tended to work as domestic servants and as railroad and steamship employees before World War II. Recent research has illuminated the lives of these black "pioneer urbanites," who formed a relatively small but surprisingly heterogeneous group in San Francisco long before the creation of black ghettos during the 1940s.[35]

During the late 1800s, blacks were scattered throughout the downtown areas, as indicated by the dispersal of the "colored" churches listed in the city directories of the period. After about the turn of the century, probably largely as a result of the disruptive earthquake and fire, blacks began moving into the Western Addition. By the 1920s many black families were clustered around Ellis and Scott streets, in the northwest corner of the district.[36] In 1940 the Works Projects Administration described this incipient black community in these terms:

---

[34]Writer's Program of the Works Projects Administration in Northern California, *San Francisco: The Bay and Its Cities* (New York: Hastings House, 1940), p. 272; and Averbach, "S.F.'s South of Market," pp. 202-204.

[35]Douglas H. Daniels, *Pioneer Urbanites: A Social and Cultural History of Black San Francisco* (Philadelphia: Temple University Press, 1980).

[36]Jerry Flamm, *Good Life in Hard Times: San Francisco's '20s and '30s* (San Francisco: Chronicle Books, 1978), p. 72.

The greater number of San Francisco's 7,000 Negroes live in the neighborhood west of Fillmore between Geary and Pine streets. Among them are representatives of every State in the Union, of Jamaica, Cuba, Panama, and South American countries. Of those from the South, the greater number are Texans who arrived after the World War; these still celebrate "Juneteenth," Emancipation Day for the Texas Negroes, who did not learn of the Emancipation Proclamation until June 19, 1863. The colony's social life revolves around it handful of bars and restaurants, its one large and noisy nightclub, its eight churches of varying faiths, and the Booker T. Washington Community Center on Divisadero Street, where trained social workers guide educational and recreational activities for children and adults. Occasionally, in churches and clubs, are heard old Negro folksongs surviving the days of slavery.[37]

According to 1940 U.S. Census statistics, about two-thirds of San Francisco's 4,860 blacks resided in the Western Addition, but they still constituted only a very small percentage of the population in that part of town and less than 1 percent of the city's total population. Although relatively small, and not rapidly growing, this nascent black concentration in the Western Addition was an essential predisposing factor in the area's massive racial turnover during the 1940s and 1950s.

EUROPEAN IMMIGRANT GROUPS

European immigrants and their offspring were more mobile in both social and spatial terms than nonwhite ethnic groups in San Francisco, but they still tended to cluster in working-class sections of the city. White residents of immigrant stock were certainly not as strikingly ethnic as the Chinese, being more readily acculturated, but ethnic ties still provided essential community supports: jobs, housing, religion, and a social life. European immigrants sought out associates of a similar ethnic background; their activities and occupations followed certain rather predictable ethnic patterns.

The reservoir of ethnicity in San Francisco based on European immigrant stock was large. In 1870, nearly half of the city's population was foreign born, and four-fifths of all residents had parents born abroad; by 1900, still over a third of the city's residents had been born abroad themselves, and three-fourths were of foreign parentage. The Chinese may have been the most segregated, but they were not the largest of the immigrant groups: the Irish and Germans were the more sizable ethnic communities

---

[37]Writer's Program, *San Francisco,* p. 285.

throughout the late nineteeth century, together accounting for nearly half of the city's first- and second-generation groups by the turn of the century (see Tables 5 and 6).

The Irish immigrated to America in the hundreds of thousands during the potato blight and economic depression of the late 1840s and 1850s. This began a massive emigration from Ireland, in which the Emerald Isle ultimately sent a greater proportion of its population to the United States than did any other country. In the abrupt transition from a traditional rural society to an expansive urban industrial society, Irish immigrants were thrust into teeming cities where ethnic ties took on great importance.[38] The potato famine and exodus from Ireland coincided with the California Gold Rush, and Irish immigrants proceeded to become San Francisco's most important nineteenth-century ethnic group. In 1870, first-generation Irish constituted over 35 percent of all those born abroad and about 13 percent of San Francisco's total population; among laborers, including all types of wage earners, Irish immigrants composed over 21 percent of the work force.[39] By 1880, there were over 30,000 first-generation and at least 43,000 second-generation Irish in San Francisco, meaning that about one-third of the total population was of Irish stock.[40] By 1900, over a quarter of the city's population was still of Irish descent.[41]

Although a number of Irish struck it rich in the Gold Rush, such as James Flood, the vast majority were working-class. The Irish entered near the bottom of the social pyramid, and their gradual ascent served as something of a model for other immigrant groups. Initially, Irish men often worked as laborers and in the construction trades, while the women frequently were domestic servants. Both the plumber's union and the carpenter's union came to be controlled by the Irish, who tended to restrict membership to family and friends. The Irish valued loyalty to their kind, and they put ethnic bonds to good use in gaining upward social mobility. Through their growing political influence, the Irish became predominant in public employment, working as city streetcar drivers, civil service bureaucrats, policemen, firemen, schoolteachers, and so on.

In addition to being the city's largest nineteenth-century ethnic group, the Irish were clearly the most highly politicized as well. Lacking a long-standing Anglo-

---

[38]KPFA, Padraigin McGillicuddy, "From the Mission to Marin: The Irish in San Francisco," radio documentary, May 17, 1983.

[39]Lawrence, *Behind the Palaces,* p. 10.

[40]Burchell, *The S.F. Irish,* pp. 3-4.

[41]KPFA, McGillicuddy, "From the Mission to Marin."

TABLE 5

San Francisco's Foreign-born Population, by Selected Countries of Origin, 1860-1970

Year	Germany		Great Britain		Ireland		Italy		Scandinavia		Other Countries	
1860	6,346	22.3%	3,071	10.8%	9,363	32.9%	No Data		No Data		9,674	34.0%
1870	13,602	18.4	7,134	9.7	25,864	35.1	1,621	2.2%	1,763	2.4%	23,735	32.2
1880	19,928	19.1	10,152	9.6	30,721	29.5	2,491	2.4	3,520	3.4	37,532	36.0
1890	26,422	20.8	13,366	10.5	30,718	24.2	5,212	4.1	6,775	5.3	44,318	34.9
1900	35,194	30.1	12,342	10.5	15,963	13.6	7,508	6.4	9,591	8.2	36,287	31.0
1910	24,137	18.4	13,483	10.3	23,151	17.7	16,981	12.9	13,856	10.6	39,329*	30.1*
1920	18,513	13.2	14,121	10.1	18,257	13.0	23,924	17.1	12,978	9.2	52,407*	37.3*
1930	18,608	12.1	15,696	10.2	16,598	10.8	27,311	17.8	15,016	9.8	78,412*	45.6*
1940	14,977	11.5	11,763	9.0	12,049	9.2	24,036	18.4	10,989	8.4	66,209*	47.2*
1950	12,394	10.3	9,464	7.9	9,014	7.5	20,051	16.6	8,472	7.0	60,998*	50.6*
1960	No Data		No Data		No Data		No Data		No Data		No Data	
1970	8,041	5.2	5,419	3.5	4,808	3.1	9,746	6.3	3,040	2.0	123,453	79.9

Note: Great Britain includes England, Scotland, and Wales; Ireland encompasses both Eire and Northern Ireland after partition; and Scandinavia includes Denmark, Norway, and Sweden.

*Foreign-born whites only.

Source: U.S. Census, various years.

TABLE 6

San Francisco's Population of Foreign Parentage, by Selected Nationalities, 1910-1970

Year	German		British		Irish		Italian		Scandinavian		Others	
1910	59,401	20.8%	28,644	10.1%	66,784	23.4%	29,081	10.2%	20,602	7.2%	80,143**	28.1%**
1920	53,924	16.7	32,928	10.2	63,299	19.6	45,599	14.1	23,082	7.1	104,011**	32.2**
1930	55,316	15.4	48,361	13.4	49,747	13.8	58,021	16.1	30,505	8.5	117,721**	32.7**
1940	42,537	13.5	31,023	9.8	43,529	13.7	56,096	17.7	25,649	8.1	117,137**	37.0**
1950	36,639	11.7	26,194	8.4	36,019	11.5	53,011	16.9	23,957	7.6	136,783**	43.7**
1960	29,073	9.0	22,108*	6.9*	22,948*	7.1*	41,089	12.7	17,451	5.4	189,133	58.7
1970	19,610	6.2	13,000	4.1	17,855	5.6	29,040	9.1	10,574	3.3	238,666	75.2

Note: The population of foreign parentage includes all persons, whether born in the U.S. or abroad, who have one or both parents of foreign birth; also termed "foreign stock" in census reports, this category in effect includes foreign immigrants and their native-born offspring. British stock includes English, Scotch, and Welsh; Irish are from both Eire and Northern Ireland since partition, except in 1960, when census data were aggregated for the United Kingdom as a whole; and Scandinavians are of Danish, Swedish, and Norwegian descent.

*Northern Irish were included as British in 1960. **White foreign stock only.

Source: U.S. Census, various years.

American political and social elite, as in Boston and New York, San Francisco offered greater opportunities for political involvement; and the Irish, entering the city early and in large numbers, had the added advantage of being English-speaking immigrants. They quickly learned how to operate politically. An Irish Catholic, Frank McCoppin, was elected mayor of San Francisco in 1867, long before such political acceptance would have been possible in eastern cities; the Irish "blind boss," Christopher A. Buckley, dominated San Francisco politics in the 1880s; the long list of Irish politicians in San Francisco stretches to the present.

San Francisco's anti-Chinese agitation, led by the Irish, ironically took the place of the anti-Irish agitation that dominated eastern cities. The hostility of the local Irish toward the Chinese was not simply a case of color prejudice, but was accentuated by the fear of being undercut by cheaper Chinese labor in competition for jobs. An Irish demagogue, Denis Kearney, led the anti-Chinese demonstrations of the Workingman's Party of California, which swept city elections in 1878 and 1879 with the slogan "The Chinese must go."[42] Even a social-activist Irish priest, Father Peter C. Yorke, who led a 1901 general strike, had a blind spot concerning the Chinese in his vision of social justice; his "Catholic universalism" apparently was overcome by his "Irish tribalism."[43]

Indeed, the Irish served as the backbone of the city's Catholic Church. Along with the local pub, the Church provided an essential institution for the Irish community. Although the English and French had been more influential in the early U.S. Catholic Church, by the time of the California Gold Rush the Irish were clearly predominant on the basis of the massive Hibernian immigration under way. The Irish so dominated the Church in the late nineteenth century that, as will be discussed later, special "national churches" were created for the other immigrant groups: rather than ministering to those residing in a specific parish, a national church served all those Catholics speaking a specific foreign language.

At the turn of the century, three-fourths of the Catholic clergy were Irish-born.[44] Anti-Catholic sentiment often denoted anti-Irish sentiment, and vice versa, in nineteenth-century San Francisco. But attacks on the Catholic Church, common in some other parts of the U.S., could not get far among the largely Catholic, immigrant population of San Francisco. Although local nativist-oriented organizations, such as the

---

[42]Cherny and Issel, *San Francisco,* pp. 31-32.

[43]KPFA, McGillicuddy, "From the Mission to Marin."

[44]James P. Walsh, *Ethnic Militancy: An Irish Catholic Prototype* (San Francisco: R and E Research Associates, 1972), 145 p.

American Protection Association of the 1890s, did form in the city, the religious strife commonplace in the East generally was muted in San Francisco.

While there were Irish living in all parts of San Francisco, they were most heavily concentrated in working-class neighborhoods south of Market Street. In 1880, 53 percent of the population of the Seventh Ward, located near the waterfront south of Market, was made up of first- or second-generation Irish, while over 49 percent of the Eleventh Ward, in the southerly Mission District, was Irish-American; on the other hand, only 10-20 percent of the population north of Market Street was Irish.[45] As San Francisco expanded in the late 1800s, the Irish and other European immigrants tended to move away from the waterfront and settle the burgeoning working-class neighborhoods in and around the Mission District.

The settlement patterns of San Francisco's Irish were reflected in the establishment of their Catholic churches, which tended to follow the street grid as it developed southwestward from the South-of-Market area into the Mission District. The Irish national church, St. Patrick's, was founded in 1851 at Market and New Montgomery streets; in 1872 it was moved to its present site at about Mission and Fourth streets, when the Palace Hotel was constructed on the original location. St. Ignatius Church was dedicated in 1855 on the south side of Market Street, between Fourth and Fifth streets (the site of the present-day Emporium Department Store), although it was later relocated in the Western Addition. In 1861, St. Joseph's Church was established on Howard Street, between Tenth and Eleventh streets (see Map 3).

Mission Dolores became a predominantly Irish church, and several new parishes were founded in the developing Mission District during the late nineteenth century: St. Peter's Church was dedicated in 1867, followed by St. Paul's in 1880, St. Charles in 1887, and St. James in 1888. The earthquake and fire served to further reinforce this flow of Irish into the Mission District, which became the most heavily Irish area of San Francisco. During the early twentieth century, the basic southwestward trajectory of Irish settlement was extended to adjacent neighborhoods: St. Phillip's Church was founded in Noe Valley in 1911, St. Kevin's in Bernal Heights in 1922, and St. Finn Barr's in Glen Park in 1926 (see Map 3).

About equal to the Irish in numbers during the late 1800s were San Franciscans of German immigrant stock. Unlike the Irish, however, who generally shared the Catholic religion and a common heritage, the Germans were split into Protestant, Catholic, and Jewish camps, and further fragmented by differences in linguistic dialects and regional

---

[45]Burchell, *The S. F. Irish,* pp. 47-49.

MAP 3. THE FOUNDING OF IRISH—CATHOLIC CHURCHES SOUTH OF MARKET STREET IN SAN FRANCISCO.

customs. Germans thus had less cultural cohesion and political power than did the Irish. Those German-Americans who did well in city politics—like Adolph Sutro, a German-born Jewish entrepreneur and philanthropist who was elected mayor in 1894—tended to do so more as outstanding individuals than as ethnic representatives. Yet the Germans, like the Irish, did form a great number of ethnically based organizations (often along religious lines), such as benevolent societies, social and fraternal groups, and trade unions. The city had eight German-language newspapers and periodicals in 1880, including daily morning and evening papers.[46] The Germans were also inclined to specialize in certain working-class professions: San Francisco's brewery workers, for example, are said to have been mainly German.

Like the Irish, Germans tended to settle in working-class neighborhoods of the city. They clustered initially in neighborhoods South of Market and around Union Square, but by the late nineteenth century were moving out of both these areas, flowing to the west into the Tenderloin District, Polk Gulch, and the Western Addition, and to the south into the Mission District. Lower Polk Street, south of California, was so heavily German in the early part of the century that it was commonly called "Polk Strasse." German neighborhoods differed somewhat according to their religious orientation. Since German Catholics often resided in neighborhoods with a large Irish presence, the establishment of national churches helped to maintain religion as an important ethnic force: the first German national church, St. Boniface, started downtown and moved to the Tenderloin during the late nineteenth century; the second German national church, St. Anthony's, was established during this period in the Mission District, which became a local bastion of German Catholicism. German Protestant churches, especially Lutheran, proliferated in several neighborhoods.

German Jews, very influential in the city's business sector, became the elite of San Francisco Judaism. They included such notables as the Strauss, Zellerbach, and Fleishhacker families.[47] Well-to-do Germans, often Reform Jews, began moving out to the Western Addition in the late nineteenth century. The district attracted more working-class, Orthodox Jewish elements after the earthquake and fire displaced many from the South-of-Market area. Along with Russians and other Eastern Europeans, Germans dominated the numerous Jewish synagogues, schools, orphanages, and hospitals in the Western Addition for several decades before World War II; the greatest concentration was around Fillmore and McAllister streets, which were lined with

---

[46]Cherny and Issel, *San Francisco,* pp. 29-30.

[47]Irena Narell, *Our City: The Jews of San Francisco* (San Diego: Howell-North, 1981).

Jewish businesses.[48] The most visible remnant of the Jewish influence here is Mount Zion Hospital.

The Italian population of San Francisco was relatively small until the influx of "new immigrants" to the U.S. from southern and eastern Europe, beginning in the last decade of the nineteenth century. In 1890, the city's largest foreign-born populations were from Ireland (30,719), Germany (26,422), and Great Britain (13,666); Italy (5,212) was far behind. By 1920, however, San Franciscans born in Italy (23,924) constituted the largest group of foreign immigrants. First- and second-generation Italians numbered 58,021 by 1930, after which their numbers began to decline. But in 1940 nearly one of every five San Franciscans was still of Italian stock (see Tables 5 and 6).

San Francisco's largest and most visible Italian enclave grew up in North Beach. Nestled diagonally between Russian and Telegraph hills, Broadway, and Fisherman's Wharf, North Beach originally sat near the northern end of Yerba Buena Cove, before the inlet was filled in by the expanding business district. Located close to the port serving as the gateway to the West during the Gold Rush, North Beach developed an exotic foreign flavor early on: St. Francis of Assisi Catholic Church, founded there in 1849, initially served a French congregation; the Latin American "Chile Town" of the early 1850s, located on the slope of Telegraph Hill, was succeeded by settlements of Mexicans and other Spanish-speakers in North Beach; Italian fishermen, mainly from Genoa, settled here in the 1860s and introduced the lateen-rigged *felucca* sailboats which remained the standard fishing boats on the Bay until the turn of the century; and many Irish, Germans, and others also resided in North Beach during the city's early years.

Gradually the Romance-language groups gained ground, so that by the late nineteenth century North Beach came to be called the "Latin Quarter." The diverse Latin groups had certain cultural similarities drawing them together in North Beach, although inter-ethnic rivalries remained, particularly between the Hispanics and Italians.[49] This local ethnic conflict had ecclesiastical repercussions, as was the case elsewhere in the country. Like the Germans before them, the Italian immigrants arriving in the late nineteenth century encountered an unwelcome Irish predominance in the U.S. Catholic Church.[50]

---

[48]Flamm, *Good Life,* pp. 72-83.

[49]See the description of group conflicts recounted in Writer's Program, *San Francisco,* pp. 240-241.

[50]Oscar Handlin, *The Uprooted: The Epic Story of the Great Migrations that Made the American People* (New York: Grosset and Dunlap, 1951), p. 135.

Separate national parishes ultimately were set up within the Catholic Church, providing services in foreign languages. A Spanish-language congregation formed in 1875, and in 1880 erected Nuestra Señora de Guadalupe (Our Lady of Guadalupe) Church at Broadway and Mason streets, in what became known as the Mexican quarter. This southwest corner of North Beach, at the base of Russian Hill, was the main focal point of San Francisco's Spanish-speaking community until after World War II, when the Mission District assumed that role.

Sts. Peter and Paul Church was dedicated in 1881 (about two blocks east of the present structure, built on Washington Square in 1922) to serve the Italian colony, which was forming around upper Dupont Street (later Grant Avenue). The Italian community proceeded to expand more than that of the Spanish-speakers in North Beach, but before 1906 Italians were still not as predominant in the Latin Quarter as is often assumed. As late as the turn of the century, families with Italian surnames constituted a minority of the population even in the heart of North Beach, although by then they were the largest single group in the area.[51] With the evacuation of North Beach following the earthquake and fire, however, many of the Germans, Russians, Eastern Europeans, and others (frequently property owning) moved out permanently; Italian immigration continued thereafter, and rebuilt North Beach presumably became more thoroughly Italian.

By the 1920s the area was known as "Italian North Beach" or even as "Little Italy." Italian shops, restaurants, cafes, newspaper offices, and other commercial establishments proliferated along Columbus Avenue, the main thoroughfare of North Beach, where diverse Italian dialects filled the air. A. P. Giannini's Banca d'Italia, later to become the giant Bank of America, was founded in 1904 and grew up in North Beach, lending out money more on the basis of an individual's reputation in the Italian community than with regard to property ownership and financial resources. Italians first dominated the city's scavengers (garbagemen), and later the teamsters. Fisherman's Wharf, moved to its present site from Filbert Street by state mandate in 1900, was known as "Italy Harbor" before the 1920s; Italians operated the fishing fleet, docks, food-processing plants, and diverse industries in the area. The commercial acumen of San Francisco's Italian immigrants has often been attributed to their origins

---

[51]Based upon an examination of the 1900 census enumeration forms by a team of geographers at San Francisco State University in 1982. Interview with Prof. Max Kirkeberg, Aug. 25, 1983.

among the enterprising townsfolk of northern Italy. The bulk of San Francisco's Italian immigrants were from the North, especially from the regions of Genoa and Tuscany. Although immigrants from southern Italy did increase during the early twentieth century, southerners never came to dominate the community, as they did in New York, Chicago, New Orleans, and other cities.[52]

After about the turn of the century, San Francisco Italian immigrants also formed a residential concentration in the Mission District, Bernal Heights, and Potrero Hill, where unskilled laborers could find work in the area's factories, warehouses, workshops, railroads, and other commercial firms. There were enough Italians here to create a second national parish in the Mission District in 1898. After 1906, when North Beach was destroyed, many of the 20,000 or so Italians temporarily displaced moved permanently to the Mission District, which was left mostly intact. The first branch of the Bank of Italy opened in the Mission District in 1907.

Another largely Italian district sprang up in the Outer Mission District. Here, a relatively insular colony of Italian truck and dairy farmers had settled much earlier: the independent agriculturalists formed their own association in 1874, and proceeded to operate a market in the city's central produce district.[53] As the area was being converted to residential use after World War I, real estate developers called it the Outer Mission in an effort to attract families through the image of a warm climate like that of the Inner Mission—which the Outer Mission definitely does not have, being located in a notable fog gap. The district became heavily Italian in the 1920s, and Corpus Christi Catholic Church in the Excelsior District became virtually a national church.

The wealthier Italians tended to settle in the Marina District, created on the landfill originally brought in for the Panama-Pacific Exposition of 1915, as single-family homes were being built there in the 1920s. But before the World War II the middle-class Marina was less ethnic in character than the working-class districts. Ironically, the Marina District is now said to have the largest concentration of people of Italian ancestry in San Francisco, reflecting the transformation of North Beach and both the Inner and Outer Mission districts by new occupants since World War II.[54]

---

[52]Dino Cinel, *From Italy to San Francisco: The Immigrant Experience* (Stanford University Press, 1982), p. 21.

[53]Deanna Paoli Gumina, *The Italians of San Francisco, 1850-1930* (New York: Center for Migration Studies, 1978), pp. 31-35.

[54]Interview with Prof. Max Kirkeberg, Aug. 25, 1983.

In addition to the Irish, Germans, and Italians, smaller European immigrant groups also formed vibrant ethnic communities in San Francisco's working-class neighborhoods before World War II. Like the larger groups, they could be found dispersed around the city to some degree, but nonetheless they had certain definite areas of ethnic concentration. Map 4 shows the approximate locations of some areas of marked ethnic presence in prewar San Francisco; though the ethnic groups cited were not necessarily predominant in these neighborhoods, there was a clustering of cultural institutions and a residential presence thereabouts.

Russians and other Eastern European groups were most prominent in the Western Addition, and during the interwar period began to appear increasingly in the Richmond District as well; the Molokan religious sect and other dissenters from the predominant Russian Orthodox Church clustered on the summit of Potrero Hill.[55] The Slovenians, a Catholic Yugoslavian group, could be found on Potrero Hill's western flank. Scandinavians entered San Francisco in significant numbers, but were never numerous enough to dominate a neighborhood; they began South of Market, then moved west into the northern Mission District, Eureka Valley, and Upper Market Street, where a number of Danish, Swedish, and Norwegian businesses and Protestant churches were centered. A Maltese community grew up in southeastern San Francisco, in the Bayview District, where their national church is still located. The heart of the Greek colony could be found South of Market, around Third and Folsom streets; a growing Latin American population, mainly male waterfront workers, was also becoming evident in this district.[56]

Among these smaller groups, San Francisco's Basques provide an illustrative case of community morphogenesis. The city emerged as a major center of Basque immigrant reception during the late nineteenth century, when San Francisco was the main port of entry for those arriving by sea on the West Coast. The city also served as both California's chief center of wool exporting and its largest mutton market, in which Basques played an important role. San Francisco developed social institutions to reinforce ethnic ties, such as the Basque hotels and restaurants of North Beach, along Broadway and Vallejo streets, which catered to the seasonal influx of ethnic brethren, mainly shepherds in transit from sheep stations in Nevada and Idaho. The local resident Basque population was employed mainly in blue-collar occupations. So the ethnic

---

[55]Michael W. Tripp, *Russian Routes: Origins and Development of an Ethnic Community in San Francisco* (Master's thesis, Dept. of Geography, San Francisco State University, 1980).

[56]For brief profiles of the city's older ethnic groups, see Leonard Austin's now-dated guide book, *Around the World in San Francisco* (San Francisco: Fearon, 1959).

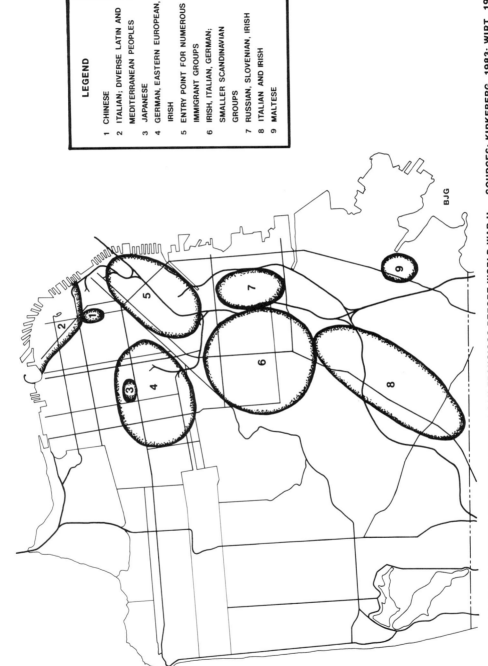

MAP 4. AREAS OF ETHNIC CONCENTRATION IN SAN FRANCISCO BEFORE WORLD WAR II.   SOURCES: KIRKEBERG, 1983; WIRT, 1974.

LEGEND

1 CHINESE
2 ITALIAN; DIVERSE LATIN AND MEDITERRANEAN PEOPLES
3 JAPANESE
4 GERMAN, EASTERN EUROPEAN, IRISH
5 ENTRY POINT FOR NUMEROUS IMMIGRANT GROUPS
6 IRISH, ITALIAN, GERMAN; SMALLER SCANDINAVIAN GROUPS
7 RUSSIAN, SLOVENIAN, IRISH
8 ITALIAN AND IRISH
9 MALTESE

community originally arose in the city because of specific urban functions, but then became self-perpetuating and culturally autonomous as social ties were cemented.[57]

BOHEMIAN QUARTERS

In addition to ethnic concentrations, unconventional communities sprang up early in San Francisco. In fact, one of America's first bohemias arose in the city. In a strict sense, bohemians were cultural radicals of a literary and artistic bent. Although true bohemians were relatively few, and certainly their subcultures were more fluid than those of ethnic groups, they were influential beyond their numbers. In a way, the wider San Francisco community was imbued with a touch of bohemianism, a tradition of nontradition dating from the Gold Rush. The city savored its naughty side and cherished its eccentrics, such as Joshua Norton, who in 1859 proclaimed himself "Emperor of the United States and Protector of Mexico." In the late nineteenth century, Rudyard Kipling called San Francisco "a mad city—inhabited for the most part by perfectly insane people whose women are of remarkable beauty."[58] Ambrose Bierce went so far as to comment:

> Of all the Sodoms and Gomorrahs in our modern world, [San Francisco] is the worst. There are not ten righteous (and courageous) men there. It needs another quake, another whiff of fire—and more than all else—a steady trade wind of grapeshot. . . . That moral penal colony of the world.[59]

Bohemia as an artistically inspired social movement actually began after the Revolution of 1830 in Paris, where struggling young artists in the Latin Quarter were likened to roving gypsies from *La Bohème* in eastern Europe. Henri Murger popularized this usage in his stories about poor, romantic artists and writers, *Scènes de Bohème*, and his subsequent play, *La Bohème*. William Makepeace Thackeray introduced the term "bohemian" into English with his 1848 novel, *Vanity Fair*. The California Gold Rush insured that San Francisco would receive a large number of restless bohemians.[60]

---

[57]See Jean Francis Decroos, *The Long Journey: Social Integration and Ethnicity Maintenance among Urban Basques in the San Francisco Bay Region* (Reno, Nevada: Associated Faculty Press, 1980), pp. 20-34.

[58]Kipling is quoted in Peter Yapp (ed.), *The Travellers' Dictionary of Quotation* (London: Routledge and Kegan Paul, 1983,) p. 958.

[59]Quoted in Yapp (ed.), *The Travellers' Dictionary of Quotation*, p. 958.

[60]Richard Miller, *Bohemia: The Prototype Then and Now* (Chicago: Nelson-Hall, 1977), p. 68.

As early as 1860 Bret Harte began writing articles for the San Francisco press under the pseudonym "The Bohemian." His first book of prose, published in 1867, was *Bohemian Papers*. Later, in *Bohemian Days in San Francisco,* Harte described the gambling saloons, the miners, and the Chinese of the Gold Rush. This loose usage of the term "bohemian" was adopted by other writers and artists, who began congregating in the Latin Quarter of North Beach, on the fringe of Chinatown and the Barbary Coast, as early as the mid-1860s. San Francisco's famed Bohemian Club was founded in 1872: membership initially was limited to writers, but it was immediately expanded to include artists, and by the late 1870s the club was becoming a bastion of the bourgeoisie, patrons of the arts.[61] Kevin Starr has maintained that San Francisco's nineteenth-century bohemia evolved quickly from a simple sense of frontier camaraderie to a more "continental" aesthetic community.[62]

As the Greater Bay Area proceeded to urbanize in the late nineteenth century, San Francisco became The City, distant from its suburbs in both physical and cultural terms. The arrival of the transcontinental railroad in 1869 made the East Bay a more convenient nexus for U.S. land transportation, tying the area to mainstream American culture, while San Francisco cultivated further what James Vance calls "its role as a center of cultural detachment."[63]

Within San Francisco, bohemians congregated in the older downtown neighborhoods of North Beach and Telegraph and Russian hills, adjacent to Chinatown and the Barbary Coast. By the 1890s the white middle classes had moved out to the newer neighborhoods in the Mission District and the Western Addition, leaving these central areas with low rents and older, picturesque settings, appealing to the romantic bohemian sensibility. The Latin Quarter beckoned with its cheap housing, unpretentious eating places and cafes, and ethnic flavor. For example, the bohemian literati were fond of Luna's Mexican restaurant, where the hearty "supper Mexican" cost only fifty cents during the week and seventy-five cents on weekends. Frank Norris,

---

[61]Albert Parry, *Garrets and Pretenders: A History of Bohemianism in America* (New York: Dover, 1933), pp. 212-227.

[62]Kevin Starr, *Americans and the California Dream, 1850-1915* (Oxford University Press, 1973), p. 241.

[63]James E. Vance, Jr., "Man and super-city: The origin and nature of the intricate social geography of the Bay Area," in Michael E. Eliot Hurst (ed.), *I Came to the City* (Boston: Houghton Mifflin, 1975), pp. 17-18.

Joaquin Miller, and other fledgling writers and artists frequented Luna's during the early 1890s. Norris set much of his novel *Blix* there, at Dupont (later Grant Avenue) and Vallejo streets.[64]

On the southeastern edge of the Latin Quarter was the Barbary Coast, long a bawdy waterfront area catering to sailors in port. The core of the district was along "Terrific" (Pacific) Street, between Kearny and Montgomery streets, where the tightly packed saloons, dance halls, brothels, flophouses, and gambling dens created an atmosphere of debauchery and moral license. This appealed to bohemian elements, some of whom were known to slum there, taking in the revelry and mingling with the underworld.[65]

Nearby was the Montgomery Block, the most notable bohemian haven in the city. A four-story structure at Washington and Montgomery streets, on the site of the present-day Transamerica Pyramid, the Block was built on redwood pilings at the edge of Yerba Buena Cove in 1853, when nearby Portsmouth Square was the center of San Francisco's business activity. As the central business district moved south along Montgomery Street toward Market Street, the "Monkey Block" was transformed into cheap offices, studios, apartments, cafes, and restaurants. This attracted many artists and writers, some 2,000 of whom are reputed to have lived in the building before its demolition in 1959.[66]

During the late nineteenth century, the Montgomery Block served as the abode or workplace of such notable literary and artistic figures as Bret Harte, Samuel Clemens, Ambrose Bierce, George Sterling, Joaquin Miller (whose friend Jack London sometimes stayed in his studio), and Gelett ("The Purple Cow") Burgess, Ernest Peixoto, and the other creators of *The Lark* magazine. The most famous bohemian haunt in the Montgomery Block was Coppa's, a turn-of-the-century restaurant and bar, where a conspicuous center table was always reserved for the distinguished literati; the renowned walls of Coppa's were decorated with a row of black cats, murals, and irreverent, occasionally risqué comments.[67]

---

[64]Frank Norris, *Blix* (New York: Doubleday, Page, and Co., 1903), p. 156.

[65]Asbury, *The Barbary Coast*.

[66]Lawrence Ferlinghetti and Nancy J. Peters, *Literary San Francisco* (San Francisco: Harper and Row, 1980), p. 96.

[67]See Idwal Jones, *Ark of Empire: San Francisco's Montgomery Block* (Garden City, N.Y.: Doubleday, 1951); and Oscar Lewis, *Bay Window Bohemia* (Garden City, N.Y.: Doubleday, 1956).

San Francisco's remarkable assemblage of *fin de siècle* artists and writers began to abate after the turn of the century. The more famous among them, such as Frank Norris and Gelett Burgess, left for the East Coast after they became successful. George Sterling's artist colony in Carmel, set up in 1905, further depleted the bohemian ranks. The earthquake and fire was the final blow: the conflagration of 1906 not only disrupted established pastimes, but the rapidly rebuilt "City of the Phoenix" seemed sobered by the catastrophe, more business like, a "big, bustling, materialistic city."[68] Local residents noted the change in ambience between what Jack London called "old Frisco" and new San Francisco, and many were not entirely pleased, waxing nostalgic about the bygone bohemian days. It was as if the post-fire city felt morally chastened, as Starr claims: "The rebuilding of San Francisco took on dimensions of atonement. Notorious for vice and corruption, the city, many said, had passed through an ordeal by fire."[69] The Barbary Coast did briefly resume its vice operations, and what was initially a more fashionable red-light district emerged uptown in the Tenderloin, near the entertainment district. But the bordellos in both areas were closed down between 1912 and 1917, under pressure from the moral reformers of rebuilt San Francisco.[70]

With the general prosperity of the 1920s, Albert Parry noted that bohemia on Telegraph and Russian hills "suffered a temporary eclipse, thanks to a rise in rents and an invasion of advertising men and Lesbian welfare workers with a yen for the artistic." By the early 1930s, however, all was "right" again, "what with the depression and lower rents, what with at least two soulful basement-theaters producing Russian, Irish, English, and French plays in the original. . ." The Montgomery Block continued as "the abode and working place of artists, writers, printers, bookbinders, spellbinders, and boys and girls who come to San Francisco to express themselves."[71] Yet by the late 1930s more affluent residents again began to appear on Telegraph Hill. One observer, who regarded this incipient upgrading as a threat to the neighborhood's traditional charm, foresaw in 1939 the contemporary renovation of Telegraph Hill:

---

[68] Lewis, *Bay Window Bohemia*, p. 237.

[69] Starr, *California Dream*, p. 293.

[70] Asbury, *The Barbary Coast*, pp. 278-314.

[71] Parry, *Garrets and Pretenders*, p. 240.

> The greatest enemy of the Hill as it exists to-day is not . . . bohemia gone pallid, but wealth seeking new fields to contaminate. In the wake of street improvements and sewer connections have appeared "artistic" apartments with natural redwood interiors, stone fireplaces and Chinese lanterns swinging from the balconies. All of which is only once removed from apartment houses with steam-heat, lifts, and flunkies at the door.[72]

The bohemian community of North Beach already had begun to serve as "urban pioneers," opening up a working-class ethnic quarter to more affluent sympathizers, who started to move into the hills. Attracted initially by cheap rents, the ethnic flavor, and picturesque settings, the bohemian avant-garde began to give way to the stylish well-to-do. Essentially a community of voluntaristic association, San Francisco's early nonconformist congregations declined as their artistic expressions lost vitality. Bohemians showed more mobility and fluidity than ethnic communities, which were more firmly anchored to working-class neighborhoods by class and cultural barriers.

INTERWAR ASSIMILATION

The period between World Wars I and II witnessed an increasing integration of most ethnic groups into the American mainstream, gradually eroding their ethnic ties. The restrictive legislation of the 1920s limited the influx of new immigrants, and the native-born of immigrant stock became progressively more Americanized. The white foreign-born population of San Francisco fell from 34.1 percent in 1910 to 22.1 percent in 1940, and reached a low of 15.5 percent in 1950; the total population of foreign parentage fell from 68.3 percent in 1910 to 49.8 percent in 1940, again bottoming out in 1950 at 40.3 percent (see Table 3).

Patterns of ethnic community location in San Francisco before World War II were strongly conditioned by labor flows, social status, and differences in group culture. Racial minorities, particularly the Chinese and Japanese, were the most spatially segregated; European immigrant groups had more mobility, but still tended to locate in working-class districts. Intra-ethnic fragmentation accounted for certain spatial patterns, as with the German religious divisions and the differentiation of German areas such as the Mission District (heavily Catholic) and the Western Addition (heavily Jewish). During the interwar period, the more acculturated immigrant offspring began to move from the ethnic neighborhoods on the city's eastern side to the more suburban

---

[72]Charles Caldwell Dobie, *San Francisco: A Pageant* (New York: D. Appleton-Century Co., 1939), p. 181.

areas of western San Francisco, the San Francisco Peninsula, Marin County, and the East Bay. But the economic stagnation of the 1930s, when the population of San Francisco experienced no real growth, hindered widespread mobility. The traditional ethnic clusters remained in place until World War II, after which the pent-up demand for new housing and the arrival of new low-income minorities rapidly transformed the character of ethnic San Francisco.

The bohemian presence in prewar San Francisco did come to constitute a distinctive community, enjoying some renown for its artistic and literary endeavors. Bohemia congregated in areas of financial feasibility and aesthetic appeal, clearly gathering through individual choice of social refusal rather than through long-standing family traditions and constraints to group mobility. Prewar bohemians may have begun to constitute a minority of sorts, but they were much more fluid than ethnic communities and already showed a tendency to attract more well-do-do imitators, who began to promote the renovation of deteriorated inner-city areas. Bohemia remained in place in San Francisco's Latin Quarter between World Wars I and II, but as a socio-artistic and literary movement it lost the focus and innovative flavor of the turn of the century; the next burst of nonconformist energy awaited the conclusion of the World War II.

The cultural geography of postwar San Francisco was to bear some resemblance to that of the earlier city: social and spatial structures inherited from the prewar city conditioned the morphogenesis of contemporary minority communities. The wealthy still occupied the hilltop residences on the northern shores and the newer "suburban" housing stock on the western side, pursued closely by the middle classes. Both ethnic and nonconformist communities settled mainly in the older, working-class neighborhoods of central and eastern San Francisco, though for somewhat different reasons and with correspondingly different consequences for the ordering of urban space, as explained in the next chapter.

Plate 9. A view of the Mission District, 1860. The area surrounding the old Spanish Mission, linked to the downtown district by horse-car lines, had by this point become a largely recreational area for the burgeoning "instant city" of San Francisco. The Mission District featured saloons, theaters, hotels, and a race track. (Photograph courtesy of the Caifornia Historical Society, San Francisco.)

Plate 10. San Francisco Chinatown, turn of the century. Of all San Francisco's ethnic districts, Chinatown was the most insular: Chinese were prohibited from living outside of the confines of Chinatown, which was a virtual medieval quarter, governed by its own set of rules and customs, enforced by the "Six Companies." (Photograph courtesy of the California Historical Society, San Francisco.)

Plate 11. A view of Mission Street about 1920, showing the small businesses which grew up along this important transportation corridor. Typically there were stores and services on the ground floors, below apartments on the upper floors. (Photograph courtesy of the San Francisco Public Library.)

4

POSTWAR SAN FRANCISCO
Morphological Adaptation and Subcultural Succession

> If California is the lunatic fringe of the United States, and San Francisco is the lunatic fringe of California, then the Haight is the lunatic fringe of San Francisco—the heart of the heart. And I say this with all due bias of a San Franciscan who loves his neighborhood.[1]
>
> Calvin Welch, 1987

World War II marked a historic watershed for San Francisco: only the Gold Rush, and arguably the earthquake and fire, had greater impacts on the cultural landscape. The city's population and economy, stagnant during the Depression of the 1930s, boomed to a degree probably not known for nearly a century. Local industry, especially the shipyards around the Bay, played a major role in the war effort, boosting industrial employment in the Bay Area from 101,000 in 1941 to 269,000 in 1943. Crowding and congestion were the norm as the Bay Area became a major military staging area for the Pacific theater: 1,644,000 military personnel and 23,389,000 tons of war materiel were transported through the Golden Gate during World War II.[2]

The acute labor shortage prompted the in-migration of large numbers of black and, to a lesser degree, Hispanic workers, who settled with their families in working-class neighborhoods. A significant number of military recruits of a nonconformist inclination, such as homosexuals, returned after the war. In short, World War II unleashed forces that ultimately served both to erode a number of older white ethnic communities, which quickly abandoned their city neighborhoods for the lure of the suburban life, and to create many of San Francisco's contemporary minority communities.

---

[1]Burr Snider, "CALVIN: *Nothing* comes between him and his City," *San Francisco Examiner*, Sunday, January 25, 1987, p. E-1.

[2]T. H. Watkins and R. R. Olmstead, *Mirror of the Dream: An Illustrated History of San Francisco* (San Francisco: Scrimshaw Press, 1976), p. 249.

Processes of urban initiation and adaptation are interrelated and constantly ongoing, thereby resisting neat historical demarcation. Still, the postwar period in San Francisco can be viewed in terms of morphological adaptation, as the massive population flux entailed putting the city's built environment and spatial structure to new uses. Along with the postwar group succession came both a new round of subcultural intensification and the evolutionary morphogenesis of contemporary minority areas—processes still very much at work in the city. As before the war, ethnic and nonconformist groups responded to a downward filtration of the housing stock in the working-class districts, often clustering in close proximity and thereby revising neighborhood social identities. Basic subcultural relationships, both internal and external, again help to explain both the periodicity of neighborhood structural change and the evolving patterns of community location.

JAPANESE-AMERICANS

San Francisco's Japanese community was the most adversely affected by the War. Japanese-Americans on the West Coast, without any evidence of disloyalty to the United States, were removed from their homes and detained in "relocation centers" by virtue of Executive Order 9066 in 1942. Japantown, which before the war had housed almost all of San Francisco's Japanese population, was left largely vacant by the detention; it was quickly occupied by the growing black population of the area.

Upon being released from the internment camps after the war, the Japanese returned to find their property frequently confiscated or destroyed, with little compensation provided. They never fully regained their former neighborhood after the war, instead moving out into other parts of the city, especially the Richmond District (see Map 5). Ironically, this dispersal was aided by the housing demolition required for construction of the Japan Center, a postwar development project serving both Japanese business interests and as a cultural center, which occupied three square blocks on the northern side of the Geary Boulevard, between Laguna and Fillmore Streets. Ironically, also, the demolition was backed largely by investors from Japan and strongly opposed by many in the local Japanese-American community.

Table 7 shows that the Japanese population of San Francisco grew steadily from 5,579 (0.7 percent) in 1950 to 12,461 (1.8 percent) in 1980, but this relatively modest increase was dwarfed by the larger gains of other Asian groups. In terms of the residential distribution of San Francisco's ethnic groups, Japanese-Americans appear to be more spatially concentrated than whites, Filipinos, and Hispanics, but less so than

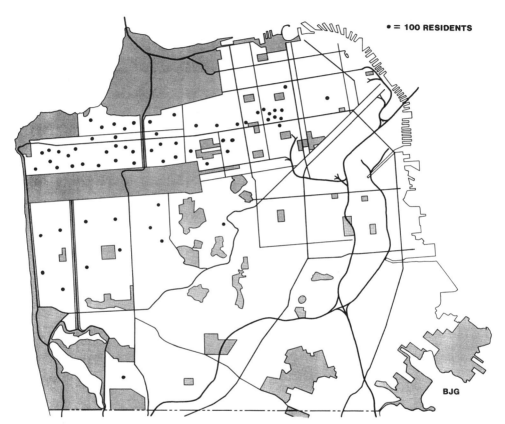

MAP 5. SAN FRANCISCO'S JAPANESE POPULATION. SOURCE: U.S. CENSUS, 1980.

TABLE 7

The Population of San Francisco by Race and Ethnicity, 1940-1980

Group	1940		1950		1960		1970		1980	
White	602,701	95.0%	693,888	89.5%	604,403	81.6%	409,285	57.2%	402,131	59.2%
Black	4,846	0.8	43,502	5.6	74,383	10.0	96,078	13.4	86,190	12.7
Chinese	17,782	2.8	24,813	3.2	36,445	4.9	58,696	8.2	82,244	12.1
Japanese	5,280	0.8	5,579	0.7	9,464	1.3	11,705	1.6	12,461	1.8
Filipino	3,483	0.5	See "Others"		12,327	1.7	24,694	3.5	38,690	5.6
Hispanic	No Data		No Data		51,602	7.0	101,901	14.2	84,194	12.4
American Indian	224	0.0	331	0.0	1,068	0.1	2,900	0.4	3,566	0.5
Others	220	0.0	7,244	0.9	2,226	0.3	10,415	1.5	53,692	7.9
Total	634,536	99.9	775,357	99.9	740,316	99.9	715,674	100.0	678,974	99.8

Note: Care should be taken in comparing the decennial counts for Hispanics and whites, since the criteria for both groups have changed continually over the years. The Spanish-surnamed population, included as part of the white population, was first counted for the city as a whole in 1960 (it had been tabulated only in selected census tracts in 1950); in 1970, persons of Spanish surname and language were considered a separate racial group and therefore not included in the white population figures; and in 1980 persons self-designated as of "Spanish origin" were also asked to identify themselves by race, which means that the Hispanic count overlaps that of other groups, especially whites.

Source: U.S. Census, various years.

Chinese-Americans and blacks.[3] These statistical correlations are generally confirmed by cartographic analysis, as shown in Maps 5 through 9.

BLACKS

If San Francisco's Japanese suffered the most displacement during World War II, blacks made the most dramatic inroads into the city's neighborhoods. The recruitment of workers in the rural South, particularly in small-town Louisiana, led to a large-scale black migration to the labor-scarce wartime economy of the Bay Area, followed by subsequent migrations of family and friends; the number of San Francisco blacks with family origins in Louisiana remains striking. This wartime migration caused San Francisco's previously small black population to increase tenfold during the 1940s, rising from under 5,000 (0.8 percent) in 1940 to over 43,000 (5.6 percent) in 1950 (see Table 7). Several districts in the city became heavily black during and shortly after the war, leading to the development of a number of dispersed residential clusters (see Map 6). Jean Vance's assessment of black settlement in the Bay Area generally applies equally well to San Francisco individually:

> Two conditions need to be emphasized as being distinctly different from the national experience of urban minority populations: this large black population has arrived over a very recent time span; and clusters of black population occur in a widely distributed pattern. These two conditions are integral to present relationships: first, because neither blacks nor whites are bound into long-established postures, and second, because there is no single central city black concentration.[4]

The first area of the city to experience a large-scale black influx was the Western Addition, where a small black community already resided before World War II, mainly along the Geary corridor between Japantown and what were then the Laurel Hill cemetery lands. In 1940, more than 3,000 blacks (nearly two-thirds of all those in the city) resided in the census tracts roughly bounded by California Street on the north, Gough on the east, Fulton on the south, and Baker, Geary, and Arguello on the southeast; still, blacks constituted barely 6 percent of the area's population.[5]

---

[3] Yoshiharu Izaki, "The residential correspondence between Japanese and other ethnic groups in San Francisco," *Geographical Review of Japan* 54, 3 (1981): 115-126.

[4] Jean Vance, "The cities by San Francisco Bay," in John S. Adams (ed.), *Contemporary Metropolitan America*, Vol. 1 (Cambridge: Ballinger, 1976), p. 264.

[5] U.S. Census, "Statistics for census tracts," 1940.

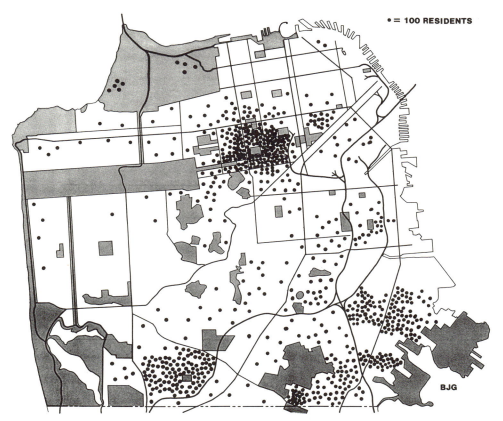

MAP 6. SAN FRANCISCO'S BLACK POPULATION. SOURCE: U.S.CENSUS, 1980.

With the Japanese relocated during the war, the growing black wartime population moved eastward into the largely abandoned Japantown. Then began a movement southward into the Fillmore District (around lower Fillmore Street), which was to become the heart of black San Francisco.[6] Although blacks were still clearly a minority in the Western Addition, by 1950 their numbers had increased dramatically and they had fatally ruptured the area's previous ethnic structure, leading to a massive and self-reinforcing "white flight." Whites of European immigrant stock fled to the nearby Richmond District, continuing a movement begun before the War, or to the Sunset District, or out of the city altogether. By 1960, the core of the Western Addition was solidly black. In terms of the stages of ethnic succession outlined earlier, the prewar and early-war period might be considered one of selective black *penetration* into the Western Addition; the mid- and late-1940s could be seen as a stage of minority *invasion,* leading to the *ethnic consolidation* of the 1950s.

Although the Fillmore was designated a blighted area by the Board of Supervisors as early as 1948, preparing the way for later redevelopment projects, its numerous black bookstores, jazz clubs, art galleries, and churches long made it a vibrant cultural center, often compared by contemporaries to New York's Harlem. The "redevelopment" demolition of the late 1950s and 1960s, which left the Fillmore's core a vacant wasteland surrounded by public housing projects and a high crime rate, is generally considered to be a classic example of misguided urban-renewal efforts.[7]

Hunters Point, in southeastern San Francisco, was the next district to attract a large black population. The U.S. Navy bought Bethlehem Steel's 47-acre ship repair and dry dock operation there in 1940, and soon expanded the facility to 500 acres for the war effort. Hunters Point became the West Coast's largest shipyard at the height of World War II, employing a racially integrated work force of about 18,500, many of them lodged in "temporary" wartime housing built on the ridges of Hunters Point. The blacks remained after the war, when the San Francisco Housing Authority took control of the wartime housing and converted it to subsidized public housing projects. Hunters Point and the adjacent Bayview District were more than 50 percent black by 1950, and

---

[6]Coro Foundation, *The District Handbook: A Coro Foundation Guide to San Francisco's Supervisorial Districts* (1979), p. 224.

[7]See Donald Canter, "San Francisco's Western Addition: How Negro removal became black renewal," *The City* 4, 3 (October-November 1970): 55-59; and Marilyn Clark, "The Tragedy of the Fillmore," *San Francisco Bay Guardian,* June 10, 1981, pp. 7-13.

since then have become almost exclusively so. The Bayshore Freeway, constructed in 1952, separated these black neighborhoods from the Visitation Valley and Portola districts to the west, which remained white working-class areas until recent years.[8]

During and shortly after the war blacks succeeded in opening up access to industrial unions and city employment, such as in municipal transit, although the craft unions and other fields remained closed to them. A growing number of blacks therefore had reasonable incomes, and they naturally sought to move into better neighborhoods. The Ingleside District of southwestern San Francisco lacked the racial covenants which, until ruled illegal by the U.S. Supreme Court in the 1948 case of Shelly vs. Kramer, prevented the sale of homes to blacks or Asians in many of the western areas of the city. Apparently aided by block-busting realtors, several parts of the Ingleside began to experience an influx of middle-income blacks in the 1940s, beginning in the southerly Oceanview neighborhood and spreading northwest into Merced Heights. The Ingleside District (not to be confused with the more exclusive Ingleside Terrace neighborhood, directly to the north) soon became postwar San Francisco's middle-class black district, as opposed to the lower-income Fillmore and Hunters Point areas. The black population in the three core census tracts of the Ingleside increased from 602 (3.7 percent) in 1950 to 7,273 (38.2 percent) in 1960, peaking at 11,171 (62 percent) in 1970 and then falling slightly to 10,894 (61 percent) in 1980.[9]

The number of blacks in San Francisco declined in both relative and absolute terms during the 1970s, falling from 96,078 (13.4 percent) in 1970 to 86,190 (12.7 percent) in 1980 (see Table 7). While some of this decline may be attributed to "black suburbanization," this does not necessarily imply upward mobility.[10] There is also reputed to be a steady black migration from San Francisco across the Bay to Oakland, where blacks increased from about a third to more than half of the total population during the 1970s. The steady escalation in San Francisco's property values and rents in recent years, and the attendant processes of gentrification and displacement in selected central neighborhoods, must be considered important factors in the city's decreasing black population.

---

[8] Coro Foundation, *District Handbook,* pp. 231-232.

[9] U.S. Census, various years.

[10] Phillip L. Clay, "The process of black suburbanization," *Urban Affairs Quarterly* 14 (June 1979): 405-424.

San Francisco's principal black core areas remained intact during the 1970s, tending to concentrate in both the Bayview-Hunters Point District and the heart of the Western Addition; the number of blacks in the middle-class Ingleside District generally stabilized, still constituting a clear majority. The erosion of the black community is most notable in revitalizing areas on the edges of the Western Addition, as will later be demonstrated cartographically.

CHINESE-AMERICANS

The Chinese also experienced widespread expansion into new areas of San Francisco shortly after World War II, initially more through a relaxation of previous segregative constraints than through new immigration. After a century of enforced ghetto existence in San Francisco's Chinatown, new conditions permitted an increasing dispersal of the Chinese during the late 1940s and 1950s. While the 1948 Supreme Court ruling against exclusionary racial covenants in real estate did not eliminate discrimination in housing, it did remove important legal barriers to nonwhite residence in much of western San Francisco. In addition, during the War the Chinese had come to be seen as allies and partners in the common struggle against the Japanese, and wartime contingencies had prompted the elimination of a number of long-standing prejudicial rules and norms.

The Chinese Exclusion Act was repealed in 1943, and the War Brides Act of 1945 was extended to Chinese wives in 1947, finally permitting an end to the "bachelor society."[11] Many of San Francisco's Chinese-Americans were of course native born by this point and, as previously noted, had begun integrating local schools earlier in the century. With the lure of the suburbs producing vacancies in most of the city's older residential areas, the Chinese began gradually to expand beyond the traditional confines of overcrowded Chinatown. The main areas of Chinese expansion during the 1950s were to the west of Chinatown, into the turn-of-the-century flats of Nob Hill; into North Beach and the eastern slopes of Russian Hill to the north; and east into the old Barbary Coast or Jackson Square area. Small numbers of Chinese also began moving into the "frontier areas" of the 1950s: the Richmond, Sunset, and West-of-Twin-Peaks districts.

As a result of new immigration laws implemented in 1965, which abolished the previous system of national quotas, San Francisco's Asian communities grew rapidly during the late 1960s and 1970s, coming collectively to constitute almost 22 percent of

---

[11]Willard T. Chow, *The Reemergence of an Inner City: The Pivot of Chinese Settlement in the East Bay Region of the San Francisco Bay Area* (San Francisco: R and E Research Associates, 1977), pp. 67-68.

the city's total population by 1980. The Chinese, by far the largest of the Asian groups, more than doubled in numbers between 1960 and 1980, reaching a total of over 82,000, 12.1 percent of San Francisco's population (see Table 7). The presence of a large Chinese population in San Francisco has helped to attract a massive influx of Asian capital in recent years. Hong Kong-based banks have proliferated in the financial district; and wealthy investors from the Far East, many nervous about the uncertain future of the British colony in Hong Kong, have sought to diversify by buying real estate in San Francisco. Overseas Chinese investors, who frequently do not speak English, have found a culturally familiar environment in San Francisco's Chinese community. In addition, the city's commercial and residential real estate is, amazingly enough, still a bargain relative to expensive Hong Kong, although the steady escalation of local property values has made San Francisco one of the highest-priced cities in the United States.[12]

This influx of Asian investments from overseas contrasts sharply with the poverty and overcrowding in Chinatown, where recent immigrants from southern China, Hong Kong, and Indochina ironically face inflated housing prices because of the bidding war for downtown property. Although the population of Chinatown was actually on the decline before 1965, the subsequent immigration reversed the trend. Chinatown's three core census tracts—bounded by Pacific, Kearny, California, Powell, and Mason streets—now average about 90 percent Chinese, a degree of ethnicity matched elsewhere in the city only by a few black areas.[13] Chinatown must be the only urban poverty area in the U.S. that is also a major tourist attraction. The population density in Chinatown is estimated at between 120 and 180 people an acre, or between 77,000 and 115,000 people per square mile—one of the highest urban densities in the United States, probably surpassed only by crowded parts of Manhattan.[14] Single-room occupancy units in residential hotels account for more than half the housing units in Chinatown—about 4,500 rooms in 120 hotels in the core area—and are occupied largely by the elderly and recent immigrants.[15] A community survey in the core area indicated that, contrary to popular stereotypes of the Chinese, 90 percent of Chinatown

---

[12]Frank Viviano and Alton Chinn, "The Hong Kong connection," *San Francisco Magazine* February 1982, pp. 54-64.

[13]U.S. Census, 1980.

[14]Victor G. Nee and Brett de Bary Nee, *Longtime Californ': A Documentary Study of an American Chinatown* (New York: Pantheon Books, 1972), p. xxii.

[15]John K. C. Liu, "San Francisco Chinatown residential hotels" (San Francisco: Chinatown Neighborhood Improvement Resource Center, 1980), pp. 5-8.

residents disliked the crowding, and 42 percent wanted to move out of the neighborhood.[16]

The more affluent and acculturated Chinese-Americans tend to do precisely that, leaving Chinatown for outlying areas of the city or for suburban locations outside of the city altogether. The movement into areas adjacent to Chinatown has generated the most controversy in recent years, particularly as North Beach has become predominantly Chinese. Something of a new Chinatown has emerged in the city's historic "Little Italy": the number of Italian-Americans in North Beach has dropped from the tens of thousands to under 4,000, and about half of the business signs in North Beach are now printed in Chinese characters.[17] Russian and Nob hills also have become heavily Chinese, predominantly so in the lower-lying area around Broadway. The Tenderloin District has become another point of entry for recent Chinese immigrants, although not to the degree that it has for the Vietnamese.

Chinese have become the dominant minority in much of western San Francisco. The Inner and Middle sections of the Richmond District are now about a third Chinese, and at current growth rates the Chinese may enjoy majority status before too long; Clement Street now boasts scores of Chinese restaurants and other businesses. The Richmond District became the focal point of the ethnic movement from Chinatown to San Francisco's western side because of a number of functional and structural characteristics. The high real estate prices in areas around Chinatown, such as Nob and Russian hills, impeded home ownership by aspiring Chinese-American families; the areas of western San Francisco were more reasonably priced and better suited for families desirous of a middle-class life-style. The housing morphology of the Richmond District—a mixture of single-family houses and multi-unit buildings (flats and apartments)—appealed to Chinese extended families, who could settle in close proximity or even under one roof. In addition, there were several direct transit lines running from the Richmond District to the vicinity of Chinatown and downtown: the #2 Clement, #1 California, and #38 Geary buses all serve this route without requiring a transfer. This transportation connection between the Richmond District and the Chinatown core has been important for a number of reasons, including the maintenance of family ties, access to ethnic foods and other products, and social institutions.

The "frontier" of Chinese settlement on the city's western side now has moved

---

[16]Gerald Adams, "Dispelling the myths about Chinatown," *San Francisco Sunday Examiner and Chronicle,* August 10, 1980, p. A-9.

[17]Gerald Adams, "Chinese spice the Italian flavor of North Beach," *San Francisco Examiner,* March 26, 1982, p. 1.

from the Richmond to the Sunset District. The Central Sunset, especially near Golden Gate Park, is about a fifth Chinese, and also growing rapidly. These Chinese communities on San Francisco's western side have evolved in time from mere satellites of Chinatown to more autonomous "suburbs" within the city. Like blacks, Chinese remain a highly concentrated and relatively insular group in residential terms. The Chinese population is most positively correlated in census tract data with the Japanese among San Francisco's major ethnic groups; there is a discernible polarity from Filipinos, Hispanics, and blacks, as indicated by the accompanying dot maps of ethnic residential distributions (see Map 7).

FILIPINO-AMERICANS

San Francisco's Filipino population, although still much smaller than the Chinese, has been growing at an even faster rate in recent years. While the city's Chinese population officially grew 40.5 percent to more than 82,000 during the 1970s, the Filipino population grew by 55 percent to more than 38,000 (see Table 7). This recent upsurge is actually the latest in a series of immigrant waves from the Philippines. The first generation of Filipinos was predominantly male and arrived during the 1920s and 1930s. San Francisco served as something of a way station between agricultural operations in Hawaii, where Filipino migrant laborers first landed, and California's San Joaquin Valley. In the early 1930s, when more than 100,000 Filipinos lived in the United States, there were 14 men for every woman; since anti-miscegenation laws hindered marriage to American women, and the migrants could not afford to bring Filipino women with them, a "bachelor society" similar to that of the Chinese was created.[18]

In San Francisco, Filipino agricultural laborers spent the winter in residential hotels on the eastern edge of Chinatown, along Kearny Street between California and Columbus, as well as South of Market and in the Mission District. Some Filipino laborers remained in the city to work in San Francisco's hotels and restaurants. By the end of World War II, 27 Filipino restaurants and numerous hotels catering to Filipino men could be found on Kearny, in what came to be called "Manilatown."[19] Although Manilatown still had about 1,500 older Filipinos of the "first generation" living in inexpensive residential hotels as late as 1971, their numbers were clearly on the

---

[18]Peter W. Stanley, "Exiled in California," *San Francisco Sunday Examiner and Chronicle,* "This World" section, July 19, 1981, pp. 16-19.

[19]Walter Blum, "Filipinos: A question of identity," *San Francisco Sunday Examiner and Chronicle,* "California Living" section, March 21, 1982, p. 8.

MAP 7. SAN FRANCISCO'S CHINESE POPULATION. SOURCE: U.S. CENSUS, 1980.

decline.[20] As the financial district expanded northward into Manilatown, and new Chinese immigration fueled an explosion of the once-declining population of Chinatown to the west, the more recent Filipino arrivals tended to settle elsewhere in the city. One of the last remnants of Manilatown was the International Hotel, where many Filipino old-timers (*manongs*) resided before their eviction (ordered by the Hong Kong-based Four Seas Investment Corporation) in 1977, which became a *cause célèbre* among local community activists.

The Filipino second generation began after World War II and marked the beginnings of Filipino family life in the United States. Veterans of the war in the Far East, both Americans and naturalized Filipinos, moved to the city with their Filipino brides and relatives. This immigrant wave, which continued until after the Korean War, constituted a lower-middle income group for the most part and settled largely in the Inner and Outer Mission districts, as well as in the Richmond District.[21] The third and largest immigrant wave began after 1965, when relaxed immigration laws permitted many more Filipinos to enter the United States. The familiar socioeconomic "push-pull" factors were sufficient to promote this migration initially, but after the declaration of martial law in the Philippines during the early 1970s an increasing number of opponents of the Marcos regime also fled to the U.S. for political reasons. For almost two decades, then, thousands of Filipinos have entered the United States every year through San Francisco. This has created an ethnic community still dominated by recent immigrants, rather than by the earlier generations.

Somewhat reminiscent of the fragmented German population of the late nineteenth century, Filipinos are of diverse dialects (Tagalog predominates) and regional customs, creating a relatively disparate population in both social and spatial terms. There are scores of Filipino social clubs in the city, often organized by town or region of origin. Like the scattered archipelago whence they come, Filipinos are fairly dispersed throughout San Francisco, and their index of residential concentration is less than that of other ethnic groups in the city, although they have settled heavily in the southern part of the city and in Daly City.[22]

The most significant residential cluster is South of Market, an entry point for recent immigrants, where two census tracts are now about 28 percent Filipino. The

---

[20] San Francisco Human Rights Commission, "San Francisco ethnic neighborhood problem packet" (June 1974), pp. 4-5.

[21] *Ibid.*, pp. 4-5.

[22] Izaki, "Residential correspondence," pp. 115-126.

distribution of Filipino residents most closely follows that of Hispanics in the city, with clusters dispersed throughout the Inner and Outer Mission districts (see Map 8) and extending into Daly City on San Francisco's southwestern edge. The Filipino population of Daly City skyrocketed from 2,677 (4.0 percent) in 1970 to 14,421 (18.4 percent) in 1980 and is now almost equal in numbers to the Hispanic population there.[23] Filipino small businesses—restaurants, grocery stores, bakeries, realtors, and so on—also are scattered from South of Market through the Inner and Outer Mission districts to Daly City, blending in easily with Hispanic establishments and showing little evidence of struggles over turf. On Mission Street, between 25th and 30th streets, for example, there are eight Filipino independent businesses and a senior citizen center, all of which comfortably coexist with the more numerous Hispanic establishments. A Filipino guidebook observes:

> The district is considered an ideal place for immigrants because of its mixed neighborhoods and relatively low-rent residential homes . . . Filipinos and Mexicans mix well because of common historical, cultural and religious background.[24]

The Filipino-Hispanic association is not always amiable, as indicated by youth conflicts in the city schools.[25] Yet common cultural traits, such as the Roman Catholic religion and a Spanish colonial heritage, undoubtedly do help to account for why Filipinos associate so much more with Hispanics than with what the U.S. Census categorizes as other "Asians and Pacific Islanders."

SMALLER ASIAN AND PACIFIC GROUPS

In addition to San Francisco's large Chinese and Filipino populations, there are a number of smaller groups of Asians and Pacific Islanders. According to official figures, in 1980 the largest of these was the Vietnamese, with 5,078 city residents (0.7 percent). Next came the Koreans, with 3,442 (0.5 percent), followed by East Indians with 1,568 (0.2 percent), Hawaiians with 1,048 (0.1 percent), and Guamanians with 302 (0.0

---

[23]U.S. Census, 1980.

[24]Rodolfo Necesito, *The Filipino Guide to San Francisco* (San Francisco: Technomedia, 1978), pp. 7-8.

[25]H. G. Reza, "Latinos vs. Filipinos: Ethnic feuds at Wilson High," *San Francisco Chronicle,* Jan. 30, 1980, pp. 1, back.

MAP 8. SAN FRANCISCO'S FILIPINO POPULATION. SOURCE: U.S. CENSUS, 1980.

percent).[26] There is also a smattering of even smaller groups that, although not showing up in large numbers in census statistics, stand out in their particular roles in the city. For example, East Indians own many of the residential hotels in the city, and Palestinians own and operate nearly half of San Francisco's combination liquor-grocery stores.[27] As with previous immigrant waves, inner-city San Francisco serves as a "way station" for the recently arrived of these Asian and Pacific Islander groups. They tend to settle initially in low-income areas of the city, moving on to other parts of San Francisco or the Bay Area after learning language and job skills. This continual shuffling of the immigrant population creates an ongoing dynamic of ethnic flux in areas of initial immigrant settlement.

A good case in point is the recent influx of Southeast Asian refugees, mainly from Vietnam, but also from Cambodia and Laos. There are now over a half a million Vietnamese in the U.S., about 35 percent of these located in California. Massive emigration began with the elites, who fled Vietnam after the downfall of Saigon in 1975, fearing a Communist bloodbath. In 1978 and 1979 came the "boat people," many of whom were ethnic Chinese.[28] The number of Southeast Asians locally is uncertain, but journalists generally put it over 50,000 in the five-county Bay Area, with approximately half of them located in San Francisco. In mid-1981, there were 28,000 former "boat people" on public assistance in the city, with continuous new arrivals from resettlement centers elsewhere in the U.S., as well as several hundred monthly departures to other parts of the Bay Area.[29] Most of those leaving San Francisco went to the South Bay, where many began working in the electronics and semiconductor industries of "Silicon Valley."[30]

Southeast Asian immigrants tend to cluster initially in San Francisco's Tenderloin District, attracted by the relatively low rents and high rates of tenant turnover in the area's apartment houses and residential hotels. Located roughly between the Civic Center and Union Square, the Tenderloin gained an early reputation for its grand

---

[26]U.S. Census, 1980.

[27]Vlae Kershner, "S.F. Palestinians—The City's grocers," *San Francisco Sunday Examiner and Chronicle,* "Sunday Punch" section, April 8, 1984, pp. 5-6.

[28]"Saigon U.S.A.," KQED television documentary, July 13, 1983.

[29]Sydney Kossen, "Dramatic rise forecast in S.F. welfare costs," *San Francisco Examiner,* June 25, 1981, p. A-ll.

[30]Tran Tuong Nhu, "Resettling the Vietnamese," *San Francisco Sunday Examiner and Chronicle,* Sept. 27, 1981, "California Living" section, pp. 4-13; Dexter Waugh, "Southeast Asians blending in all over the Bay Area," *San Francisco Examiner,* March 30, 1981, p. B-1, B-10.

theaters, adult entertainment, brothels, and other vice activities. The district's name came from the inevitable police payoffs, which were said to allow corrupt cops to eat a relatively luxurious diet of "tenderloin" steak, as in some other vice districts; the old Barbary Coast was sometimes called the "downtown tenderloin," as opposed to the initially more fashionable "uptown tenderloin" in the entertainment district.[31] The Tenderloin became a low-income apartment and hotel district after World War II, serving as a bastion mainly for the elderly on fixed incomes, down-and-out single people, homosexuals, artists, prostitutes, winos, drug addicts and pushers, and other social renegades.

Although there has always been a smattering of ethnics in the Tenderloin, the recent influx of Southeast Asians has made it a new ethnic core area. They have also introduced a novel family element: in 1983, there were estimated to be some 12,000 to 13,000 Indochinese refugees in the Tenderloin, bringing a new abundance of children to a neighborhood with very little open space.[32] In addition to their Tenderloin core, some Vietnamese also have settled in the Mission District, and a few have been placed in public housing projects in the predominantly black Bayview-Hunters Point area. The more affluent and acculturated tend to leave the Tenderloin, following other Asians out to the Richmond District (see Map 9).

HISPANICS

San Francisco's immigrant communities are surprisingly heterogeneous, containing a diversity of dialects and subgroups that often goes unnoticed by the casual observer. The large Hispanic population, for example, which numbers over 84,000 (12.4 percent), has multi-national roots in Latin America, lacking a majority from any one country: people of Mexican origin represent about 39 percent of the *Latino* population, but 53 percent come from Central and South America, 6 percent from Puerto Rico, and 2 percent from Cuba.[33] By all accounts the city's fastest-growing Latin American groups in recent years have been from strife-torn Nicaragua and El Salvador, which together probably outnumber Hispanics of Mexican origin. In fact, San Francisco may well be the only U.S. city with a predominance of Hispanics from Central America.

---

[31] Oscar Lewis, *Bay Window Bohemia* (Garden City, N.Y.: Doubleday, 1956), p. 22.

[32] Edvins Beitiks, "Uneasy transition for Tenderloin's refugee children," *San Francisco Examiner*, April 10, 1983, pp. B-1, B-4.

[33] U.S. Census, 1980.

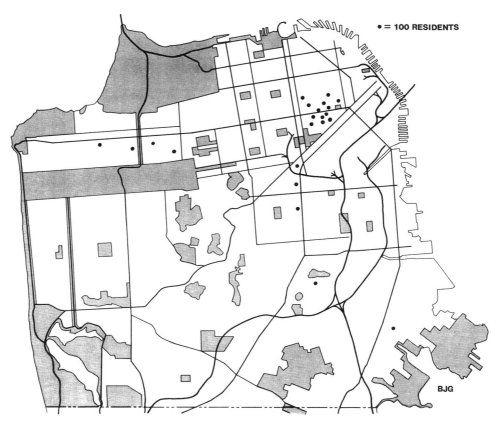

MAP 9. SAN FRANCISCO'S VIETNAMESE POPULATION. SOURCE: U.S. CENSUS, 1980.

Latin Americans have been immigrating to San Francisco in significant waves since the Gold Rush. They first clustered in North Beach, where a Spanish-language congregation dedicated the Mexican national Catholic Church, Our Lady of Guadalupe, in 1880. After World War I, increasing numbers of Hispanic immigrants also began clustering in the South of Market area, a traditional low-income point of entry for new immigrants to the city. Like other groups before them—Irish, Germans, Scandinavians—Latins followed the street grid southwest into the Mission District, beginning in the interwar period.

After World War II the still relatively small Latin colony in the Mission began to grow steadily as older white ethnic groups abandoned the area. It was not such an abrupt racial transformation as in the Western Addition, but more of a gradual ethnic turnover in a long-standing working-class neighborhood. The Spanish-surnamed population of the Mission District rose from 11 percent in 1950 to 23 percent in 1960 and 45 percent in 1970, by which time the Inner Mission was known as *El Barrio*. While the U.S. Census showed a decline in San Francisco's total Hispanic population during the 1970s, the number of Hispanics counted in the nine census tracts of the Mission District still increased slightly to about 46 percent; the Inner Mission's core area reached about 60 percent Hispanic. These figures are probably conservative, given the presence of many undocumented residents.

In recent years there has been a notable movement of Hispanics to the Outer Mission District, into such neighborhoods as the Excelsior, although the Inner Mission remains the central core (see Map 10). Like blacks in the Western Addition, Hispanics in the Inner Mission District have witnessed an erosion of their community's flanks and an intensification of its core in recent years. This has given rise to areas of social conflict, much of which has involved the influx of nonconformist groups, most notably the gay community, as recounted in numerous press reports.[34]

POSTWAR NONCONFORMISTS: BEATS, HIPPIES, AND GAYS

Bohemia reestablished itself after 1906 in rebuilt North Beach, but did not regain its former creative vitality until after World War II. Postwar San Francisco became the cultural hearth of a number of new nonconformist communities, each in its own way sharing a bohemian interest in avant-garde aesthetics, collective feelings of social alienation, and a clustering of supportive businesses and institutions in selected urban

---

[34]See Katy Butler and Gwendolyn Evans, "Gay migration into black neighborhoods," *San Francisco Chronicle,* Sept. 1, 1979, pp. 1, 5; and Phil Bronstein, "Muggings: Gay-Latino confrontations or no?" *San Francisco Examiner,* Nov. 11, 1980, p. B-1.

MAP 10. SAN FRANCISCO'S HISPANIC POPULATION. SOURCE: U.S. CENSUS, 1980.

enclaves. The city's neighborhoods were the breeding-grounds for such nontraditional subcultures as the Beat Generation, the counter-culture, and the gay and lesbian movements. The history of these successive nonconformist communities is tied to the evolutionary morphogenesis of the areas in which they congregated.

In the late 1940s and early 1950s, North Beach still had low rents. Acculturated Italian-Americans were beginning to abandon the area, as postwar suburban expansion permitted increased mobility. This declining Latin Quarter provided a propitious setting for the formation of the "beat" bohemia, which emerged in a succession of bars, cafes, bookstores, restaurants, and other gathering spots:

> Thus the North Beach underground began in the 40's with the Iron Pot, the Black Cat, the old Montgomery block; it moved up Columbus Avenue to the Vesuvio, along Upper Grant to The Place, The Cellar, Miss Smith's Tea Room, later to the Co-Existence Bagel Shop, The Coffee Gallery, Otis's, and finally down the street again to Cassandra's Hot Dog Palace and Mike's Pool Hall on Broadway, where it ended, to all intents, surrounded by topless dance clubs.[35]

Many of the most prominent beats were homosexual, and the beat and gay subcultures overlapped in both spatial and cultural terms in North Beach. A number of popular gay and lesbian bars, such as the Black Cat, had begun as bohemian haunts and continued to attract a mixed clientele. The beats legitimized nonconformity, so that homosexuals began to see themselves as social rebels rather than as deviant personalities. *Life* magazine proclaimed San Francisco the country's "gay capital" as early as 1964, by which point homosexual gathering places were starting to spread outward from North Beach into the Polk Street, Tenderloin, and South-of-Market areas.[36]

The most visible nonconformist community in San Francisco during the 1960s was the counter-culture, however. Hippies drew upon the oppositional attitudes of the beatniks, but tended to be less bohemian in a strict literary and artistic sense—less intellectual and more experiential, as evidenced by the increased use of hallucinogenic drugs. The counter-culture of the 1960s coincided with both the civil rights movement

---

[35]Thomas Albright, "The elevated underground: The North Beach period," in Robert E. Johnson (ed.), *Rolling Renaissance: San Francisco's Underground Art in Celebration, 1945-1968* (San Francisco: The Center for Religion and the Arts, 1976), p. 15.

[36]See John D'Emilio, *Sexual Politics, Sexual Communities: The Making of a Homosexual Minority in the United States, 1940-1970* (University of Chicago Press, 1983), pp. 176-195.

and youth protests over the Vietnam War, making it a more broadly based social phenomenon than the Beat Generation of the 1950s. As opposed to the melancholy beatnik demeanor, the "flower children" presented themselves in more innocent, festive, and colorful ways, as exhorted by the lyrics of a popular 1967 song written by John Phillips and recorded by Scott McKenzie:

> If you're going to San Francisco,
> Be sure to wear some flowers in your hair.
> If you're going to San Francisco,
> You're going to find some gentle people there.
>
> For those who come to San Francisco,
> Summertime will be a love-in there;
> In the streets of San Francisco,
> Gentle people with flowers in their hair.

At the height of the counter-cultural influx, thousands of hippies invaded the Haight-Ashbury in what a geographer called "one of the most remarkable mass colonizations in modern American urban history."[37] News commentator Harry Reasoner called the San Francisco neighborhood "the hippie capital of the world" in a 1967 CBS television documentary.[38] The "summer of love" of 1967 was a meteoric but short-lived phenomenon, however, as will be recounted in another chapter. By the late 1960s the area had degenerated into what the Director of the Haight-Ashbury Free Medical Clinic, David Smith, called a "heroin ghetto," and the neighborhood fell to a socio-economic nadir around 1970. In recent years the Haight-Ashbury has witnessed a remarkable revitalization, linked in part to a new influx of nontraditional households.

Since the decline of the 1960s counter-culture, San Francisco's gay and lesbian communities have stepped into the nonconformist limelight. The homosexual population of the city actually has been growing steadily since World War II, when a considerable number of military personnel from the Pacific theater were dishonorably discharged in the Bay Area for their sexual preferences; many other homosexual veterans, both male and female, remembered wartime San Francisco, a major military center, as a tolerant, wide-open city, and returned after the war.[39]

San Francisco's homosexual population continued to increase through the 1970s,

---

[37] Peter Hall, "The urban culture and the suburban culture," in Hurst, *I Came to the City*, p. 174.

[38] Harry Reasoner, "The hippie temptation," CBS News, 1967.

[39] Allan Berube, "Coming out under fire," *Mother Jones*, February March 1983, pp. 23-45.

according to one study reaching a total of "at least 115,000 people; 17% of the city's population in 1980, two-thirds of them men."[40] Others dispute such a high estimate. Sociologist Claude Fischer, after reviewing several figures for the homosexual population, concluded that 12 to 15 percent appeared "most accurate."[41] There has been speculation that the number of homosexuals in the city peaked between 1977 and 1979, since then leveling off.[42] Obviously no official statistics are available to account definitively for the demography of nonconformist elements, but subcultural business directories can point to patterns of community location (see Map 11).

Listings of homosexual-identified businesses and social gathering spots in the best long-term community guide, *Bob Damron's Address Book,* are totalled in Table 8 for each year between 1969 and 1988. The gay subculture reached its maximum point of expansion into San Francisco neighbohoods in 1982; during the six following years, the number of gay and lesbian establishments fell by a total of 84 listings, or by over a quarter of the 1982 number. This drop undoubtedly reflected a change in the "fast-lane" gay male life-style and a drop in gay tourism in San Francisco since the advent of the Acquired Immune Deficiency Syndrome (AIDS) epidemic in the early 1980s. Many gay bars and discos closed as a result of a decline in patronage, particularly in the South-of-Market and Polk Street areas; only the Castro District maintained its strong gay commercial identity (see Table 9).

Although the diminution of gay-identified places of entertainment in San Francisco does not necessarily mean a like decline in the homosexual population, the erosion of gay public space in the city implies that the community is at least no longer growing and is probably decreasing somewhat in size. Long-time residents attribute this to several causes. A widespread fear of AIDS undoubtedly has prevented the gay community from growing, but it might well have stabilized anyway. The saturation of the local job market, and the escalation of San Francisco's housing costs, have encouraged some homosexuals to leave and discouraged many others from coming to the city. In addition, by the early 1980s there were many other American cities with viable homosexual communities, making migration to San Francisco less urgent for

---

[40]Manuel Castells and Karen Murphy, "Cultural identity and urban structure: The spatial organization of San Francisco's gay community," *Urban Affairs Review,* 22 (1982): 237-259.

[41]Claude S. Fischer, *To Dwell Among Friends: Personal Networks in Town and City* (University of Chicago Press, 1982), p. 424.

[42]Paul Shinoff, "City's gay population peaks in '70s, levels off, surveys reveal," *San Francisco Examiner,* April 29, 1982, p. A-6.

MAP 11. GAY AND LESBIAN BUSINESSES IN SAN FRANCISCO. SOURCE: BOB DAMRON'S ADDRESS BOOK, 1984.

TABLE 8

Gay- and Lesbian-identified Businesses and Social Gathering Spots in San Francisco, 1969-1988

Year	Total Number	% Change Over Previous Year
1969	73	--
1970	66	-9.5%
1971	81	+22.7
1972	106	+30.8
1973	128	+20.7
1974	128	0.0
1975	164	+28.1
1976	162	-1.2
1977	188	+16.0
1978	202	+7.4
1979	213	+5.4
1980	231	+8.4
1981	270	+16.8
1982	307	+13.7
1983	291	-5.2
1984	252	-13.4
1985	257	+1.9
1986	238	-7.3
1987	218	-9.1
1988	223	+2.3

Source: Bob Damron's Address Book, various years.

TABLE 9

Gay- and Lesbian-identified Businesses and Social Gathering Spots,
by San Francisco Neighborhoods, 1984-1988

Neighborhood	1984	1985	1986	1987	1988
Castro	66	72	69	73	76
South of Market/Folsom Street	48	47	40	32	30
Haight-Ashbury/Fillmore	24	25	18	18	18
Mission District	18	20	17	11	17
Polk Street	58	56	55	48	46
Tenderloin	34	33	35	31	31
Other	4	4	4	5	5
Total	252	257	238	218	223

Source: Bob Damron's Address Book, various years.

those seeking to lead openly gay or lesbian life-styles.[43] Still, the city's homosexual population remains a strong political and social force and will continue to enjoy national prominence; in fact, the AIDS epidemic has created the basis for new forms of solidarity and mobilization in San Francisco's gay community.[44]

The most heavily gay area of San Francisco has grown up in Eureka Valley, in the general vicinity of Castro and 18th Street, a district now generally referred to simply as "The Castro." Once the political home base of slain gay supervisor Harvey Milk, the Castro District began to assume its present social identity during the *gay bohemian influx* of the late 1960s and early 1970s, when a working-class, largely Irish Catholic neighborhood with relatively low rents and low home prices was discovered by local counter-cultural homosexuals. Several local taverns were converted into gay bars, and homosexual realtors began to channel gay men into the neighborhood of small Victorian houses and flats, attractive to small households. As with the earlier hippie influx in the Haight-Ashbury, the gay population entering the Castro was widely regarded by the established local community as something of an undesirable, quasi-ethnic minority during this initial phase of subcultural expansion, raising fears of "invasion" and precipitating "white flight":

> Real estate agents were already writing obituaries for the Haight-Ashbury neighborhood over the hill. The hippies came in and wham, there went the neighborhood. Now the gays were going to do that too, right here in Most Holy Redeemer Parish... The stolid Irish families sold their Victorians at dirt-cheap prices, fearing greater loss if they waited. By 1973, the numbers of gays moving into the neighborhood amounted to an invasion. That's what the old-timers called the new men of Castro Street—invaders. . . . At least half of the people moving in were gay, while more and more of the old-timers sold out.[45]

Gay bars, bookstores, restaurants, and other businesses began to proliferate in the Castro during the *middle-class transition* of the mid-1970s; regardless of local fears, property values actually increased by about five times between 1973 and 1976. Police conservatively estimated in 1976 that about 80 gay men a week were moving into San

---

[43]Interviews with Max Kirkeberg, July 22, 1986, and Ed Boyle, Aug. 6, 1986.

[44]For a good account of the reaction of the gay community to the AIDS epidemic, see Frances FitzGerald, "A Reporter at Large," *The New Yorker,* July 28, 1986, pp. 44-63.

[45]Randy Shilts, *The Mayor of Castro Street: The Life and Times of Harvey Milk* (New York: St. Martin's Press, 1982), p. 82.

Francisco. By this point the gay counter-culture had been replaced by a more middle-class, specifically gay community on Castro Street.[46] Trendy boutiques, gift shops, and clothes stores began to replace services to the local population, such as hardware stores, wallpaper shops, and other businesses important in the earlier stages of neighborhood renovation by gay elements. According to one study, the Castro District had become a "gay ghetto" by the late 1970s, marked by a large and visible subculture with supportive businesses and institutions located nearby.[47]

After the counter-cultural and middle-class gay entrepreneurial phases in the Castro, a number of national commercial chains, able to pay the increasingly high rents, opened local franchises in the early 1980s, leading some residents to fear that the *bourgeois consolidation* of urban revitalization had gone too far. Many neighborhood-based stores were replaced by the likes of Walgreen's, Hallmark Cards, Mrs. Field's Cookies, Seven-Eleven, and Haagen-Dazs ice cream. The Castro retained its gay identity, but lost its working-class character and become a prime example of what locals began calling "guppie" (gay urban professional) culture, homosexual counterpoint to the prevailing "yuppie" (young urban professional) phenomenon.

Several other neighborhoods have been affected by a homosexual influx, reflecting an internal differentiation within the gay and lesbian communities. For example, a budding feminist community, predominantly lesbian, grew up during the late 1970s around The Women's Building and a number of female-owned bars, bookstores, and other businesses in the vicinity of Valencia Street on the western edge of the Mission District (see Map 11).

The Haight-Ashbury is a neighborhood that shows clearly the interactions and mutual influences of the beat, hippie, and gay subcultures. In the early 1960s nascent beatnik and homosexual communities were forming in the district, but soon these were overshadowed by the massive influx of hippies. If the "hippie capital" had not emerged in the Haight during the late 1960s, the area might well have assumed the present-day gay identity of the Castro District! In any case, the revitalized Haight-Ashbury has become quite heterogeneous, with a large but not predominant homosexual community, indicating that the area has evolved into what Christopher Winters calls a "self-consciously heterogeneous neighborhood."[48]

---

[46]*Ibid.*, pp. 112-113.

[47]Martin P. Levine, "Gay Ghetto," in *Gay Men: The Sociology of Male Homosexuality,* (New York: Harper and Row, 1979), pp. 182-205.

[48]Christopher Winters, "The social identity of evolving neighborhoods," *Landscape,* 23, no. 1 (1979): 8-14.

As Chapter 6 documents, the evolution of the Haight-Ashbury District suggests that postwar nonconformist subcultures, in addition to increasing in size and impact, have attained a greater sense of social cohesion and cultural tradition than was previously the case. A nonconformist group succession has emerged in San Francisco and a number of other large American cities, comparable in some ways to the ethnic succession that has long characterized metropolitan areas in the United States. This indicates that at least in some cases nonconformists have come to constitute valid minority groups in American cities, although there remain important differences between them and ethnic groups, which can be seen in terms of their respective roles in contemporary urban revitalization.

URBAN REVITALIZATION AND SUBCULTURAL SUCCESSION

Since World War II, San Francisco's economy has become increasingly specialized in tourism, the retail trade, and white-collar services associated with a regional "headquarters city"—especially in the finance, insurance, and real estate sectors. The port, manufacturing, agricultural refining, and other blue-collar functions have steadily declined in importance. This economic shift has put new pressures on the city's older working-class neighborhoods, promoting physical renovation and attendant changes in social identity. In 1980, for example, 20,300 new jobs were created in San Francisco, mainly in the white-collar and service sector, while only 852 net dwelling units were added to the city's housing stock.[49] The resulting housing shortage and affordability problems have made San Francisco one of the nation's most expensive cities to live in and contributed to problems of gentrification and displacement in the neighborhoods.[50] Some areas have been radically transformed by this wave of inner-city revitalization. South of Market, for example, has witnessed a steady encroachment of redevelopment projects, such as the Moscone Convention Center, and expansion of the burgeoning downtown financial district. This threatens to eliminate the area's remaining reservoir of low-income housing. If the cheap housing goes, South of Market certainly cannot continue to serve as a reception area for low-income immigrants, artists, and others.[51]

---

[49]Gerald Adams, "S.F. blamed for Bay Area housing crisis," *San Francisco Examiner,* Nov. 2, 1981.

[50]For an analysis of the city's contemporary housing crisis, see San Francisco City and County, *Report of the Citizen's Housing Task Force,* July 29, 1981.

[51]See Chester W. Hartman, *Yerba Buena: Land Grab and Community Resistance in San Francisco* (San Francisco: Glide Publications, 1974), and *The Transformation of San Francisco* (Rowman and Allanheld, 1984).

The similarities and differences between types of communities become clearer when viewed in relationship to these processes of urban decay and revitalization. Both ethnic and nonconformist groups have initially been the recipients of a downward filtration of deteriorating physical structures, and both have used the formation of localized communities as a means of creating specialized subcultural identities. But nonconformists have displayed more of a sense of congregation by choice, helping to account for their greater degree of mobility and fluidity. Elements of the urban built environment, generally a combination of aesthetic appeal and initially low rents, attracted the nonconformist communities, where they initiated a process of urban renovation: North Beach, the Haight-Ashbury, and the Castro District all witnessed "invasions" by nontraditional groups, and all have subsequently been gentrified. Although nonconformist groups have tended to be forerunners of gentrification in the inner city, their presence nonetheless has involved the creation of distinctive minority districts in American cities, as with ethnic groups. The development of San Francisco's major postwar ethnic groups generally can be traced to initial labor immigration, as well as to more recent political turmoil abroad that has created sizable refugee communities. The in-migration of nonconformist elements cannot be so directly related to labor immigration or political asylum; it has resulted more from the prospects of personal fulfillment in San Francisco's large nontraditional communities.

Some general patterns of ethnic flux can be found in a comparison of San Francisco's principal ethnic areas in 1970 and 1980, as shown in Maps 12 and 13. Areas in which blacks constituted 25 percent of the population were eliminated on the western side of the Western Addition, in both the Haight-Ashbury and Lone Mountain districts, as well as on Potrero Hill. Hispanics suffered a notable erosion on the western side of the Mission District, in Eureka and Noe valleys, but witnessed an increased presence in the Outer Mission. Filipinos increased both South of Market and toward Daly City, along with Hispanics, while the Chinese expanded into the Richmond District. In general, San Francisco's principal ethnic cores remained intact during the 1970s, but some outlying sectors experienced significant modifications, providing indications of contemporary subcultural flux.

The precise sequence of subcultural succession in the city's neighborhoods has depended on a number of factors, including both the availability of areas being abandoned by previous groups and the numbers, socioeconomic status, and culture of the incoming groups. So a number of internal and external variables need to be considered in explaining the evolutionary morphogenesis of different minority

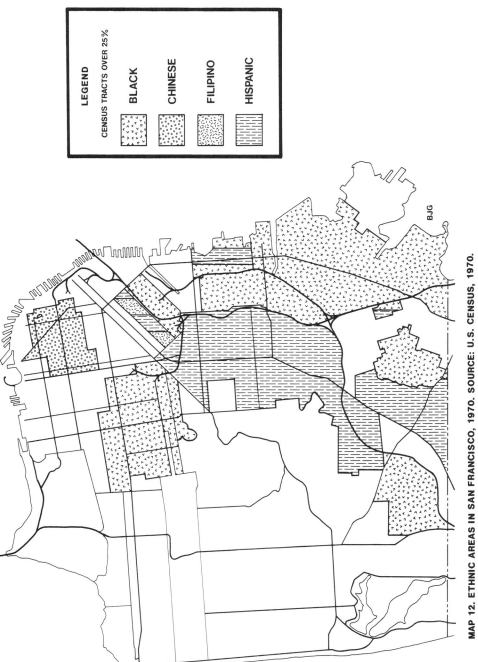

MAP 12. ETHNIC AREAS IN SAN FRANCISCO, 1970. SOURCE: U.S. CENSUS, 1970.

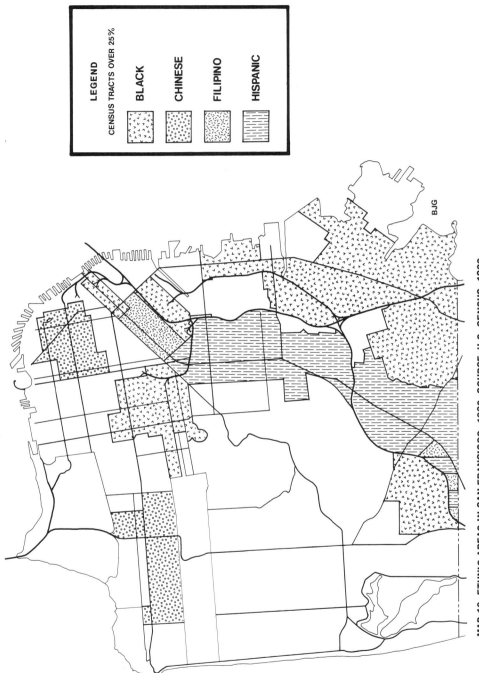

MAP 13. ETHNIC AREAS IN SAN FRANCISCO, 1980. SOURCE: U.S. CENSUS, 1980.

communities. But there are some general patterns transcending local particularities: ethnic and nonconformist communities have tended to follow different life-cycles, as will be seen in more detail in the following two case studies of neighborhood evolution.

Plate 12. Chinatown's symbolic entrance, the "Dragon Gate" at Grant and Bush streets. This popular landmark and tourist attraction, completed in 1970, was a gift of the Government of Taiwan. (Photograph by Brian J. Godfrey.)

Plate 13. The extension of San Francisco's Chinatown into North Beach. This view shows the Wing Fai Trading Company next to the Panelli Brothers, an uncomfortable ethnic juxtaposition also found in New York City and other large American cities. As Italian immigration abated and Chinese immigration resumed in recent years, the old "Little Italy" districts have been affected by the expansion of Chinatowns across the United States. (Photograph by Brian J. Godfrey.)

Plate 14. Mission Dolores, with a Gray Line tour bus in front. This former Spanish mission has accompanied the ethnic vicissitudes of San Francisco: the congregation became largely Irish-American in the late nineteenth century, and largely Hispanic-American in the late twentieth century. (Photograph by Brian J. Godfrey.)

5

THE MISSION DISTRICT
Evolutionary Morphogenesis of a Hispanic *Barrio*

> The Mission's traditional role in San Francisco has been as a stopping-off place for successive waves of foreign-born. When they made enough money, or mastered the language, or otherwise got to feel more at home in their new country, they moved out of the sheltering ghetto to the Parkside or Sunset, or the Peninsula.[1]
>
> David Braaten, 1962

San Francisco's Mission District has a long history of ethnic succession, predating development of the inner city's "sheltering ghetto." Costanoan Indians, Spanish, and Mexicans settled the sparsely populated area around Mission Dolores by the early nineteenth century. Yankee squatters occupied rural lots in the area during the Gold Rush. As the Mission District was urbanized in the late nineteenth and early twentieth centuries, waves of Old World immigrants and their offspring poured into the area, particularly the Irish, Germans, Italians, and Scandinavians. Latin American immigration mounted after the Second World War, in a sense recapturing past turf. Although Hispanics remain clearly predominant in the Mission's inner core, heart of the *barrio,* in recent years the western and northern parts of the district have experienced a significant influx of other ethnic groups, as well as nonconformist elements, intensifying the various subcultural enclaves.

The origins and evolution of the Mission District's Hispanic community provide an illustrative case of ethnic flux in the American inner city. The development of this social area involves historic processes of urban morphogenesis, the initiation and adaptation of city form; and the physical shaping of this community reflects subcultural intensification, the making of distinctive social worlds within a larger urban setting. The importance of putting subcultural theory into a spatial context becomes apparent in

---

[1]David Braaten, "Signs of a renaissance in the Mission: New buildings rise above dowdy streets," *San Francisco Chronicle,* May 4, 1962, p. 12.

examining the evolutionary morphogenesis of the Mission's *barrio*: the emergence of Hispanic ethnic identities has been organically related to the creation of form and structure in an urban social area.

The Mission District lies in the valley surrounded by Twin Peaks, Diamond Heights, Bernal Heights, and Potrero Hill. In a generic sense, "the Mission" traditionally has been considered a general sector of the city, cutting a wide swath between Civic Center and Daly City; this broad area has been divided between the Mission District proper (also called the Inner Mission) and the more southerly Outer Mission District (see Map 14). Adjacent neighborhoods have had an ambivalent relationship with the Mission District. During the late nineteenth and early twentieth centuries, when blue-collar residents of European immigrant stock dominated the whole area, the surrounding neighborhoods tended to be included as parts of the generic Mission District. As Hispanics made inroads in the Mission after World War II, surrounding areas gradually resigned their district status, a trend accentuated by the contemporary influx of youngish, middle-class whites into the adjacent hills. Although popular conceptions of the Mission District's boundaries have varied over the years, reflecting the history of ethnic settlement, a good contemporary approximation is a planning district for city agencies called the "Mission Model Neighborhood." Map 15 subdivides this broad area into three distinct morphological zones:

1. The Mission Core roughly coincides with the contemporary Hispanic *barrio*. It is a topographically low-lying area on the district's southeast side, and consists primarily of modest single-family cottages and multi-unit buildings.[2] Renters occupy over four-fifths of the housing units; about half of these renter households are Hispanic, along with well over half of the total population. In 1980, the median value of an owner-occupied house in the Mission Core was 12 percent below the city median, and the median monthly rent was 17 percent below the citywide level (see Table 10).

2. The North Mission is composed largely of declining industry and warehouses, cheap flats, and residential hotels. Historically, it has served as a bridge between the Mission District and the South-of-Market area in both functional and social terms; this was the earliest part of the Mission to experience a large-scale Hispanic influx, and in recent years the North Mission has witnessed a large influx of Asians (e.g., Chinese, Vietnamese, and Filipinos) and alternative life-style groups (e.g., gays and lesbians,

---

[2]As defined here, the predominantly Hispanic Mission Core includes census tracts 208, 209, 228, and 229; this area is bounded by Army Street on the south, Valencia Street on the west, 17th Street on the north, and the James Lick Freeway (101) on the east.

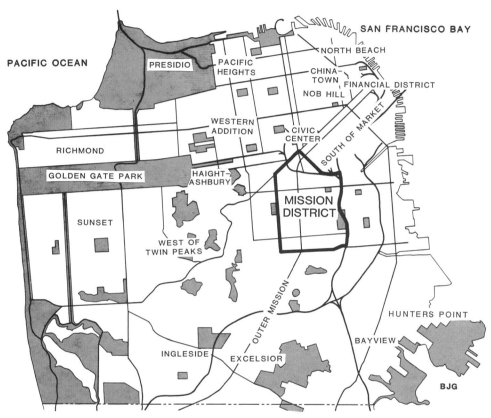

MAP 14. THE MISSION DISTRICT AND ADJACENT NEIGHBORHOODS

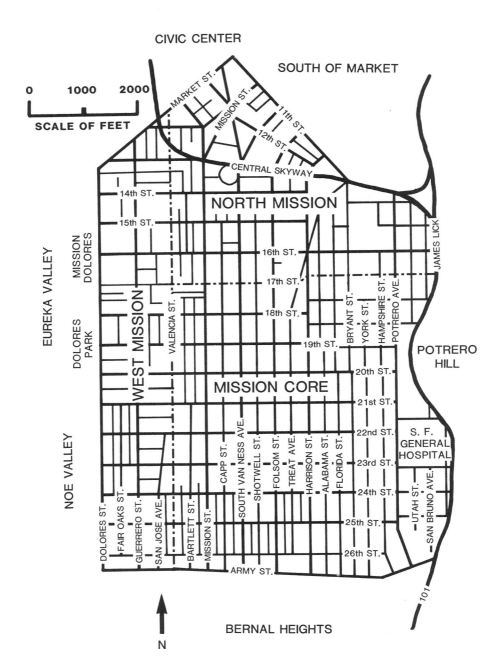

MAP 15. MISSION DISTRICT STREETS.

TABLE 10

Housing Characteristics in the Mission District, 1980

	Mission District Core	North Mission District	West Mission District	Total Mission District	Total S.F. Citywide
Percent of Units Owner-Occupied	17.4%	4.5%	11.1%	13.3%	31.8%
Percent of Owners Hispanic	39.3%	31.8%	15.1%	31.7%	8.5%
Median Value of Owner-Occupied Homes	$91,500	$87,500	$119,900	$94,900	$103,900
Percent of Units Renter-Occupied	82.6%	95.4%	88.9%	86.7%	68.2%
Percent of Renter Households Hispanic	48.0%	34.3%	23.0%	36.7%	9.5%
Median Monthly Contract Rent	$222	$185	$250	$223	$266

Source: U.S. Census, various years. The Mission District Core includes census tracts 208, 209, 228, and 229; the North Mission, 177 and 201; and the West Mission, 202, 207, and 210.

artists, and "punks").[3] Renters occupy more than 95 percent of the housing units here, with Hispanics making up more than a third of these households. This area has the lowest housing prices in the district: the median value of an owner-occupied home was 16 percent below the city average in 1980, and rents were more than 30 percent cheaper (see Table 10).

3. The West Mission, topographically and socially upscale, has witnessed the most physical renovation in recent years, largely a spillover effect of prospering Eureka and Noe valleys to the west.[4] The West Mission has experienced a significant influx of youngish, affluent whites, including sizable homosexual and quasi-bohemian components. Renters occupy almost 90 percent of the housing units here, and the median rent approached the city norm in 1980; the median value of owner-occupied homes exceeded that of the total city by 15 percent. Less than a quarter of the renter households were Hispanic (see Table 10).

The primary focus of this chapter is the morphogenesis of a Hispanic *barrio* in the Mission Core, but the North and West Mission are also referred to, since both areas have played important roles in the settlement of San Francisco's Hispanic community. The historical geography of the Mission District does not reveal a ghetto, with its negative images of ethnic isolation, exclusivity, and degradation.[5] Instead, the Mission has served as something of an incubator for subcultural identities, a way station where a succession of groups have adapted to American society. As one observer puts it, "The Mission has been a revolving door into American society."[6]

HISPANICS AS AN ETHNIC PROTOTYPE

Ethnicity is commonly conceptualized as a simple matter of allegiance to primordial religious, national-origin, or racial groups. Upon close inspection, however, ethnic identification is not such a static, clear-cut, or homogeneous phenomenon; instead, it represents an intricate and evolving set of identities, multiple but cohesive in

---

[3]The North Mission includes census tracts 177 and 201, an area bounded by 17th Street on the south, Valencia Street on the west, and roughly Market and 11th streets on the north.

[4]The West Mission encompasses census tracts 202, 207, and 210, an area bounded by Army Street on the south, Dolores Street on the west, Market Street on the north, and Valencia Street on the east.

[5]For a review of the inapplicability of the traditional "ghetto model" to the Hispanic *barrio,* see Ricardo Romo's *East Los Angeles: The History of a Barrio* (Austin: University of Texas Press, 1983), pp. 3-13.

[6]Randolph Delehanty, *San Francisco: Walks and Tours in the Golden Gate City* (New York: Dial Press, 1980), p. 154.

nature. Ethnicity is socially constructed in time and space. It constitutes a variable process of human adaptation to specific environments.

The spatial and temporal contexts within which ethnic identities emerge often are not appreciated. Yet immigrants cannot help coming to perceive themselves in terms of both their background and the nature of their contacts with the receiving society; this interactive process fosters the acquisition of new group identities. A study of West Indians in London, for example, found that an ethnic identity "based upon blackness [was] emerging," despite prior cultural and national differences.[7] On the other hand, outward ethnic similarities may disguise internal differences, as for West Indians in New York City, a largely overlooked black minority.[8] So immigrant groups manifest varying degrees of both ethnic syncretism and separation. Immigrants may form a new ethnic identity as part of a wider minority group, but still maintain a more specific sense of regional origin—in a sense, subcultures within wider subcultures. For example, Vietnamese in the United States come to see themselves to some extent as Asian-Americans, Haitians as blacks, and Salvadorans as Hispanics. The degree of subcultural cohesion and fragmentation naturally varies, depending upon factors specific to each minority group. Examination of the historical geography of immigrant settlement clarifies the nature of different ethnic identities.

Hispanic immigrants show the complexities of these countervailing cultural forces. Certain common cultural traits, most notably the Spanish language itself, tend to provide a unifying focus in American society, while national and regional differences provide the basis for differentiation. American cities have come to be associated with different Hispanic groups: Cubans in Miami, Puerto Ricans in New York City, and Mexicans in Los Angeles, for example. Recent years also have witnessed a growing recognition of the internal differentiation of Hispanic communities within American cities, such as that represented by the Dominican immigrants in New York City.[9] San Francisco's heterogeneous Hispanic community, made up of diverse Latin American nationalities, also provides a good example of the complexities attending the creation of ethnic identities. About 39 percent of the city's total *Latino* population is of Mexican

---

[7]Douglas K. Midgett, "West Indian ethnicity in Great Britain," in Brian M. Du Toit and Helen I. Safa (eds.), *Migration and Urbanization* (The Hague: Mouton, 1975), pp. 57-82.

[8]Dennis Conway and Ualthan Bigby, "Residential differentiation among an overlooked black minority: 'New immigrant' West Indians in New York," *Proceedings of the Conference of Latin Americanist Geographers,* 9 (1983): 99-109.

[9]See, for example, Glenn Hendricks, *The Dominican Diaspora: From the Dominican Republic to New York City—Villagers in Transition* (New York: Teachers College Press, 1974).

origin, 6 percent is from Puerto Rico, 2 percent emanates from Cuba, and 53 percent is what the 1980 U.S. Census categorizes as of "other Spanish origin." These "others"—or *los otros,* to use the Spanish—come mainly from Central American countries. San Francisco probably has the highest proportion of Hispanics of Central American origin of any major U.S. city.

The city's fastest-growing Central American groups in recent years have been from strife-torn Nicaragua and El Salvador, and together they probably outnumber Hispanics of Mexican origin. San Francisco has come to be a major center of Central Americans in the United States, along with Los Angeles, New Orleans, Miami, Washington, D.C., and New York.[10] Scholars have largely overlooked the history, nature, and extent of Central American migration to both San Francisco and the United States generally; only the news media have paid even cursory attention to this large-scale migration, because of the contemporary upheavals in Central America. Yet Central Americans and other Latins have migrated to San Francisco in significant waves ever since the Gold Rush, setting the preconditions for the more recent influx. This migration to San Francisco reflected both the city's traditional role as a major port of entry on the West Coast and its commercial ties specifically with Latin America. A historical geography of ethnic settlement in the city, considering both external and local variables, helps to explain both the nature of Latin American identities and the evolutionary morphogenesis of San Francisco's Hispanic *barrio*.[11]

EXTERNAL CONNECTIONS AND LATIN AMERICAN IMMIGRATION

Historical-geographic connections account for the large Central American component to San Francisco's Hispanic population, as in the mercantile model of settlement proposed by geographer James Vance.[12] This model holds that long-distance trade ties create a wholesaling entrepot, which subsequently becomes a social entrepot for migrants. When immigration continues and ethnic identities remain strong, secondary settlement centers may emerge; or, under conditions of immigrant acculturation, ethnic compounds may remain chiefly in the entrepot city instead of

---

[10]Interview with Carlos Córdova, who has taught a course at San Francisco State University on Central Americans in the U.S., May 24, 1983.

[11]For another version of this analysis, see Brian J. Godfrey, "Ethnic identities and ethnic enclaves: The morphogenesis of San Francisco's Hispanic *barrio*," *Yearbook of the Conference of Latin Americanist Geographers,* 11 (1985), pp. 45-53.

[12]James E. Vance, Jr., *The Merchant's World: The Geography of Wholesaling* (Englewood Cliffs, N. J.: Prentice-Hall, 1970).

diffusing. This social model of settlement has been applied to the eastern seaboard of the U.S., and to the internal migrations of blacks and Mexican-Americans.[13] San Francisco's role as an entrepot city for Central Americans also fits well into this scheme, given the city's historic position as a mercantile center of commercial interests on the West Coast.

San Francisco has long maintained transportation ties with Central America. During the California Gold Rush, the Pacific Mail Steamer and other vessels regularly plied a course between the East Coast and San Francisco via overland connections on the Central American isthmus, mainly in Panama and Nicaragua.[14] William Walker's expeditionary force in Central America, which invaded the region between 1856 and 1865, was formed of adventurers recruited "on the wharves of San Francisco."[15] Coffee was introduced as a cash crop in Central America during this period and a brisk export trade developed with the West Coast, where San Francisco was the chief processing center. Companies based in the city—Folger's, Hills Brothers, and MJB—fostered contacts with Central America's coffee-producing areas; once these links were established, social networks led to incipient migratory movements, both to and fro, limited at first to members of the coffee oligarchy and other elite families. Mass immigration from Central America started during the early twentieth century. Many Salvadorans, Nicaraguans, and other Central Americans were recruited to work on construction of the Panama Canal; afterwards, much of this mobile labor force joined shipping lines operating in the Canal, leading many Central Americans to come to San Francisco, the principal port on the West Coast until after World War II.[16]

Restrictive legislation checked Old World immigration during the mid-1920s, and Latin American labor helped fill the void in both agriculture and low-paying urban jobs until the Depression of the 1930s temporarily stopped this labor influx. In addition to Central Americans, many Mexicans fled the dislocation of the Revolution or were attracted to the U.S. by the prospect of jobs in the prosperous, labor-scarce 1920s; and many Puerto Ricans and other Spanish-speakers entered San Francisco from Hawaii,

---

[13]James E. Vance, Jr., *Location in a System of Global Extent: A Social Model of Settlement* (Geographical Papers, University of Reading, England, 1982).

[14]Jean Vance, "The cities by San Francisco Bay," in John S. Adams (ed.), *Contemporary Metropolitan America*, vol. 1, (Cambridge, Mass.: Ballinger, 1976), pp. 231-232; and J. S. Holliday, *The World Rushed In: The California Gold Rush Experience* (New York: Simon and Schuster, 1981).

[15]Roque Dalton, *Las Historias Prohibidas del Pulgarcito* (Mexico City: Siglo Veintiuno Editores, 1980), p. 43.

[16]Interview with Carlos Córdova.

where they had worked in plantation agriculture.[17] Census figures reflected these pre-Depression migratory waves. After decades of relative stability, the number of Mexican-born immigrants in San Francisco more than quadrupled between 1910 and 1930, reaching 7,900, or 5.1 percent of the total foreign-born population; immigrants born in Central and South America more than tripled during the 1920s to over 3,200, or 2 percent of the total foreign-born population.[18]

Many Latin American males worked as laborers near the waterfront, especially south of Market Street. The coffee companies were located there, as were canneries, agricultural refineries, and industrial plants needing manual labor. Also nearby were the United Fruit Company docks on the south side of the China Basin channel, where a banana boat arrived weekly from Central America; the United Fruit Company operated three freight and passenger steamships between San Francisco and the west coast of Central America, where banana plantations were moved in the late 1920s and 1930s to escape the Panama disease, a banana plague, on the Caribbean side.[19]

The prewar shipping lines between Central America and San Francisco contributed to larger immigrations from the region during and after World War II. During the war, shipyards and other wartime industries in the labor-scarce Bay Area recruited not only blacks from the U.S. South but also significant numbers of Central Americans, from both El Salvador and Nicaragua. Mexican immigrants tended to be absorbed into the *bracero* agricultural labor program, started in 1942, and settled more in the East Bay and South Bay regions, where agriculture still flourished.[20] These wartime labor flows accounted for the great increase in the Central American-born population of San Francisco during the 1940s. After a decline during the 1930s, the Depression era, San Francisco's Mexican-born population increased only moderately to 5,600 (4.6 percent of the total number of foreign-born) by 1950. Meanwhile, the Central and South American-born population more than doubled to 6,855 (5.6 percent), so that by 1950 it already outnumbered the number of Mexican-born. Still, during and shortly after the war, many *Chicanos* did move to San Francisco, particularly the children of migrant

---

[17] For more on Puerto Rican immigration, see R. C. Leyland, *Puerto Ricans in the San Francisco Bay Area, California: An Historical and Cultural Geography,* Master's thesis in Geography, California State University, Hayward, 1980.

[18] U.S. Census, various years.

[19] Writers' Program of the Works Projects Administration (WPA) in Northern California, *San Francisco* (New York: Hastings House, 1940), p. 270; Robert C. West and John P. Argelli, *Middle America* (Englewood Cliffs, N. J.: Prentice-Hall, 1966), pp. 388-390.

[20] Interview with Charles Wollenberg, history professor in the Peralta College District, March 29, 1984.

farm workers from the Southwest, and Mexican-Americans tended to predominate in the affairs of the Hispanic community.[21]

By the 1940s, if not before, San Francisco attracted a "critical mass" of Central American population, contributing to increasing emigration from the region, and after the War the number of Central American immigrants continued to increase steadily, as preexisting family ties helped to encourage settlement in the city. By 1970, the Central and South American-born population of San Francisco reached 16,700 (10.82 percent of the foreign born), mostly Salvadorans and Nicaraguans, more than twice the number of Mexican-born. In the 1970 census, there were 18,500 San Franciscans of Mexican stock (5.8 percent), and 27,000 (8.5 percent) of other Latin American nationalities.[22]

Until the late 1970s, the migratory process followed the familiar socioeconomic "push-pull" pattern: lack of opportunity for advancement at home led to widespread emigration to the United States. San Francisco was an attractive destination for aspiring Central American immigrants, mainly of urban working-class and professional backgrounds.[23] In the late 1970s, however, Central American immigration changed in nature and accelerated in volume. The region's political situation became increasingly oppressive and chaotic, forcing many to seek political refuge abroad. Many Nicaraguan opponents of the Somoza regime fled to the U.S. before the strongman was overthrown in 1979; after this, many opponents of the Sandinista regime came to San Francisco, bringing *contra* political activities with them. The internal crisis in El Salvador flared up in the late 1970s as well, leading the local Salvadoran population to swell. Significant numbers of Guatemalans also began to appear. Community activists estimate that the number of Central Americans in San Francisco has doubled or even tripled since 1977, although the undocumented nature of the immigration makes this impossible to quantify precisely.

San Francisco's historic connections with Latin America explain its preeminence as a destination for this contemporary immigration. The Pacific maritime routes encouraged labor flows, both before and during World War II, which in turn promoted larger-scale Central American immigration to the city. Thus the Hispanic population of San Francisco, as well as that of satellite suburban communities in nearby San Mateo

---

[21]Interview with Dorinda Moreno, a long-time Mission District resident and community activist, March 22, 1984.

[22]U.S. Census, various years.

[23]Hernan Daniel González, *La Trayectoria: A Method,* Interdisciplinary master's thesis, San Francisco State University, 1976.

and Marin counties, is predominantly non-Mexican; East Bay, South Bay, and coastal farming zones, on the other hand, were more closely tied to Mexican agricultural labor, and consequently Mexicans became the predominant group of Hispanic origin in those areas (see Table 11).

SETTLEMENT INCEPTION IN THE MISSION DISTRICT

Within San Francisco, the creation of a contemporary *barrio* in the Mission District must be placed within the historical context of local group succession. The area's settlement history conditioned its recent ethnic evolution. The Hispanic community's evolutionary morphogenesis reflects the adaptive processes by which emergent social groups make use of the existing built environment of the city, modifying it for new uses. To evaluate contemporary ethnicity in the Mission District, it is important first to recapitulate briefly the history of the area's spatial structure and its relationship to subcultural intensification and succession.

Although dedicated to Saint Francis of Assisi (*San Francisco de Asis*) when it was founded in 1776, the local Spanish mission soon became known as Mission Dolores, after a nearby stream. The mission was set in a location about four miles southeast of the *presidio*, an area considered appropriate for agriculture and herding, lying in a valley sheltered from the wind and fog by the peaks to the west and watered by a creek flowing into a swamp and shallow bay on its northeastern edge. The population of Mission Dolores reached a peak of about 1,500, composed mostly of local Indian neophytes, but it was subject to the ravages of new diseases and a high rate of desertion from mission life; between 1804 and 1806, for example, the Indian population of Mission Dolores dropped from 1,103 to 886.[24] Missions better suited inclined to agro-pastoral pursuits were established elsewhere in Northern California, such as Santa Clara and Sonoma, and San Francisco's mission settlement stagnated in the early 1800s.[25]

After gaining independence from Spain, Mexico secularized the California mission lands during the early 1830s, turning them over to Mexican soldiers and settlers, the *Californios*. The names of some Mission District streets—such as Guerrero and Valencia—recall Mexican settler families, but the Hispanic origins were all but obliterated in the late nineteenth century. Now on the district's northwestern edge, at

---

[24]Zephyrin Engelhardt, *San Francisco or Mission Dolores* (Chicago: Franciscan Herald Press, 1924), p. 137.

[25]Oscar Lewis, *San Francisco: Mission to Metropolis* (Berkeley: Howell-North Books, 1966), pp. 12-16.

TABLE 11

Total Hispanic and Mexican-origin Populations in the Bay Area, 1980

County	Total Population	Total Hispanic Population		Total Mexican-Origin Population	
Alameda	1,105,379	129,962	11.7%[a]	80,230	61.7%[b]
Contra Costa	656,380	55,977	8.5	36,266	64.7
Marin	222,568	9,241	4.1	4,110	44.4
Napa	99,199	8,636	8.7	6,327	73.2
San Francisco	678,974	83,373	12.2	32,633	39.1
San Mateo	587,329	73,362	12.4	36,541	49.8
Santa Clara	1,295,071	226,611	17.4	176,838	78.0
Solano	235,203	24,773	10.5	15,144	61.1
Sonoma	299,681	20,850	6.9	13,832	66.3
Totals	5,179,784	632,785	12.2%	401,881	63.5%

a. Percentage of total population.
b. Percentage of Hispanic population.

Source: U.S. Census, 1980.

Dolores and 16th streets, Mission Dolores was the principal landmark as the valley began to be urbanized, and the surrounding area took on the name "Mission District."

As San Francisco expanded from Yerba Buena Cove during the Gold Rush, the city's transportation corridor to the south, blocked by Mission Bay and Potrero Hill, developed in a more southwesterly direction through the Mission District. In 1851, a private contractor completed a 2.5-mile plank road from Yerba Buena Cove to the old mission; a road along Folsom Street into the Mission District was completed in 1853. The city's first regular public transportation service began on the Mission Plank Road in 1852 with initiation of the horse-drawn Yellow Omnibus line. With increasing traffic several competing lines opened up and by 1862 the fares were uniformly reduced. The first streetcar line in San Francisco, horse-drawn on rails along Market Street out to Mission Dolores, was extended to 25th and Valencia streets in 1863.[26] Completion of the San Bruno Turnpike in 1858 provided a new level road from the Mission District to the Peninsula, and the San Francisco-San Jose Railway Company opened in 1863, soon thereafter acquiring a station at 25th and Valencia streets in the Mission District.

As an area on the urban fringe, the Mission District initially developed recreational facilities and resorts, featuring theaters, racetracks, formal gardens, and zoos. The largest and most popular attraction, Woodward's Gardens on Mission and 14th streets, opened in 1866 and closed in 1894. The intervening years witnessed the gradual transformation of the Mission District from countryside to cityscape, as larger holdings were progressively subdivided for the construction of housing to accommodate San Francisco's growing population. A street grid platted in the "Mission Addition" in the 1860s and 1870s opened the way for residential growth.[27] Throughout this period, Yankee settlers squatted on the former *ranchos* in the area; by the 1860s, land titles in the Mission had been regularized, largely through legitimizing the claims of the squatters over those of Mexican landgrant holders. The Mission District fell into the hands of many landowners, thereby hindering the larger-scale housing-tract development of some later neighborhoods. The title settlement encouraged growth, as indicated by the increasing population of the city's 11th Ward, in which the Mission

---

[26]Anita Day Hubbard, "Cities within the city," *San Francisco Bulletin,* August-September, 1924. (Transcribed version available at the San Francisco History Room of the Public Library, vol. 2, pp. 105-161.)

[27]Charles Lockwood, *Suddenly San Francisco: The Early Years of an Instant City* (San Francisco: A California Living Book, 1978), pp. 152-153.

The Mission District 145

constituted the main settled area: from only about 3,000 in 1860, the ward grew to a population of some 23,000 by 1870.[28]

Housing production proceeded in earnest during the 1870s, spurred by the availability of both abundant redwood and cheap labor in the craft and construction trades during periodic economic depressions. Homesteading associations formed to develop tracts of lands, initially in flatter areas of the Mission District, since the hills posed transportation problems before cable-car lines became widespread. The Real Estate Associates was a major developer during this period, advertising in the local newspapers "handsome blocks of flats" and "Mission houses" for working- and middle-class households. The diversity of the district's "Victorian" architecture, which includes Italianate, "Stick," Queen Anne, and Edwardian styles, reflects the steady, organic urban growth of the Mission. The Mission District remained an attractive residential area during the late nineteenth century, noted for its good weather, convenient transportation facilities, and quasi-suburban atmosphere. Although the district never took on the ostentatious air of Nob Hill, some wealthy San Franciscans settled in the Mission and built mansions during this period, particularly along Howard Street (now South Van Ness Avenue). By the turn of the century, however, the district had become more densely populated and took on a more working-class air, populated largely by Irish, Germans, Scandinavians, and Italians.

The founding of local churches during this period reflected the mixed social and ethnic character of the neighborhood. Two Episcopal churches, St. John's (1857) and Holy Innocents (1903), catered to the Anglo-Saxon middle and upper classes. German and Scandinavian Lutheran settlers set up the first foreign-language churches. The Irish came to dominate the area's Catholic parish churches: Mission Dolores, reactivated as a parish church in the 1850s; St. Peter's, founded on 24th and Florida streets in 1867; St. Charles, established on South Van Ness Avenue and 18th Street in 1887; and St. James, on Guerrero and 23rd streets, in 1888. Germans congregated in St. Anthony's Catholic Church, on Army Street. This abundance of Catholic parishes in the Mission District proved to be important in the Hispanic influx after World War II, since the churches then converted to Spanish-language usage among the predominantly Catholic Latin population.

An enduring land-use pattern emerged in the Mission District by the turn of the century. Industrial activity—including foundries, breweries, tanneries, warehouses, and factories producing bottles, furniture, and mattresses—was concentrated in the northeast

---

[28]The 11th Ward covered the entire area south of Duboce, Market, and Seventh streets to the San Mateo County line; U.S. Census, various years.

sector of the Mission and extended into the South-of-Market and Potrero Hill districts toward the Bay. The rest of the Mission became a heterogeneous mixture of single-family dwellings and multi-family structures, with combined residential and commercial buildings (stores and services on the ground floors) along the major transportation arteries of Mission, Valencia, 16th and 24th streets.[29]

The conflagration of 1906 spared most of the Mission District. The fire stopped in front of Mission Dolores, thereby destroying only the northern quadrant of the district between Dolores and Howard (South Van Ness) streets north of 20th Street.[30] Although Mission Street benefited initially from increased retail activity, as downtown was rebuilt, the earthquake ultimately ended the District's pretensions of affluence. The housing shortage in the city encouraged the development of increased densities in the Mission: the larger old houses were steadily subdivided and the remaining vacant lots were developed, often with higher-density flats and apartment buildings, to house refugees from the ravaged areas. Many displaced Italians from North Beach, as well as Irish and Scandinavians from the South-of-Market area, moved into the Mission District. This lowered the social standing of the district, making it a more strictly working-class area. By 1910 the population of the Mission District exceeded 50,000, reaching about its present level. One-third of the Mission's 1910 population was foreign-born, including 3,800 Irish, 3,200 Germans, and over 1,000 Italians, Swedes, and English.[31] Although it remained a respectable area, the Mission District clearly was going downhill in social cachet:

> The Mission was already becoming a working-class neighborhood before the turn of the century, and the pell-mell building boom after the fire made it permanently so, its crowded rows of flats and backyard cottages offering few of the amenities that appeal to those in search of social status.[32]

Foreign immigration slowed down briefly during World War I, and then again more enduringly during the late 1920s. The Mission District became chiefly an area of secondary ethnic settlement, a place to establish familial roots after immigrants had

---

[29]Judith Waldhorn, "Historic preservation in San Francisco's Inner Mission" (U.S. Department of Housing and Urban Development, Washington, D.C.: U.S. Government Printing Office, 1973).

[30]See Lewis, *San Francisco,* pp. 191-193.

[31]U.S. Census, 1910.

[32]David Braaten, "S.F.'s Mission: A place of many voices," *San Francisco Chronicle,* May 1, 1962, pp. 1, 7.

already arrived in the city. It was not so much an ethnic ghetto as what the Chicago School's urban ecologists labeled a "zone of working men's homes." The Mission's blue-collar status had a functional basis: the district was centrally located, with convenient access to public transportation routes leading to the blue-collar employment centers south of Market Street, especially those along the waterfront, on the northern slope of Potrero Hill, and in "Butchertown" near Islais Creek to the east. The Mission District remained a stable working-class neighborhood during the interwar period, inhabited for the most part by increasingly acculturated European ethnic groups whose children intermingled in school and often intermarried. The development of a characteristic local accent in the "Mish," sometimes compared to Brooklynese, reflected the area's relative stability.[33] A long-time resident recalled in these terms the tightly knit, highly localized basis of community life in the interwar Mission District:

> We were dominated completely by family and church and we were absolutely secure. Every one of our relatives from both sets of grandparents to each of our many cousins lived within walking distance of each other's houses. We were Irish Catholics, mostly civil service employees. My father still tries to persuade his sons-in-law to "get on the list" just in case.
>
> Our neighborhood was our world. Although there were occasions when we took the J Streetcar or the 26 or 14 bus downtown, we rarely visited other districts of The City and it was clearly understood that one only went to Oakland in case of emergency. Our church and school were only a few blocks away and nearby Mission Street offered complete shopping and entertainment... There was an overpowering sense of continuity.[34]

Despite the relative stability of the interwar period, the Mission District gradually was becoming a lower-income and increasingly dilapidated residential area of San Francisco. By the late 1930s, the area to the east of South Van Ness Avenue, topographically the lowest-lying part of the Mission, already was among the city's lowest in socioeconomic status, just a step up from South of Market. The North Mission was the worst off: half the housing units were considered "substandard," owner occupancy was less than 20 percent, and average monthly rents were below $20 (more than a third under the city average of $31.50). Conditions in the District Core were not yet so bad, but already were well below par. For example, in the eight city

---

[33] Interviews with Dorinda Moreno and with John Keating, a retired San Francisco policeman and lifetime resident of the area, Feb. 24, 1984.

[34] Geraldine Fregoso, "Growing up in the Mission," *San Francisco Sunday Examiner and Chronicle*, "California Living" section, April 21, 1974.

blocks surrounding Alabama Street, between 20th and 24th streets, average monthly rents were about $23, owner occupancy was only 33 percent, and more than a third of all the structures were either in need of "major repairs or unfit for use."[35]

By the beginning of World War II, the Mission District had experienced a steady downward filtration of the housing stock and was ready for a process of ethnic succession. Between 1910 and 1950, the percentage of the Mission's population born abroad gradually declined from over 33 percent to under 19 percent, consistently under the citywide average. But with the influx of Latin American immigrants after 1950, the proportion of foreign-born in the District rose to new heights: 22.0 percent in 1960, 33.5 percent in 1970, and 37.8 percent in 1980 (see Table 12).

MORPHOLOGICAL ADAPTATION: THE MAKING OF A *BARRIO*

San Francisco's Latin American population historically clustered first in North Beach, where in 1875 it founded the Mexican national Catholic Church in San Francisco, Our Lady of Guadalupe. But the Hispanic community of North Beach was unable to expand greatly during the twentieth century. Italian immigration mounted in the early part of the century, and development of the bohemian nightclub and restaurant complex after World War II raised rents and forced the growing Hispanic population to move into other parts of the city.

Before the war, increasing numbers of recent Hispanic immigrants already had begun gathering in the South-of-Market area, a traditional low-income point of entry for new arrivals to the city. Many Latin American males worked on or near the docks, close to the United Fruit Company docks, the coffee companies, canneries, warehouses, and light industry. Like other immigrant groups before them—such as the Irish, Germans, Scandinavians—Latin Americans began during the interwar period to move southwestward from the South-of-Market area, following the street grid into the Mission District, clustering initially in the North Mission. Latins lived around Howard Street (now South Van Ness Avenue) in the North Mission by the early 1930s, although residents of European stock still greatly outnumbered them.[36] Construction of the Bay Bridge and its approaches during the 1930s displaced a small but growing Hispanic community on Rincon Hill, in the South-of-Market area, further accelerating this

---

[35]Figures drawn from the census tract and block statistics in the U.S. Works Projects Administration (WPA), *1939 Real Property Survey,* San Francisco, 1940.

[36]Interview with John Keating (who graduated from Mission Dolores Grammar School in 1933).

TABLE 12

Foreign-born Population in San Francisco and the Mission District, 1910-1980

Year	Mission District	San Francisco
1910	33.7%	34.1%
1920	25.9	29.4
1930	24.3	27.1
1940	21.6	22.1
1950	18.7	15.5
1960	22.0	19.2
1970	33.5	21.6
1980	37.8	28.3

Source: U.S. Census, various years.

incipient Latin American influx into the North Mission.[37] By 1940 the first Spanish-language religious congregation appeared in the North Mission.[38] Flats in this area were among the cheapest in San Francisco, renting for less than two-thirds the city average (see Table 13).

The still-small Hispanic colony in the Mission District grew steadily during the late 1940s, as the older groups steadily abandoned the area and rents remained low. Sixteenth Street in the North Mission became the first thoroughfare in the district with a significant Latin American cluster, attracting Hispanic restaurants, bakeries, and specialty shops in the early postwar years.[39] Census-tract data for Hispanics in 1950 (the first year available) show the highest concentration still in the South-of-Market and North Mission districts, after which the Latin American population continued its southward migration into the Mission Core (see Map 16).

The perception of the Mission District as a poverty area solidified after World War II. Latin American men labored at blue-collar occupations in small manufacturing shops, warehouses, and other locations close by in the North Mission, South-of-Market, and waterfront areas; Spanish-speaking women worked at the Liggett and Myers cigarette packing plant at 4th and Brannan streets and the Levi Strauss plant on Valencia and 14th. Although the Mission District already had become solidly working class, the influx of new immigrants made it appear to be going further downhill in social terms, and white residents of European ancestry increasingly moved out. Yet the postwar ethnic succession did not occur as rapidly as in the Western Addition, where a classic "white flight" developed and blacks quickly came to dominate the area; neighborhood change proceeded at a more gradual pace in the Mission District. In terms of the general stages of ethnic flux hypothesized in Chapter 2, the 1930s and 1940s constituted an incipient period of Hispanic *penetration* in the Mission District. The 1950s were the real stage of ethnic *invasion,* as the Spanish-surnamed population rose from 11 percent in 1950 to 23 percent in 1960. The *consolidation* of this ethnic community occurred during the 1960s, as the Hispanic population increased to 45 percent by 1970. Although the U.S. Census showed a 17 percent decline in San Francisco's total Hispanic population during the 1970s, the percentage of Hispanics in

---

[37]Lynn Ludlow and Mireya Navarro, "Winds of change sweep a polyglot neighborhood," *San Francisco Examiner,* Oct. 19, 1981, p. A-6.

[38]El Buen Pastor Church, at Sixteenth and Guerrero streets.

[39]Based upon the storefront listings in *Polk's San Francisco Directory* beginning in 1953, the first year that streets were indexed.

TABLE 13

Average Monthly Rents and House Sale Prices in the Mission District, 1940-1980

	Mission District Core	North Mission District	West Mission District	Total Mission District	S.F. Citywide
1940					
Rents	$27	$22	$31	$27	$37
% of Citywide	73%	59%	84%	73%	
1950					
Rents	$34	$31	$37	$34	$45
% of Citywide	76%	69%	82%	76%	
House Prices	$9,151	$8,021	$11,388	$9,645	$12,209
% of Citywide	75%	66%	93%	79%	
1960					
Rents	$58	$50	$61	$58	$74
% of Citywide	78%	68%	82%	78%	
House Prices	$16,125	$16,000	$18,000	$16,800	$19,200
% of Citywide	84%	83%	94%	87%	
1970					
Rents	$107	$90	$114	$105	$135
% of Citywide	79%	67%	84%	78%	
House Prices	$24,950	$23,100	$28,833	$25,833	$30,600
% of Citywide	82%	75%	94%	84%	
1980					
Rents	$222	$185	$250	$223	$266
% of Citywide	83%	70%	94%	84%	
House Prices	$91,525	$87,500	$119,933	$94,000	$103,900
% of Citywide	88%	84%	115%	90%	

Source: U.S. Census, various years. Average monthly rents are figured from census-tract medians for renter-occupied units; average house prices are figured from census-tract median values for owner-occupied homes.

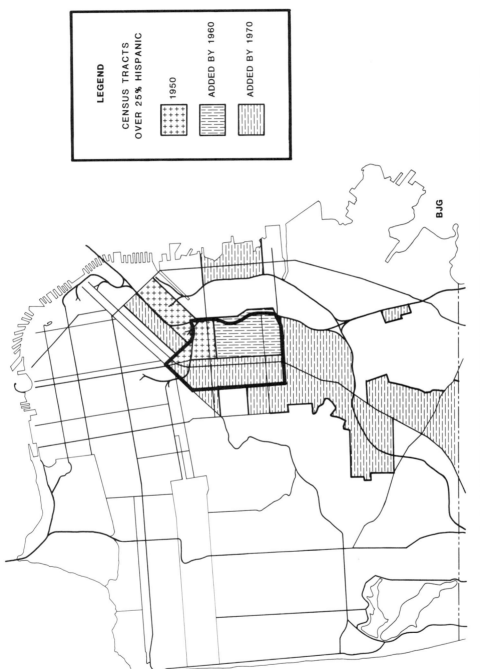

MAP 16. EXPANSION OF SAN FRANCISCO'S HISPANIC POPULATION, 1950–1970. SOURCE: U.S. CENSUS, 1950–70.

the Mission District still increased, particularly in the Mission Core (see Table 14).

The area in the Mission Core east of South Van Ness Avenue reached an official average of over 60 percent Hispanic in 1980; but given the presence of many undocumented residents, these official figures are probably conservative. It is therefore difficult to determine with precision the actual number of Hispanic residents. Residential listings in the city directories show that along Alabama Street, between 21st and 23rd streets in the heart of the *barrio,* the proportion of heads of household with Spanish surnames rose from 29 percent in 1953 to 55 percent in 1963 to 72 percent in 1973 and to 74 percent in 1982.[40] These percentages, based upon heads of household, presumably underrepresent the total Hispanic population, given its larger-than-average household size.

The reasons most commonly given for the Mission's continuing role as a reception area for Latin American immigrants include the presence of a preexisting *Latino* population with external family and social connections, so that Spanish is widely spoken, in addition to the relatively low-cost housing and the warmest climate in San Francisco.[41] New immigrants tend to settle initially with relatives, which can entail considerable cramping of living quarters in the densely populated Mission. Besides family, a variety of support services exist for new immigrants: resettlement programs, community and church groups, language and vocational training schools. Still, the lack of employment among Hispanic immigrants remains a major problem in the Mission. Former professionals often find themselves working as janitors or in restaurants, which creates great difficulties in personal adjustment.[42]

Although many immigrants initially view their stay in the U.S. as temporary, they generally become permanent residents in time, as happens elsewhere.[43] After some years in the Mission—usually working in the service sector, janitorial services, or the construction trades—the more successful immigrants tend to move to outlying parts of the city or to suburban areas, such as the Outer Mission, South San Francisco, or Daly City, which all have experienced a notable influx of Hispanics in recent years. Movement out of the Inner Mission is often regarded as a sign of upward social

---

[40]Figures compiled from *Polk's San Francisco Directory,* beginning with 1953, the first edition indexed by streets.

[41]See González, *La Trayectoria,* pp. 37-38; and Leyland, *Puerto Ricans.*

[42]Interview with Carlos Córdova.

[43]Michael J. Piore, *Birds of Passage: Migrant Labor and Industrial Societies* (Cambridge University Press, 1979).

TABLE 14

The Hispanic Population in the Mission District, 1950-1980

Year	Mission District Core		North Mission District		West Mission District		Total Mission District	
1950	3,543	12.3%	1,344	17.7%	644	5.7%	5,531	11.6%
1960	7,589	26.9	1,798	27.5	2,235	13.5	11,622	22.7
1970	15,489	52.3	2,333	39.8	5,361	32.6	23,183	44.6
1980	15,862	55.9	2,744	41.9	4,373	28.5	22,979	45.7

Source: U.S. Census, various years. The Mission District Core includes census tracts 208, 209, 228, and 229; the North Mission District, 177 and 201; and the West Mission, 202, 207, and 210.

mobility and acculturation. The continual shuffling of the immigrant population maintains the Mission District as an ethnic enclave and makes the Mission's *Latino* population "more mobile than other San Franciscans and than the total Spanish population of the City."[44] A study of Central American immigrants found:

> The inner cities in the United States, and neighborhoods like the Mission, can be conceptualized as "airports" where Central American emigrants "land" and "take off" to other geographical parts of the city and Bay Area.[45]

Twenty-fourth Street in the Mission Core has become the banner street of the *barrio*. St. Peter's Catholic Church, at 24th and Florida streets, now has an overwhelmingly Spanish-speaking congregation and is a more important religious congregation for Latin Americans in San Francisco than the traditional national church in North Beach.[46] Local businesses also reflect the population of the surrounding *barrio* streets. As opposed to the higher-rent properties on Mission Street, where national chain stores and larger commercial operations predominate, the businesses on 24th Street are smaller, more often family run, and highly ethnic in character. There were 11 businesses indicating Spanish surnames or products on lower 24th Street in 1953, constituting roughly 7 percent of the storefronts along the 13-block thoroughfare. There were 32 such Hispanic-identified storefronts by 1963 (21 percent of the total), 60 in 1973 (40 percent), and 82 in 1982 (54 percent). The most common businesses have been restaurants, grocery stores, and specialty shops; a wide variety of nationalities have been represented, but the most common have been Mexican, with a smaller number of Salvadoran and Nicaraguan, as well as a scattering from South American and Caribbean countries.[47]

Although specific Latin American national groups are not strictly segregated within the Mission District, there are areas of concentration. Mexican-Americans cluster most in the heart of the Mission Core. Door-to-door surveys taken by a local Catholic priest on streets near St. Peter's Church found about two-thirds of the population to be

---

[44]Joint Mission Coalition Organization/Stanford University Community Development Study, "Summary of trends in housing and population in the Mission Model Neighborhood 1940-1970," 1972.

[45]González, *La Trayectoria,* p. 38.

[46]There are now about a dozen Catholic churches in San Francisco offering masses in Spanish, including most of those in the Inner Mission District and many in the Outer Mission.

[47]Figures drawn from commercial listings in Polk's San Francisco Directory for 1953, 1963, 1973, and 1982.

Hispanic; of these, about 57 percent were either from Mexico or of Mexican ancestry, 21 percent were from El Salvador, 11 percent were Nicaraguan, and the rest were from diverse Caribbean and South American countries.[48] The 1980 U.S. Census data for Spanish-origin subgroups also showed Hispanics of Mexican origin to predominate in much of the Mission Core. On the other hand, *los otros*—of origins other than Mexican, Puerto Rican, and Cuban—more heavily populate the western and northern parts of the Mission, as well as the Outer Mission District (see Map 17). This spatial differentiation reflects a degree of social-class differentiation by nationality within San Francisco's Hispanic community. Central Americans predominate in the more affluent and less Hispanic areas of the West Mission and Outer Mission districts, while Mexican-Americans concentrate more in the lower-income core of the *barrio*. These geographic patterns confirm the widespread local view that Central Americans are generally more upwardly mobile in San Francisco, as might be expected of longer-distance migrants; the farther away the sending areas, the more selective would be the immigration in the social class of the participants.[49]

The diversity of the Hispanic population has hindered effective participation in local politics. Recent immigrants naturally have been more preoccupied by political struggles in their homelands than by forming effective political alliances in San Francisco; changes of regime in Central America have contributed to the development of rival factions among emigres in the city. Not surprisingly, the Mission District has had a poor voter turnout in recent years. Yet the internal differentiation of San Francisco's Latin American population does not preclude the development of a wider pan-Hispanic cohesion among the diverse nationalities, which over time forges a Hispanic minority identity. This heightened ethnic solidarity is visibly apparent in many ways in the Mission. At least 50 major public murals have been painted in the area since the early 1970s, inspired by Latin American muralists and emphasizing the Hispanic presence in the *barrio*. The Cinco de Mayo parade has been an annual event for the *Latino* community of the Mission since 1965; although it really celebrates a Mexican holiday, the defeat of the French at the Battle of Puebla in 1862, Central American groups have floats and are highly visible in the annual parade in the Mission District. A Latin American Carnaval celebration, equivalent to Mardi Gras, has taken place since 1980 and also emphasizes the common cultural roots of diverse groups. The most heavily Hispanic part of the Mission, the area around lower 24th Street (east of Mission Street), has sponsored a mainly *Latino* street fair in recent years.

---

[48] Ludlow and Navarro, "Winds of Change."

[49] González, *La Trayectoria,* pp. 35-37.

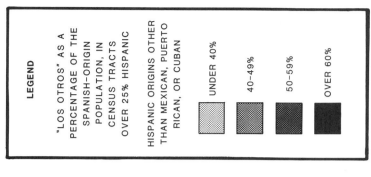

MAP 17. "LOS OTROS" IN SAN FRANCISCO'S HISPANIC AREAS, 1980. SOURCE: U.S. CENSUS, 1980.

The emergence of a Hispanic minority group among Latin American immigrants in the U.S. is in part a generational process: Glazer and Moynihan contend that "the specifically *national* aspect of most ethnic groups rarely survives the third generation in any significant terms."[50] This is the case in the Mission District, where the *Latino* presence has become identified in the public eye with the activities of young people, especially low-riders and gangs, who have attracted the attention of the news media and the ire of the police. There are at least seven Hispanic youth gangs in the Mission District, organized by neighborhood turf areas.[51] One professional observer notes:

> Mission Street is the stage to act out a drama. The liberalization of the Church and family has affected Hispanic culture, and with Hispanics being the fastest growing group in the country, there has been an increase in social conflict, given the lack of social planning. There have been no provisions for support of this young population, coupled with the breakdown of traditional sources of authority such as the Church, family, and school... With the trend toward freedom, there has been less emphasis on the setting of limits on behavior. Youths are charged with making decisions for which they are not prepared.[52]

The Mission District does have a high proportion of youth—about a third of the neighborhood's population—compared with other parts of the city. With the general crowding of living quarters in the Mission, a widely acknowledged lack of recreational facilities, and high unemployment, the street is a logical place for young people. A local group called the "Real Alternatives Program" (RAP) claims that "Mission youth by their presence are threatening the 'new' Mission; they are declaring that it is still the Barrio. This is the real reason they are seen as such a threat."

Community efforts to defend the territorial autonomy of the Mission date from the 1950s, when public housing projects were proposed for the district. A few were built, but local residents were aware of the displacement of blacks and Japanese in the Western Addition and resisted massive redevelopment in the Mission District. During the 1960s, however, the construction of the Bay Area Rapid Transit (BART) subway

---

[50] Nathan Glazer and Daniel P. Moynihan, *Beyond the Melting Pot,* 2nd ed. (Cambridge, Mass.: The M.I.T. Press, 1970), p. 113.

[51] Mireya Navarro, "Showdown between Latino gangs ends in peace pact," *San Francisco Sunday Examiner and Chronicle,* July 10, 1983, pp. B-1, B-4.

[52] Comments by Carmen Carillo, Director of Mental Health for San Francisco's District 1, which encompasses the Mission District, on a KQED television documentary, "Mission Street: Four Blocks of Trouble," Sept. 27, 1980.

line up Mission Street proved nearly as traumatic for the district as redevelopment had been in the Western Addition. Controversies over height limits and densities ultimately prompted the implementation of controls on development near the BART subway stations at 16th and 24th streets. The Mission Coalition Organization (MCO), active during the anti-poverty programs of the late 1960s and early 1970s, became a powerful voice for neighborhood preservation; but the MCO became defunct during the mid-1970s, split apart largely by the unresolved conflicts posed by the Mission's dual identity as both a *barrio latino* and a working-class district of diverse groups.[53]

Despite the efforts of community activists, rents in the Mission District did tend to rise faster than the citywide average during the 1970s, raising fears of displacement (see Table 13). The northern and western areas of the Mission District so far have been the most "gentrified." The in-movers have started new businesses and restored many older residences in one of San Francisco's principal "Victorian" neighborhoods, thereby enhancing the area's socioeconomic status and physical appearance to conventional eyes. Many types of people are involved in this revitalization process, but several social groups stand out. Artists have converted lofts and former warehouses into studios and dwelling units in the North Mission, along with the "punk" and "new wave" sets along Sixteenth Street. Fashionable "yuppies" (young urban professionals) have moved into the western edge of the Mission District, congregating in coffeehouses, bookstores, and bars. The homosexual population of the Castro District spilled over somewhat into the adjacent Mission District during the late 1970s, and a growing women's community has formed in recent years along Valencia Street in the western area of the Mission District itself. Although most of these supposed "gentry" also rent their living quarters, without large families to support they can afford higher rents; their affluence is in part conditional, contingent upon the greater disposable income resulting from smaller households.

The West Mission has been an area of occasional social conflict in this potpourri of specialized communities. The number of *Latinos* here declined in both absolute and relative terms during the 1970s, although it increased in the Mission District Core (see Table 14). Undoubtedly this has been a factor in the widely publicized conflict of recent years between Hispanic youths and homosexuals.[54] The specter of displacement

---

[53]For a detailed analysis of the rise and fall of the Mission Coalition Organization and the impact upon the neighborhood, see Manuel Castells, *The City and the Grassroots* (Berkeley: University of California Press, 1983), pp. 99-137.

[54]See Phil Bronstein, "Muggings: Gay-Latino confrontations or no?" *San Francisco Examiner,* Nov. 11, 1980, p. B-1.

Figure 2. Housing—another neighborhood-breaker. Source: *El Tecolote*, February 1978.

on the edges of the Mission has served to kindle more cohesion among Hispanics in the district.[55]

San Francisco's Hispanic population has become increasingly concentrated in the Mission District. Less than 23 percent of the Spanish-surnamed population of San Francisco resided in the Mission District in 1960 and 1970; this percentage increased to more than 27 percent in 1980, although the Hispanic population of the city was reported by the U.S. Census to have dropped 17 percent.[56] Along with the intensification of the ethnic core and the erosion of the flanks within the Mission District, this increased citywide Hispanic concentration in the *barrio* contributes to the formation of what sociologist Gerald Suttles calls a "defended neighborhood," a community protecting itself from invasion through youth gangs and a forbidding reputation.[57]

The *Latino* community's sense of being under siege heightens the feelings of ethnic solidarity. Despite prior differences in Latin American nationality, there are shared social and cultural traits, especially the Spanish language and extended family patterns. Constraints on social mobility, and competition with non-Latin groups over such scarce resources as jobs, housing, and inner-city territory, increase pan-Hispanic solidarity. The presence of an established Hispanic minority in the *barrio* checks but does not entirely prevent neighborhood revitalization and displacement, which would prove to be destructive to the ethnic community in the Mission, as it has in other cities.[58]

URBAN SPATIAL STRUCTURE AND THE ETHNIC COMMUNITY

The experience of Latin Americans in the Mission District shows how the historical geography of ethnic settlement can illuminate the ways in which immigrants adapt to and modify American cities. The impetus for immigration came from external commercial relationships, as in the mercantile model of settlement: the historic trade routes of the Pacific encouraged the development of a large Central American population in San Francisco. Within the city, Hispanic settlement reflected long-term

---

[55]See a series of articles about "Gentrification in the Mission" in *El Tecolote,* a Hispanic community publication, during July, August, and November of 1978; and "El Barrio de la Mision: La Puerta de Oro," *La Verdad Hispana,* Dec. 10, 1980, pp. 6-7.

[56]U.S. Census, various years.

[57]Gerald D. Suttles, *The Social Construction of Communities,* (University of Chicago Press, 1972, pp. 21-43.

[58]Roman Cybriwsky, "Social aspects of neighborhood change," *Annals of the Association of American Geographers,* March 1978, pp. 17-33.

processes of neighborhood succession. An evolutionary morphogenesis took place as the new minority group entered the area, adapting the churches, businesses, housing, and other urban forms to its own community uses.

The first area to experience a significant Latin American influx was the North Mission, where immigrants found low rents, housing vacancies, and proximity to blue-collar jobs. The ethnic community formed initially in response to functional land-use characteristics. Yet land values and other economic factors, though an important consideration, do not suffice to explain subsequent neighborhood change. Rent theory would imply that the *barrio* developed through a steady decline in housing values. Although comparative census data are not available on this until 1940, the neighborhood's previous social history would indicate that a downward filtration of the housing stock was indeed an essential element in initiation of the Hispanic influx into the Mission District; but once established, the ethnic community became self-perpetuating, influencing as well as reacting to the physical environment. Despite a steady rise in both rents and house prices since 1940, in both absolute and relative terms, the Hispanic *barrio* still has steadily solidified in the Mission Core (see Figure 3).

This counter-intuitive correlation between economic and demographic variables in the Mission District since World War II could reach a breaking point in the future, since the ethnic community is not impervious to structural change. Ethnic intensification did slow down in the 1970s, probably in part reflecting rising rents. Still, erosion of Hispanic territory has been limited mainly to the western flank. This suggests that social networks and cultural traditions, as well as economic status, become bound up with an area's spatial structure, giving a place a persistent subcultural meaning. That meaning is socially constructed in space and time, and its evolution can be traced through historic phases of neighborhood change.

The morphogenesis of the Hispanic community in the Mission District reflects an organic relationship between ethnic subcultures and urban spatial structure. Minority communities form in specific places in the city: *barrios* and other specialized districts are in a sense incubators of subcultures. Ethnicity, far from being a static entity, is best conceptualized as a multi-faceted but coherent force among immigrant groups, involving both ethnic solidarity and differentiation; the emergence of ethnic identities can be understood in terms of the historical geography of group settlement and the evolutionary morphogenesis of ethnic enclaves in the inner city. The Mission's *barrio* is thus a place of subcultural formation, where a cohesive ethnic identity forms out of diverse regional and national origins. This case study indicates that the ethnic enclave

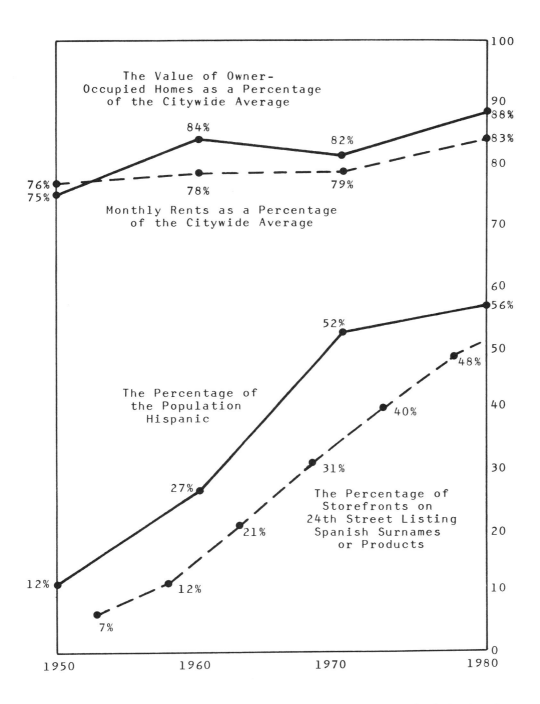

Figure 3. The relationship between the percentage of Hispanics and relative housing prices in the Mission District core, 1950-1980.

may arise initially on the basis of long-distance connections and local land-use characteristics, but that as the ethnic community grows in size and gains a distinctive subcultural identity it plays an important role in its own right in the allocation of urban social space.

Plate 15. A view of the deteriorated Mission Dolores in 1856. After the independence of Mexico from Spain, the California missions were secularized and the mission lands were divided up and granted to the Mexican soldiers and settlers. (Photograph courtesy of the Bancroft Library, University of California, Berkeley.)

Plate 16. The entrance to Woodward's Gardens. This popular amusement park, located on Mission Street between 14th and 16th streets, opened in 1866 when the Mission District was still semi-rural and closed in 1894 when the area had for the most part been developed. (Photograph courtesy of the San Francisco Public Library.)

Plate 17. The J.D. Spreckles Mansion, located at Howard and 21st streets, 1887. Although during the late nineteenth century the Inner Mission District attracted some rich families like the Spreckles, who built impressive mansions, by the early twentieth century the area had lost its social cachet and had become solidly middle- or working-class in character. (Photograph courtesy of the California Historical Society, San Francisco.)

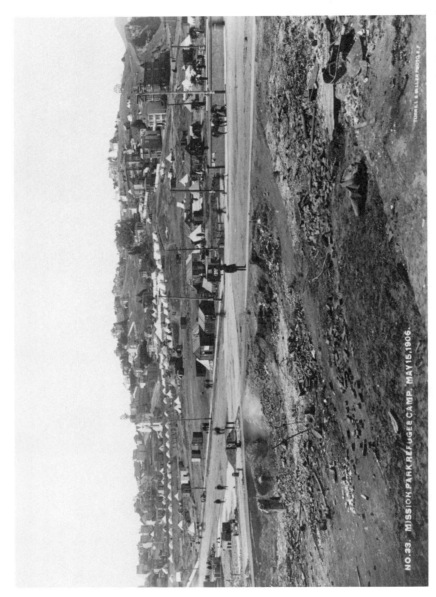

Plate 18. A view of the refugee camp set up at "Mission Park," present-day Dolores Park, after the Earthquake and Fire of 1906. In the Mission District, the fire swept across Market Street and destroyed the area east of Dolores Street, north of Twentieth Street, and west of an oblique line from Valencia to Howard and Eighteen streets. (Photograph courtesy of the San Francisco Public Library.)

Plate 19. Banco Comercial Agrícola de El Salvador, Mission at 25th streets, 1987. This San Francisco branch of a Salvadoran bank attests to the size and importance of the Central American expatriate colony in the city. (Photograph by Brian J. Godfrey.)

Plate 20. Crowds on 24th Street at the Cinco de Mayo Parade, 1982. Although Cinco de Mayo technically is a Mexican holiday, celebrating the defeat of the French at the battle of Puebla in 1862, the parade has become an important pan-Hispanic communal celebration in the Mission District, in which Central American groups play an important role. (Photograph by Brian J. Godfrey.)

Plates 21-22. Neighborhood graffiti in the Inner Mission District. These graffiti refer to the "Hampshire Street" and "West 24th Street" youth gangs and serve to mark territorial associations with group signatures. (Photograph by Brian J. Godfrey.)

6

THE HAIGHT-ASHBURY DISTRICT
Subcultural Succession and Inner-City Revitalization

It's no particular reason, but an entire situation. Smyle on.

Leaving only this terse explanation posted on a window, the Psalms Cafe went out of business at the end of 1979. This venerable remnant of the counter-culture, at the northeast corner of Haight Street and Masonic Avenue, was supplanted by a more stylish restaurant, the Yellow Rose, which in turn was later replaced by Dish, another fashionable eatery. The metamorphosis of this corner business was symptomatic of broader changes in the neighborhood: it was, indeed, "an entire situation."

San Francisco's Haight-Ashbury showed clear signs of being a neighborhood in transition. Not long before the closing of the Psalms, the *Wall Street Journal* had proclaimed that "The Haight," as the area commonly was called, was turning "into a bastion of the middle class."[1] This upswing in the neighborhood's fortunes was indeed a newsworthy development, given the Haight-Ashbury's previous social history. After attracting widespread attention as a vibrant hippie haunt during the "Summer of Love" of 1967, this district of San Francisco degenerated into what David Smith, the Medical Director of the Haight-Ashbury Free Clinic, called a "heroin ghetto." It was thus surprising to many people when, in the mid-1970s, the neighborhood began to experience a widespread rejuvenation. A rash of new businesses opened their doors on Haight Street, countless "Victorian" buildings were renovated, and a more well-to-do population became noticeable. As the physical appearance of the neighborhood improved to conventional eyes, however, property values and rents skyrocketed, increasingly forcing out both lower-income residents and small businesses.[2]

---

[1] Marilyn Chase, "The Haight-Ashbury turns into a bastion of the middle class," *Wall Street Journal*, July 24, 1978, p. 1.

[2] For another version of this case study of gentrification, see Brian J. Godfrey, "Inner-city revitalization and cultural succession: The evolution of San Francisco's Haight-Ashbury District," *Yearbook of the Association of Pacific Coast Geographers,* 46 (1984), pp. 79-81.

The newly "gentrified" Haight thus is representative of yet another important contemporary trend in America—the renovation of deteriorated inner-city neighborhoods by youngish, relatively affluent whites, and the displacement of the less affluent population. The neighborhood also illustrates the importance of nontraditional social identities in this process of neighborhood gentrification. As neighborhood activist Calvin Welch explains:

> Haight Street is an urban lifestyle archaeological dig in which you can find all the urban social movements of the last 40 years manifested in one way of another. Mostly in the faces of the people. There are punks, hippies, remnants of the beats, anti-war health faddists, pro-war joggers, skinhead skateboarders . . . name it.[3]

BOHEMIANISM AND THE SOCIAL DYNAMICS OF GENTRIFICATION

Gentrification—the process of converting working-class areas into middle-class neighborhoods through a renovation of the housing stock—is now affecting most American inner cities to some degree. The nature and extent of gentrification vary considerably from one city to the next, though, and even within the same city only selected neighborhoods are being substantially rehabilitated. Gentrification is not a uniform, homogeneous process of neighborhood rehabilitation, but takes on many forms. This chapter relates the variability of gentrification to the social dynamics of the local community being gentrified, while at the same time finding an underlying structural logic to the successional sequences involved in gentrifying neighborhoods.

The burgeoning literature on urban revitalization, gentrification, and displacement tends to stress the common characteristics of the gentrifiers. In-migrants to gentrifying neighborhoods are often pictured as a rather undifferentiated group of "young, white professionals." For example, one comparative analysis of displacement in American cities contends that the in-movers constitute "a relatively homogeneous group in terms of prior location, age, race, income, family structure, and occupation." They are overwhelmingly young, white, affluent, and well-educated, working as professionals and managers; their family structure tends "toward small households, both singles and couples (but without children)."[4] This assessment of in-movers as "a relatively

---

[3]Quoted in Burr Snider, "CALVIN: *Nothing* comes between him and his City," *San Francisco Examiner,* January 25, 1987, pp. E-1, E-3.

[4]Richard LeGates and Chester Hartman, *Displacement* (Berkeley: California Legal Services Anti-Displacement Project, 1981), p. v.

Figure 4. Attention: Entering Haight-Ashbury gentrified zone. Source: *San Francisco Bay Guardian,* January 6, 1982, p. 8.

homogeneous group" may be accurate in a general sense, but it plays down the often divergent social identities of gentrifying neighborhoods. Few studies have examined cultural differentiation among revitalized communities. One of the few that has done so is by Christopher Winters, who observes:

> In cities where several neighborhoods are being rejuvenated, each tends to acquire a *different* reputation. These reputations are self-fulfilling, because new people move into the neighborhood that appears likely to be the most congenial. Thus, different neighborhoods end up with distinct populations and increasingly divergent social characters. The result of the sorting process is the development of entirely new types of neighborhoods in several large cities.[5]

These "new types of neighborhoods" include the self-consciously heterogeneous, chic, gay, artist, family, black revitalized, and working-class revitalized districts. Winters does not analyze how and why these distinctive neighborhoods develop in the first place, however—a topic examined in the present study. The historical geography of the Haight-Ashbury indicates that urban revitalization should be considered in culturally specific terms, rather than as the "homogeneous" phenomenon depicted in much of the literature on gentrification and displacement. At the same time, this San Francisco neighborhood reveals certain characteristic patterns of nonconformist community morphogenesis that appear to apply to oppositional areas in other American cities.

To understand how the Haight's very idiosyncrasy illustrates broader patterns, it is useful to review briefly two main poles of understanding in the gentrification literature. One emphasizes *sociocultural* factors: gentrification, according to this view, can best be understood in terms of consumer desires for greater personal and community self-fulfillment. The disillusionment among many with suburban life-styles led to a return to inner-city life by a new middle class; the "yuppy" is, after all, the young *urban* professional. Actually, surveys indicate that most in-movers already lived in the same city, although more often than not they were raised in rural, small town, or suburban environments. So in this sense gentrification is more of a "stay in the city" than a "back to the city" movement.[6] Still, gentrification does imply a widespread change in values, substituting for the "suburban dream" a more urban one.

---

[5]Christopher Winters, "The social identity of evolving neighborhoods," *Landscape*, 23, no. 1 (1979): 8-14.

[6]LeGates and Hartman, *Displacement*, p. v.; and Brian J. L. Berry, "Islands of renewal in seas of decay," in Paul E. Peterson (ed.), *The New Urban Reality* (Washington, D.C.: Brookings Institution, 1985), pp. 76-79.

Other sociocultural explanations for gentrification stress changing life-styles and demographic trends, such as a breakup of the nuclear family, later marriages and higher divorce rates, an increasing number of single people, and an increasing pool of childless couples. These social, cultural, and even demographic factors undoubtedly are important to consider in understanding the behavior of in-movers, who are typically less concerned about schools and risk-taking in "marginal" inner-city neighborhoods.[7] Chapter 1, for example, showed the large number of nonfamily households in American big cities—such as New York, Boston and San Francisco—indicating a plausible connection between singles and gentrification. But sociocultural explanations by themselves do not provide satisfying rationales for changes in consumer tastes and life-styles.

Political-economic explanations, on the other hand, tend to view gentrification as market induced, not solely the result of consumer demand. One variant of this approach stresses the structural evolution of the postwar urban economy in America. Cities most affected by gentrification are those with strong downtown white-collar office sectors—reflecting the transformation of much of the American urban economy from an industrial to a postindustrial or corporate managerial base, concentrating corporate activities and key services in selected cities.[8] "Headquarters cities" like New York City, Washington, Boston, San Francisco, and Seattle therefore are high on the list of gentrifying central cities; low on the list are Detroit, Cleveland, St. Louis, Newark, and other cities where white-collar jobs have not been found in sufficient numbers to replace lost blue-collar functions. In addition to downtown expansion, political-economic explanations stress the dynamics of urban housing markets. Suburbanization entailed disinvestment in the inner city, creating potential profits from eventual reinvestment there. The hidden profit motive—the "rent gap," in Neil Smith's terminology—is the difference between the "actual" and "potential" land rent in revitalizing cities.[9]

These "headquarters city" and "rent gap" theories are insightful, particularly on a macro-geographic scale. Chapter 1, for example, showed how the San Francisco downtown and housing markets have been transformed since World War II, putting

---

[7]Pierre De Vise, "The expanding singles housing market in Chicago: Implications for reviving city neighborhoods," *Urbanism Past and Present* 9 (Winter 1979-Spring 1980): 30-39.

[8]Berry, *The New Urban Reality*, pp. 69-96.

[9]Neil Smith, "Toward a theory of gentrification: A back to the city movement by capital, not people," *American Planning Association Journal*, October 1979, pp. 538-547.

pressure on older working-class neighborhoods for conversion to higher status. Still, the political-economic approaches tend to be too mechanistic to account for the finer features of the processes of inner-city upgrading. Why do some inner-city areas gentrify while other areas do not? Or why does gentrification begin in certain areas, before spreading? Political-economic processes are mediated by social groups and their culturally influenced perceptions, as well as their conscious economic benefit. The broad economic restructuring of the American economy, as well as the evolution of the land market, explain in a general sense the metropolitan areas most affected by gentrification. But on a local level, we need to look more closely at the social dynamics of community formation and neighborhood change; the "laws of land rent" operate in conjunction with social and cultural forces in the processes of community formation and neighborhood change.

The articulation of political-economic and sociocultural forces becomes apparent in the general life-cycle of gentrifying neighborhoods, a successional sequence proceeding through phases of *bohemian influx, middle-class transition, and bourgeois consolidation.* In the first stage, a bohemian fringe discovers a neighborhood's special charms—e.g., social diversity, subcultural identification, architectural heritage. Nontraditional "footloose" elements are favored, such as single people, counter-culturals, homosexuals, artists, feminist households, or college students. These "urban pioneers" make a run-down or even dangerous area livable and attractive to others who would not normally venture there; they constitute the unintentional "shock troops" for gentrification and encourage the beginnings of housing speculation. These social elements are not necessarily wealthy in objective terms, but they do often enjoy a conditional affluence, at least insofar as they have more disposable income to spend on renovation because of smaller households and fewer traditional pursuits. In addition to more disposable income, these smaller households are willing to take risks in locating their households and generally seek out social and ethnic diversity.[10]

The bohemian phase is most pronounced in the earliest gentrifying neighborhoods: Greenwich Village, SoHo, and the East Village in New York; North Beach, the Haight-Ashbury, and the Castro District in San Francisco. In later gentrifying neighborhoods, the bohemian elements can be less notable, especially if a large-scale development

---

[10]For another assessment of risk-taking in gentrification, see Dennis E. Gale, "Neighborhood resettlement: Washington, D.C.", in Shirley Bradway Laska and Daphne Spain (eds.), *Back to the City: Issues in Neighborhood Renovation* (Pergamon Press, 1980), pp. 95-115.

project has impacted an area, such as the Lincoln Center on Manhattan's Upper West Side. After the bohemian influx of variable duration, a middle-class transition subsequently occurs. At this point, the word gets out about the neighborhood and we see the rise of both an entrepreneurial class on the local shopping strip and a residential middle-class within the community. Property speculation begins. This stage is followed by a bourgeois consolidation, when outside firms enter the area, catering to a wealthier clientele; the residential population becomes increasingly homogeneous, as rents and property values rise, displacing lower-income residents. The original bohemians often move on to new areas.

Gentrification, then, can be seen as having a positive initial impulse, reflective of a search for a distinctive identity in American culture. But in the end, this search for identity is overwhelmed by increasingly large-scale commercial forces. Gentrified neighborhoods become victims of their own success. But we should not ignore the degree to which the search for subcultural identities conditions the evolution of gentrified neighborhoods and is reflected in the character of the businesses and populations there.

NEIGHBORHOOD INCEPTION AND GROWTH

Where does gentrification begin? Usually in neighborhoods of upper-class or upper-middle-class social origins, with special architectural charm or historic interest, as well as a relatively central location with good transportation access to downtown. The previous social history thus is important, both in providing an original built form and in conditioning the subsequent succession in the neighborhood. The importance of local conditions in channeling the broad forces of inner-city revitalization is apparent in the history of San Francisco's Haight-Ashbury District. During the late nineteenth and early twentieth centuries the neighborhood's basic physical structure was established, later to be adapted to new uses as new communities formed there. The Haight's recent renovation needs to be understood in terms of historical phases of urban morphogenesis, beginning with the initial period of neighborhood inception and growth. To appreciate the specific forms taken by contemporary revitalization in the Haight-Ashbury, it is necessary to examine briefly the district's past.

Now located at the virtual geographic center of densely populated San Francisco, the Haight-Ashbury began to be settled little more than a century ago, as a rural outpost of an expanding "instant city." Although the Indians of nearby Mission Dolores previously had been known to forage for berries, acorns, and edible roots in this area, the Spanish dismissed it as *tierra de las pulgas*—land of the fleas. Formal property ownership began in 1845 with a Mexican land grant to Jose de Jesus Noe, whose

Rancho San Miguel was broken up after San Francisco was incorporated as an American city in 1850. As the city expanded during and after the Gold Rush, small farmers producing for the local market began moving into the "Outside Lands" to the west of Van Ness Avenue, then the city limit. William Lange, a German immigrant, bought a nine-acre parcel of land in 1870 and set up a dairy farm in what is now the southerly Cole Valley section of the Haight-Ashbury.

In the late 1860s the San Francisco Board of Supervisors appointed a Committee on Outside Lands to plan for the westward expansion of the city, settle land tenure disputes, and develop a grand park along the lines of New York's Central Park. Golden Gate Park was originally planned to begin farther to the east and extend across much of the Haight-Ashbury, but a number of squatters in the area could not be dislodged. Hence the street grid was extended to the west and the Haight was platted at the park's entrance (see Map 18). The members of the Committee on Outside Lands included Supervisors Charles Clayton, Monroe Ashbury, R. Beverly Cole, A. I. Shrader, and Charles Stanyan—all of whom were immortalized in local street names. Haight Street, which was to become the main neighborhood thoroughfare, apparently was named after California Governor Henry H. Haight. Although several of Haight's relatives were prominent locally, it appears most likely that Haight Street was named after the governor, also a San Franciscan, who expedited the complex land deal between the city, property owners, and squatters that permitted the establishment of Golden Gate Park.

The development of the park prompted the opening of a cable-car line along Haight Street in 1883, followed by lines along the parallel streets of Oak and Hayes. These lines terminated at the carbarn at Haight and Stanyan streets, where the Park and Ocean Railroad began its run out to the beach. The area at the eastern end of the park, along Stanyan Street, developed as a resort area with hotels, restaurants, saloons, billiard parlors, livery stables, and bicycle shops. Local tradition has it that many a clandestine rendezvous occurred here, away from the downtown crowds. As an area on the urban fringe, near the park, the Haight-Ashbury attracted other recreational facilities during the late nineteenth century. Between 1885 and 1895, crowds numbering in the thousands would ride out Haight Street for games at the California League Baseball Grounds, at Stanyan and Waller.[11] The Chutes, a 60-foot-high water sled, on Haight between Cole and Clayton streets, opened in 1895. The Chutes proved to be immensely popular, adding an zoo, carnival booths, twin roller coasters, and a vaudeville theater by

---

[11] Greg Gaar, "Baseball in the early Haight," *Haight-Ashbury Newspaper,* November 1981, p. 1.

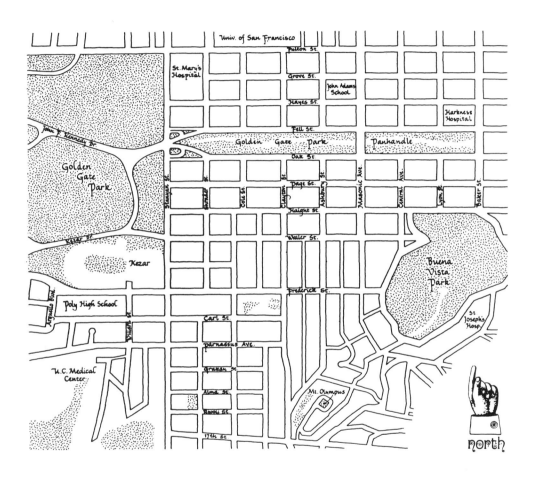

MAP 18. THE HAIGHT—ASHBURY DISTRICT.
SOURCE: S.F. DEPT. OF CITY PLANNING, 1972.

the late 1890s. The site was soon inadequate for further expansion, however, so it was sold in 1902 and the amusement park was moved to the Richmond District.[12]

With the development of Golden Gate Park and the streetcar system, land speculators and real estate developers increasingly bought up land in the Haight-Ashbury. Property values increased about fivefold between the early 1880s and 1891. In 1892 the Lange Land Company was established to subdivide the family dairy into lots for residential development.[13] The Haight became popular with the affluent "horse and buggy" set, because of its suburban ambience and proximity to the park; around the turn of the century there were about 25 livery stables in the neighborhood. Wealthier residents tended to buy corner lots, where they built impressive mansions, leaving the middles of blocks for contractors to construct small tracts of middle-class housing. The Rowntree brothers, for instance, marketed a number of their "Queen Anne" row houses as "gracious suburban villas" in the 1890s. The predominance of the Queen Anne style among houses in much of the Haight—particularly in the lower-lying areas around the Panhandle of Golden Gate Park, where widespread building commenced—reflects this late nineteenth-century building boom.

The earthquake and fire of 1906, which ravaged downtown San Francisco, left the western part of the city unscathed and led to another wave of new construction in the Haight-Ashbury. Tens of thousands of the displaced moved into temporary tent villages in nearby Golden Gate Park, while the well-to-do took rooms in the resort hotels on Haight Street. Many of the wealthy quake victims proceeded to build mansions on the heights around Buena Vista Park and Mount Olympus, an area that became nicknamed "Nob Hill West." In the flatlands below, many duplexes and multi-family apartment buildings filled in the remaining vacant lots during the post-quake boom. The district was still without basic services, however, prompting property owners and merchants to form the Panhandle and Ashbury Heights Improvement Club, which lobbied the Board of Supervisors for paved streets and streetlights. Nearly 90 percent of the Haight's present housing stock was built by 1923.[14]

After the earthquake and fire, San Francisco high society briefly considered Ashbury Heights to be a fashionable area: the elite's *San Francisco Blue Book* listed

---

[12]Greg Gaar, "Shoot the chutes," *Haight-Ashbury Newspaper,* April 1982, p. 4.

[13]Greg Gaar, "Cows in Cole Valley," *Haight-Ashbury Newspaper,* July 1983, p. 4.

[14]San Francisco Department of City Planning, "Housing in the Haight Ashbury," August 1972.

194 local residents in 1906 and 204 in 1909, but only 188 in 1911, 130 in 1919, and 71 in 1922.[15] Although already declining in socioeconomic status by the end of World War I, the social-class origins of the Haight-Ashbury (as the district was becoming known) provided for a durable housing stock, the basis for recent physical renovation. By the 1920s the Haight had lost much of its high-class cachet, but still was regarded as a solid middle-class residential area, leading one commentator to write:

> There is a comfortable maturity about the compact little city that San Francisco knows as Haight-Ashbury. Not the maturity that is suspicious of down-at-the-heel old age, but a nice upholstered, fuchsia garden sort of grown-up-ness, just weathered enough to be nice, and new enough to be looking ahead to the future instead of sighing futilely at the past.[16]

PHYSICAL DETERIORATION AND COMMUNITY FLUX

The Haight-Ashbury witnessed a gradual but steady decline in physical appearance and socioeconomic status during the Depression and World War II, beginning a downward filtering of the housing stock to lower-income groups. A number of technological developments helped to erode the earlier localized basis of the community. The opening of the Twin Peaks Tunnel in 1917 and the Sunset Tunnel in 1928 provided alternate access to the growing districts of western San Francisco, where rival commercial districts developed. Increased use of the automobile, instead of public transportation, lessened the importance of the Haight's proximity to the entrance of Golden Gate Park.

Building maintenance suffered, absentee ownership rose, tenant turnover increased, and single-family houses and flats increasingly were subdivided into smaller units during the 1930s and 1940s. The *Real Property Survey* of 1939, carried out by the Works Projects Administration (WPA), documented the incipient deterioration of property in the neighborhood. Single-family residences accounted for only about 10 percent of the total dwelling units by this time; most of the population consisted of tenants, living in multi-unit buildings, with an average residence of only 1.9 years. The most dilapidated part of the Haight-Ashbury was the flatlands area south of the Panhandle, near Haight Street in the census tract between Waller and Oak streets, where

---

[15]Sister M. Bernadette Giles, "Topography and history of the Haight-Ashbury District," an extract from *A Changing Parish—A Study of Mobility in St. Agnes Parish, San Francisco, California,* July 1959, pp. 3-4.

[16]Anita Day Hubbard, "Cities within the city," *San Francisco Bulletin,* August-September, 1924.

owner occupancy was under 13 percent, rents were about 24 percent under the city average, and between 15 and 30 percent of the units were classified as "substandard."[17] By the time the United States entered World War II, the Haight's housing stock already was well below par for San Francisco: monthly rents, for example, averaged about 14 percent below the citywide figure (see Table 15). Increased pressure for housing during the war, when large numbers of wartime industrial workers and military personnel entered San Francisco, furthered the subdivision and physical deterioration of housing in the Haight. While the number of buildings showed virtually no increase, the number of living units went from 4,750 in 1919 to 8,040 in 1940 and 8,770 in 1950—an increase of 85 percent.[18]

As the United States began a postwar period of widespread prosperity and suburban expansion, the Haight-Ashbury epitomized the decay and downward filtering of an inner-city neighborhood. Although the Haight did not suffer the blight of some such neighborhoods—like San Francisco's South-of-Market, Tenderloin, or Mission districts—it did become very working-class in character, and the social and racial composition of its population began to change. As property deteriorated, minority groups moved in, particularly into the flatlands area south of the Panhandle of Golden Gate Park, around Haight Street, where rents were the lowest in the district (see Table 15). It is important to note that the Haight's influx of both ethnic and nonconformist groups did not precede, but rather followed the area's incipient physical decline; in this sense, the subsequent "invasion" of minorities was more an effect than a cause of neighborhood deterioration.

The black population of the district rose from less than 2 percent in 1950 to 17 percent in 1960 (see Table 16), as redevelopment projects displaced many in the nearby Fillmore District. A significant number of nontraditional households also began entering the district during this period: "beatniks" displaced from North Beach, as well as homosexuals, settled around the Panhandle. Many college students attending San Francisco State settled in the district, where run-down flats and houses could be rented cheaply and convenient streetcar service connected with the campus. A number of cafes, bars, restaurants, and other businesses catered to these black, bohemian, student, and gay elements in the Haight.

---

[17]WPA, 1939 *Real Property Survey,* San Francisco.

[18]Coro Foundation, *The District Handbook: A Coro Foundation Guide to San Francisco's Supervisorial Districts,* 1979, p. 225.

TABLE 15

Average Monthly Rents and House Prices in the Haight-Ashbury District, 1940-1980

	North of Panhandle	Flatlands	Cole Valley	Total Haight	S.F. Citywide
1940					
Rents	$34	$28	$33	$32	$37
% of Citywide	92%	76%	89%	86%	
1950					
Rents	$43	$38	$43	$41	$45
% of Citywide	96%	84%	96%	92%	
House Prices	$12,937	$11,738	$12,440	$12,371	$12,209
% of Citywide	106%	96%	102%	101%	
1960					
Rents	$74	$65	$76	$72	$74
% of Citywide	100%	88%	103%	97%	
House Prices	$22,080	$21,000	$19,000	$20,693	$19,200
% of Citywide	115%	109%	99%	108%	
1970					
Rents	$129	$126	$139	$131	$135
% of Citywide	96%	93%	103%	97%	
House Prices	$32,900	$31,300	$35,400	$33,200	$30,600
% of Citywide	108%	102%	116%	108%	
1980					
Rents	$273	$279	$304	$285	$266
% of Citywide	103%	105%	114%	107%	
House Prices	$130,100	$164,400	$155,700	$150,066	$103,900
% of Citywide	125%	158%	150%	144%	

Source: U.S. Census, various years. Monthly rents are figured from census-tract medians for renter-occupied units; average house prices are figured from census-tract median values for owner-occupied homes. The North-of-Panhandle area is tract 165; the Flatlands, 166; and Cole Valley, 171.

TABLE 16

Racial Composition of the Haight-Ashbury, 1940-1980

Year	Total Population	White	Black	Other
1940	21,775	99.1%	0.1%	0.8%
1950	22,387	97.2	1.8	1.0
1960	21,519	75.1	16.6	8.3
1970	20,080	48.8	33.1	18.1
1980	17,083	69.0	19.9	11.1

Source: U.S. Census, various years. The Haight-Ashbury District, as designated by the San Francisco Department of City Planning, encompasses the three census tracts bounded by 17th Street on the south, Stanyan Street on the west, Fulton Street on the north, and Baker Street, Buena Vista Park, and Upper Terrace on the east.

THE BOHEMIAN INFLUX

By the early 1960s, the Haight-Ashbury was "a liberal, sometimes radical, successfully integrated, bohemian, working-class, deviant, residential area."[19] The progressive ethos of this working-class district of San Francisco, where labor activists had been influential in local affairs since the 1940s, both prevented racial flux from becoming a highly divisive issue and encouraged the formation of radical political and cultural groups. Despite occasional intergroup tensions, social diversity was widely acclaimed as a virtue in the Haight, defusing much of the potential local conflict.

The Haight-Ashbury's reputation for social activism also crystallized during this period, largely in response to the threat of official redevelopment. In 1959, the State Division of Highways proposed to build crosstown freeways linking the Golden Gate and the San Francisco-Oakland Bay bridges, one of which would pass through the Panhandle of Golden Gate Park. This fostered a vigorous neighborhood movement of opposition, led by the newly formed Haight-Ashbury Neighborhood Council (HANC), which was to become the enduring voice of the neighborhood's liberal establishment. In unison with other neighborhood groups in the city, HANC launched San Francisco's successful "Freeway Revolt." This grassroots organization's ultimate success, by the mid-1960s, in preventing the completion of a funded freeway project, against virtually the entire political and institutional establishment, encouraged later forms of neighborhood activism in the Haight-Ashbury.

The "Hashbury," as it was nicknamed by the news media, gained worldwide notice as the focal point for the psychedelic movement of the hippies during the 1960s. The community developed here as a result of the convergence of diverse structural and cultural forces in the neighborhood. Although overshadowed by the new tribe, the preexisting beatnik, student, and gay groups had found some degree of tolerance here for nontraditional elements; these groups were not accepted without reservations by the older community, of course, and had at times an uneasy coexistence even with each other. In fact, one local resident observed:

> It was interesting to see the gay bars on Haight Street slowly disappear. . . . The Haight was a developing gay neighborhood, and it might have become what the Castro is, had it not been for the influx of the Hippies.[20]

---

[19]Sherri Cavan, *Hippies of the Haight* (St. Louis, Mo.: New Critics Press, 1972), p. 47.

[20]Quoted in Randy Alfred, "On live," *The Sentinel,* San Francisco, March 21, 1980, p. 6.

Still, the social diversity and relative tolerance for alternative life-styles did encourage the formation of an oppositional area. In addition to the influx of nonconformist groups in the Haight during the early 1960s, the growing black population put the neighborhood in a state of racial flux and fostered a quiet but steady "white flight." The Haight's commercial decline and low rents allowed for the entry of a subculture opposed to the pursuit of material affluence. Its proximity to the black ghetto of the Fillmore, on the neighborhood's eastern side, as well to the recreational areas of adjacent Buena Vista and Golden Gate parks, made the Haight especially attractive to the emerging counter-culture: "The neighborhood offered easy access to two necessary ingredients for a new experiment in Utopia—the beauty of nature and a beginning contact with the life of the poor."[21]

A series of counter-cultural celebrations and street activities began in late 1965 and 1966, reaching a peak during the "Summer of Love" in 1967, when tens of thousands of young people descended upon the Haight. The Haight became the headquarters for the "San Francisco sound" that so influenced the "acid rock" music of the 1960s: such legendary artists as the Grateful Dead, Jefferson Airplane, Janis Joplin, and Jimi Hendrix lived and performed in the Haight. The "Gathering of the Tribes for a Human Be-In" attracted some 20,000 to nearby Golden Gate Park on January 14, 1967, garnering widespread attention in the national media.[22] The local parks served as sites for free performances and other events, while Haight Street was dominated by more than 30 counter-cultural establishments, including "head shops" selling psychedelic paraphernalia; cafes, restaurants, and take-out food shops; and stores selling clothing and sandals, art supplies, and other wares. The neighborhood constituted the artistic and cultural center of the counter-culture, as opposed to more politically inclined Berkeley, across the Bay. There was even an abortive attempt during this period to rename Haight Street "Love Street."[23]

Despite serious qualms about the disruption of normal life perceived to be occurring in the neighborhood because of the hippies, the older liberal community of "straight" property-owners in the Haight-Ashbury found themselves in an ideological bind. They could not bring themselves to forsake a xlong-standing liberal tolerance for alternative life-styles, even if for a while they appeared to be losing control of the

---

[21]Helen S. Perry, *The Human Be-In* (New York: Basic Books, 1970), pp. 27-28.

[22]Gene Anthony, *The Summer of Love: Haight-Ashbury at its Highest* (Millbrae, California: Celestial Arts, 1980), 184 p.

[23]"Hippie plea—make it love, not Haight," *S.F. Examiner,* Feb. 23, 1967, p. 7.

neighborhood. The ultimate result was an ambivalent relationship, reflected in a social polarization without much outright organized resistance to the youthful influx; in fact, the straight community, as represented by HANC, even felt compelled to defend the hippies from harassment by city agencies, as after a police sweep for drugs on Haight Street in 1968.

By this time, the hippies had carved out their own territory in the neighborhood, centered in the "flats" around Haight Street. This new community did not represent the entire district, but still a profound change had occurred in its character and composition. Virtually overnight, the Haight-Ashbury became a mecca for disenchanted youth from all over America, who tended to occupy flats and homes in the flatlands, or just "crash" in the park. The influx of youthful seekers was fluid and transient, precluding any precise numbers, but by all accounts it was massive. Police estimated that 75,000 youthful pilgrims descended on the neighborhood during 1967, although the permanent population was never that large: spatial mobility was a watchword of the counter-culture, as many people prided themselves on their ability to get up and move on short notice. The number of resident hippies in the Haight probably reached a total of about 7,000, representing about a third of the neighborhood population.[24] In a 1967 CBS documentary entitled "The Hippie Temptation," Harry Reasoner even focused on the Haight-Ashbury as the "hippie capital of the world":

> [The hippies'] main colony has grown up in a low-rent district of San Francisco which is called Haight-Ashbury. This place has become a mecca for young people from all over the nation, to come in search of something new and significant for themselves. It is a mecca too for tourists, who come to look at the hippies. The quiet residential and shopping district has become a milling turmoil of seekers, many of whom are seeking the drug LSD. . . . In a sense, the hippies have taken over the community, by superimposing their own subculture and values upon it. . . . The aggressive determination of hippies to start a new society has made its mark upon San Francisco's Haight-Ashbury. Part of the neighborhood is occupied by ordinary people, bewildered by what's going on; part of it is occupied by a growing population of hippies. There are a lot of "for sale" signs in Haight-Ashbury; there are a lot more houses being occupied by hippies.[25]

---

[24]These figures are based on several estimates recounted in Cavan, *Hippies,* pp. 55-56; and Charles Perry, *The Haight-Ashbury: A History* (New York: Random House, 1984), pp. 238, 245.

[25]Harry Reasoner, "The hippie temptation," CBS News documentary, 1967.

The youthful idealism and innocence of the "flower children" in the neighborhood quickly faded. On October 6, 1967, a mock funeral procession commemorated "The Death of the Hippie, Son of Media, and Birth of the Free Man." This marked the beginning of the dispersal of the original free spirits of the Haight, many of whom began to move to rural areas, and the ascendancy of more hardened elements, drug pushers, and criminals. By early 1968 the drug scene had escalated and it became clear that the tribal love-feast had gone sour: the use of amphetamines, barbiturates, and even heroin reached alarming proportions and contributed to serious social and medical problems.[26]

The late 1960s and early 1970s constituted the socioeconomic nadir of the Haight-Ashbury, as property values fell and crime and random violence rose. Tourism, upon which Haight Street had grown to depend, dropped off, and local businesses began to fold: in 1965, there were only 7 vacant storefronts (4 percent) on the six-block shopping strip of upper Haight Street; by 1969 there were 49 commercial vacancies (30 percent); and in 1971, the worst year, 57 businesses (35 percent) were boarded up.[27] The neighborhood gained a reputation for being extremely dangerous after a series of well-publicized violent assaults. The 1400 block of Waller Street, between Clayton and Ashbury streets, even became known in the press as "terror terrace":

> Some of the crash-pads of the street—once neatly-maintained dwellings—are foul, litter-infested, evil-smelling latrines. Dog feces, festering garbage and broken bottles abound next to living establishments that are meticulously maintained. It is from many of the hovels that the predatory types emerge at night—like hungry rats—to loot, forage, and violate.[28]

THE MIDDLE-CLASS TRANSITION

The recent upswing in the fortunes of the Haight-Ashbury cannot be precisely dated, but attempts to turn things around began around 1970. In that year, the *San Francisco Examiner* ran an editorial on the "Haight revival," noting that the "attempt to restore the one-time hippie haven to the safe, family-oriented neighborhood it once was

---

[26]David E. Smith and John Luce, *Love Needs Care: A History of San Francisco's Haight-Ashbury Free Medical Clinic and Its Pioneer Role in Treating Drug-Abuse Problems* (Boston: Little, Brown, 1971.)

[27]San Francisco Department of City Planning, "Haight Street shopping area: A background study," November 1972, p. 5.

[28]"In the Haight-Ashbury: Violence stalks in a street called Terror Terrace," *San Francisco Examiner*, Dec. 15, 1969, p. 4.

deserves every cooperation from City Hall and the community at large."[29] Soon thereafter, in August of 1970, Mayor Alioto announced the formation of a "Mayor's Committee to Restore the Haight-Ashbury," which was charged with developing a plan for revitalization of the Haight. Perceiving a threat of higher-density development that would displace local residents and businesses, concerned citizens successfully concluded a struggle to downzone the Haight to conform with existing land-use patterns in 1972.[30]

By this point the *Examiner* could write: "Students of tragic events are developing a renewed interest in the late great Haight Street."[31] Commercial vacancies on Haight Street fell to 40 (24 percent), and a rash of self-help building renovation began. New home-owners and speculators began to purchase and restore battered old buildings, many of which were sold for a pittance. After the downzoning of 1972, property values soared. The average value of property in the Haight increased from $33,000 in 1970, about 8 percent above the median price of a house in San Francisco, to over $150,000 in 1980, about 44 percent above the median price (see Table 15).

In addition to increased property values, the social composition of the Haight also was changing. A study by a proposed Savings and Loan in the neighborhood found that between 1973 and 1976 the incidence of violent crime decreased by 21 percent; there was a 29 percent drop in recipients of Aid to Families with Dependent Children and a 48 percent decrease in food-stamp purchases locally. Between 1970 and 1977, the number of households in the Haight-Ashbury earning more than $15,000 a year increased from 15 to 24 percent.[32] The experience of a local resident reflected such changes in the character of the neighborhood, as noted in a 1980 interview:

> When I bought my house in the Upper Ashbury from a black family in 1970, there was a hippie commune living in the other unit of the building; fortunately, they left a couple of days after I moved in. There were a lot of families with kids around then, and a lot of blacks. Now there are hardly any left. My street has been bought mainly by young white professionals, many

---

[29]"Haight revival," *San Francisco Examiner,* April 28, 1970, p. 36.

[30]SPUR (San Francisco Planning and Urban Research Association), "Haight-Ashbury 'protective rezoning'," April 1972.

[31]Dexter Waugh, "Salvaging the Haight," *San Francisco Examiner,* Jan. 9, 1972.

[32]California Department of Savings and Loan Assns., "Public hearing: In the matter of the proposed neighborhood savings and loan association for the approval of the articles of the incorporation," transcript of the tape recording of Exhibit C, San Francisco, Nov. 24, 1976.

of whom work at UC Hospital or downtown; often they used to live in Marin or in the suburbs and have moved back to the city not to have to commute. A lot of the new residents are young couples who don't want children; and a lot of them, I'd say about 40 percent, are gay.[33]

Interestingly, the same respondent indicated in 1986 that many of the gays on his block had sold their homes, profiting from greatly increased housing prices, and proceeded to move on to other neighborhoods.[34] This bears out the contention that homosexuals are disproportionately represented in the early stages of gentrification. Although there has been some concern about the influx of homosexuals in the Haight-Ashbury, intermittent fears about their turning the neighborhood into a "gay ghetto" have abated. After a period of rapid proliferation during the late 1970s, the number of gay and lesbian bars in the Haight has stabilized at five, of about fifteen local taverns. The long-time Medical Director of the Haight-Ashbury Free Clinic, David Smith, estimates that a quarter of the neighborhood's total population is gay, including a disproportionate number of the owners of local businesses.[35]

Low-income black, senior-citizen, and hippie tenants are the main groups being displaced by rising property values and rents in the Haight-Ashbury. From 1970 to 1980, the number of blacks in the three census tracts of the district fell from 6,658 (33.1 percent) to 3,394 (19.9 percent); this racial turnaround was even more notable in the flatlands south of the Panhandle, around Haight Street, where the census tract between Oak and Waller witnessed a decrease in the black population from 2,596 (41.5 percent) in 1970 to 936 (18.9 percent) in 1980. The in-movers are mainly what might be called the "hipoisie"—youngish, white, relatively affluent, socially liberal, but still somewhat varied in personal orientations and life-styles.

The evolution of business on Haight Street, the focal point for the neighborhood, both reflects and presages broader changes. Beginning in the mid-1970s a wave of real estate speculation hit the street: between 1976 and 1978, one-third of all the property on the Haight business strip changed hands.[36] Certainly the Haight has experienced a remarkable commercial revival. Listings for Upper Haight Street in Polk's *San*

---

[33] Interview with Ed Boyle, long-time owner of a clothing store on Haight Street, Feb. 20, 1980.

[34] Interview with Ed Boyle on Aug. 6, 1986.

[35] Richard Saltus, "Haight clinic still fighting '60s wars," *San Francisco Examiner,* Oct. 10, 1982, pp. B-1, B-3.

[36] "Real estate speculation: What's it doing to the Haight," *Haight-Ashbury Newspaper,* March 1978, pp. 4-5.

Francisco Directory, as well as personal observations, indicate that the number of vacant storefronts steadily declined from 34 (21 percent) in 1975 to 20 (12 percent) in 1980, and to 3 (2 percent) in 1983.

Commercial development has become a controversial political issue locally, however, particularly as it relates to the displacement of community-service-oriented businesses by the proliferating restaurants, fast-food outlets, bars, boutiques, and trendy specialty shops. Black-owned businesses have faced particular pressure, a number moving to the lower-rent and predominantly black Fillmore District. Especially upsetting to community activists has been the increasing presence of national chains on Haight Street: McDonald's opened a franchise in 1978, Round Table Pizza replaced the venerable Grand Piano Cafe in 1985, and The Gap jeans and clothing store opened in 1986. Another source of local controversy has been the expansion of such nearby institutions as the University of California Medical Center, the University of San Francisco, and St. Mary's Hospital, which has been strongly opposed by HANC and local activists.

Perhaps the most vivid symbol of the demise of the counter-culture on Haight Street was the demolition of the "Straight Theater" in 1979. Originally called the Haight Theater, it was built about 1910 at Haight and Cole streets as a matinee movie-house. After World War II it suffered hard times, like many neighborhood movie-houses, largely because of the competition with television. It was closed down in 1964, after a brief final stint as a gay theater and movie-house, which had provoked intense local opposition. In 1966 a group of young people leased and reopened the Haight Theater as a counter-cultural concert hall, discotheque, and movie-house, renaming it the Straight Theater, presumably a tongue-in-cheek reference to both the theater's previous gay identification and to the local "straight" community. The theater was sold in 1969, however, and the new owner closed it down. In the early 1970s, local groups attempted, to no avail, to raise funds to convert the building to a community center. Over a storm of local protest, the owner succeeded in demolishing the building in 1979, leaving a vacant lot at a busy intersection, commonly called the "hole on Cole." Finally, in 1987, construction began on a building planned to accommodate a Thrifty Drug Store and upper-story apartments; community activists protested the entry of yet another national chain and even picketed Thrifty Drug stores elsewhere in the city. But by the late 1980s the Haight's commercial revival could not be stopped.

THE BATTLE FOR HAIGHT STREET

Figure 5. The battle for Haight Street. Source: *Haight-Ashbury Newspaper*, February 1980, p. 1.

THE BOURGEOIS CONSOLIDATION: NEIGHBORHOOD IMAGE AND REALITY

There is a general feeling among residents that the Haight is moving toward a residential community composed primarily of professional people, auguring well for local commerce. On the other hand, there is widespread concern that the neighborhood is losing the social and racial diversity for which it is so renowned. As one community activist remarked: "We have to ask ourselves whether we saved the Haight from the developers only to see it turned over to a new social class not in need of protection."[37]

Despite the recent transformation of the Haight, the counter-culture has left its mark on the neighborhood. When owners of a local business whitewashed a landmark "rainbow mural" of the 1960s, planning to replace it with something "more in tune with the changing community," the resultant furor was such that they asked the original artist to repaint the psychedelic statement.[38] The Haight-Ashbury's voting record is still consistently among the most liberal in the city, and the only precinct to favor an ouster of Mayor Dianne Feinstein in the ill-fated recall movement of 1983 was located in the neighborhood, home of the radical sponsors, the White Panthers.[39] The Haight-Ashbury has evolved into what Christopher Winters calls a "self-consciously heterogeneous neighborhood," marked by local pride in a diverse population and liberal ethos.[40] Like New York City's Upper West Side and East Village, Adams-Morgan in Washington, D.C., and the South End in Boston, residents of the Haight generally extol the virtues of social and racial diversity. The neighborhood might not be functionally as integrated as its proponents imply, but the widespread agreement on the desirability of a heterogeneous community nonetheless creates a distinctive social identity.

This neighborhood self-perception has grown out of the Haight's history of group succession. By the time of the bohemian influx of the early 1960s, the neighborhood already had budding ethnic and nonconformist communities—a fact generally overlooked in explaining the subsequent counter-cultural explosion of the mid-1960s. Residents already bragged of being one of the most racially integrated neighborhoods in America; in 1967, defending the hippies against media diatribes, the Haight-Ashbury

---

[37]Interview with Richard Ross, since the 1960s on the staff of a local community center, "409 House," Feb. 27, 1980.

[38]Ken Wong, "Rainbow mural glows again after whitewash 'backlash,'" *San Francisco Examiner*, Nov. 16, 1983, pp. A-3.

[39]Carl Irving, "The lone precinct that voted to oust Feinstein," *San Francisco Examiner*, May 18, 1983, p. A-2.

[40]Winters, "Social identity," pp. 8-14.

Neighborhood Council commended the neighborhood's "cosmopolitan character, its congenial climate, its tolerance of diverse peoples and life-styles."[41] Similarly, the Department of City Planning has noted that "most community residents are extremely proud of [the Haight-Ashbury's] diversity and want to keep it the way it is."[42] Even gentrified Haight Street has been seen as "one of the weirdest mixes of businesses and life-styles in an American retail area."[43] A resident waxed enthusiastic in the *Haight-Ashbury Newspaper,* comparing the neighborhood with

> a confetti of races, ages, politics, life-styles, orientations, and appetites. And, like any bag of confetti, the overall effect is pretty festive, despite an undercurrent of chaos which results in occasional discords.[44]

Inner-city revitalization and displacement may continue to affect the socioeconomic composition of neighborhoods like the Haight-Ashbury, but that does not necessarily imply either the demise of specialized social identities or the emergence of blandly uniform "yuppie" communities. Although this San Francisco district provides evidence of common problems of displacement, the evolution of the Haight also indicates that the local history of cultural succession greatly influences how a neighborhood proceeds to "gentrify."

Although the counter-culture's heyday was relatively brief in the Haight-Ashbury, it both reflected and contributed to a continuing nontraditional identification in the neighborhood. The "Summer of Love" of 1967, while constituting the most remarkable event in the neighborhood's cultural history, also was in a sense merely the culmination of a long-term process of social diversification. Street people and run-away youth still abound on Haight Street, drawn by the area's reputation, the neighborhood free lunch program (attended by about 250 people a day), and diverse shelters, half-way houses, and other social services. Given increased rents and property values in the neighborhood, this transient population of counter-cultural descendents generally does not take up permanent local residence any more, instead living in the local parks or commuting in during the day; but still the street population has remained a staple of

---

[41] Helen Perry, *The Human Be-In,* pp. 23-25.

[42] San Francisco Department of City Planning, "Housing in the Haight-Ashbury," p. 2.

[43] W. A. Van Winkle, "The state of the Haight, 1979," *San Francisco Bay Guardian,* May 3, 1979, p. 16.

[44] Tim Deniger, "A tree grows in Haight-Ashbury," *Haight-Ashbury Newspaper,* May 1982, p. 6.

daily life, despite the misgivings of many merchants on Haight Street. In addition, the youthful flavor of the Haight has been maintained by the large population of students from nearby institutions of higher learning—the University of California Medical Center, the University of San Francisco, and San Francisco State University—who often form groups of roommates to lease large flats and hence can afford higher rents than many families.[45]

The cultural history of the Haight-Ashbury illuminates certain characteristic patterns of nonconformist community morphogenesis. Group succession in the revitalizing Haight-Ashbury has drawn much upon the district's "Summer of Love" image, which can never be eradicated. In fact, local renovation has proceeded largely because the neighborhood's avant-garde reputation (if not the lingering street people themselves) appeals to the new gentry. As opposed to the ethnic community—in which long-distance socioeconomic and political ties often lead to persistent immigrant flows, directed to neighborhoods within the city largely on the basis of functional land-use characteristics—the nontraditional area forms more on the basis of a social dynamic of detachment from mainstream national culture. To be sure, functional characteristics are also important in the morphogenesis of an oppositional area, in this case including the once-low rents, the availability of housing, and the proximity of parks for recreation; but also important have been the general "funky" ambience and the sense of local social tolerance.

In contrast to the ethnic community, which perpetuates itself through long-standing family traditions and social ties, the nonconformist community is more fluid in its composition and mobile in its trajectory. It forms out of a selective appeal to individuals dissatisfied with certain elements of mainstream American culture. In this sense, the nontraditional community is more voluntaristic in its generating mechanisms. As a result, it is less a captive of the inner-city environment, being able to choose attractive elements of the urban landscape as a basis for in-migration, rather than being so firmly anchored to an urban social space by preexistent community standards and constraints. These basic subcultural differences have important consequences for the evolution of American urban spatial structure: as communities of preference, oppositional groups tend not to be as enduring as ethnics in the city, but are more volatile in their appearance and rapid in their inter-group succession. This point is illustrated in the case of the Haight by a comment of one observer of the counterculture:

---

[45]Interview with Ed Boyle on Aug. 6, 1986.

> As a physical center of people, the Haight worked like a cyclone—tugging them in from all over, whirling them in the air and scattering them in every direction. Very few people stayed continuously in the Haight through the mid-seventies. The move was in the direction of the country, but the distance varied; a lot of spare-changers never got past Telegraph Avenue in Berkeley.[46]

San Francisco's Haight-Ashbury provides evidence of both the common transience of specific nontraditional subcultural forms, based on group mobility and fluid composition, and the frequent persistence of a general oppositional identification in parts of the American inner city. This neighborhood's cultural history cannot be considered typical of most of the modern American metropolis, not even of most of San Francisco, but it does show in a tangible way how the general society has become socially and spatially fragmented into special-identity groupings. Oppositional areas have become a visible feature of the American city to a greater degree than ever before.

Despite their typical differences in character from ethnic communities, nonconformist groupings still have shown themselves to constitute an important type of minority community in the American inner city, and the morphogenesis of oppositional areas therein has reflected this minority status. Certainly subcultural detachment from the national mainstream must be appreciated in neighborhood studies. Even as the Haight-Ashbury has passed through the phases of bohemian influx, middle-class transition, and bourgeois consolidation, the neighborhood has maintained a liberal political orientation and an oppositional social identity; despite the increases in rents and the entry of national firms, the Haight has gentrified in its own inimitable way. This indicates that the processes by which distinctive social areas form in the city need to be understood in specific sociocultural terms, as well as in terms of the broad evolution of urban political-economic structure.

Contemporary gentrification of the Haight-Ashbury has created increasing strains between the social ideals and realities of the neighborhood, but subcultural identification remains an important force in neighborhood change, reacting to, but also to some degree affecting economic processes. Highly generalized models of spatial structure cannot explain the finer points of community change: studies of ground rent and capital movement should not ignore the importance and variability of the human agents involved in urban processes. Although gentrified neighborhoods in the end

---

[46]Charles Perry, *The Haight-Ashbury,* p. 291.

become victims of their own success, as previous residents are displaced, we should not ignore the degree to which the initial search for a subcultural identity and the subsequent sorting by social class condition the life-cycles of inner-city areas in transition.

Plate 23. The Haight-Ashbury District, looking toward the entrance of Golden Gate Park, 1902. At the turn of the century, the district was becoming an affluent suburban neighborhood, linked to downtown by several streetcar lines, but still spacious enough to permit numerous livery stables for recreation and the display of carriages for formal promenades through the Panhandle of Golden Gate Park. (Photograph courtesy of the California Historical Society, San Francisco.)

Plate 24. Haight Street, circa 1947. This view shows the Haight Street Theater and the numerous small businesses lining the street. (Photograph by Tom Gray, courtesy of Greg Gaar.)

Plate 25. The corner of Haight and Ashbury streets, 1969. This view of the crossroads of the counter-culture shows a boarded-up store front, typical during the commercial nadir of the street. (Photograph courtesy of the California Historical Society, San Francisco.)

Plate 26. Demolition of the Straight Theater, 1979. Although local community groups had battled to obtain city funding to convert the Theater into a community center, the owner of this highly visible site at the corner of Haight and Cole streets succeeded in demolishing the structure; the lot then sat vacant long after gentrification of the neighborhood warranted some kind of development. (Photograph courtesy of Greg Gaar.)

Plate 27. Haight Street, 1987. This view shows Round Table Pizza, a chain operation, which replaced the venerable Grand Piano, a popular cafe from the counter-cultural era. (Photograph by Brian J. Godfrey.)

Plate 28. A row of tastefully restored houses, 1987. These renovated "Queen-Anne-Tower" houses on Central Avenue, between Haight and Page streets, were inhabited by the late 1970s almost exclusively by single people and childless couples, who could afford the substantial home prices and high rents. (Photograph by Brian J. Godfrey.)

7

SUMMARY AND CONCLUSIONS
Subcultural Succession and Community Morphogenesis

> ... San Francisco has grown by more than 10 percent since 1980. While heterosexual whites pack into the Marina District and gays fill the Castro, Vietnamese refugees are rejuvenating the Tenderloin, Filipinos swell the southern neighborhoods and Salvadorans make the Mission the third-largest Salvadoran community in the world. We are a city of refugees, says supervisor Harry Britt. Refugees from Saigon and San Salvador and Saginaw.[1]
>
> Tim Schreiner, 1986

Detachment from mainstream American culture has come to play an increasingly important part in the processes of U.S. urban community morphogenesis—the emergence of physical forms and spatial structures within inner cities of the United States. Cultural pluralism in the U.S. traditionally has denoted ethnic diversity, which still is very much a force in the internal differentiation of cities. But the increasing size and visibility of nonconformist communities since World War II has led to a broader conception of pluralism, closely related to the emergence of new types of specialized urban neighborhoods. With the growth of oppositional enclaves in the American city, pluralism has come to encompass a complex of alternative life-style groups in addition to ethnic communities. This study has examined the roles of these two different types of subcultures in the making of distinctive neighborhoods in the American city. Its thesis is that ethnic and nonconformist subcultures, as minority groups, share a cultural detachment from mainstream American society that helps to explain their joint tendency to cluster in the inner city; characteristic subcultural traits, however, also make for certain general differences in their respective spatial and historical patterns. This final chapter contrasts these two types of communities in terms of their respective patterns of subcultural succession and social mobility.

---

[1] Tim Schreiner, "The Bay Area exception," *San Francisco Chronicle*, December 14, 1986, "This World" supplement, p. 15.

At this point, some conceptual recapitulation is in order. In this study, *urban spatial structure* is viewed as the geographic arrangement and interrelation of human activities and physical forms in the city. *Culture* in a general sense encompasses people's ways of life, characteristic patterns of human thought and behavior that are embedded in geographical conditions but not strictly limited to them; *subcultures*, then, are specialized social worlds involving distinctive ways of life, with discernible morphological expressions, within a larger pluralistic society. *Social class,* on the other hand, refers to a group's relative position within a stratified society, particularly in terms of the social relations of production and consumption. It has been argued here that an economistic view of the city, assuming a simplistic primacy of economic variables in neighborhood change, tends not to grant enough theoretical autonomy to sociocultural processes of community formation. Specialized communities not only react to urban spatial structure, as many economic studies of land rent have it,[2] but both ethnic and nonconformist subcultures also come to influence the evolution of spatial structure, although generally in somewhat different fashion.

Ethnic communities have long been important in the American city, occupying significant portions of the metropolitan core. Defined by their adherence to racial, national-origin, or religious groups outside of the dominant nativist society, ethnic quarters have always been regarded with mixed feelings by both American scholars and the general public. Although this country historically welcomed immigrants in many informal and official ways, quick integration into the mainstream was expected of them. As ethnic groups persisted in the city, they were often viewed as disorganized and even pathological urban formations.[3] Only in recent decades have ethnic communities been treated as orderly and stable subcultures in the city, as in the concept of "urban villagers".[4]

In recent years, nonconformist communities have become increasingly visible as well, tending also to cluster in the central city, often close to ethnic quarters. Rather than long-standing family ethnic traditions, oppositional areas have represented a conscious group rejection of selected elements of mainstream culture by various nonconformist subcultures. The alternative life-style complex therefore has probably

---

[2]For a review of land-rent theory, refer to Mark La Gory and John Pipkin, *Urban Social Space* (Belmont, Calif.: Wadsworth, 1981), pp. 175-182.

[3]See David Ward, "The ethnic ghetto in the United States: Past and present," *Transactions of the Institute of British Geographers,* 7 (1982), pp. 258-275.

[4]Herbert Gans, *The Urban Villagers: Group and Class in the Life of Italian-Americans* (New York: Free Press, 1962).

been even more controversial than the ethnic. Nontraditional quarters often have been viewed as deviant refuse from society, a perception initially intensified by their common proximity to urban vice districts. Increasingly, however, nonconformist communities have been recognized as possessing a certain stability and coherence; they have come to be regarded in some circles as minority communities, even as "quasi-ethnic" groupings.[5]

Despite their importance and common juxtaposition in the central city, ethnic and nonconformist communities have rarely been studied as interlocking parts of the urban fabric. This comparative study indicates that their subcultural patterns help to explain both similarities and differences in the spatial structures of the two types of communities. As minorities, both ethnics and nonconformists find in parts of the inner city socioeconomic conditions and physical structures conducive to the creation of specialized neighborhoods, which in turn become important vehicles for the maintenance of group identity. But there are important differences in the degrees of group mobility and cohesion, reflected in the siting and periodicity of such distinctive social districts.

SAN FRANCISCO AS A STUDY SITE

The development of San Francisco's ethnic and nonconformist communities provides an illustrative case study of subcultural intensification and succession in the American inner city. Chapter 1 states that San Francisco differs from a hypothetical "norm" more by degree than in kind, notwithstanding the city's colorful image as a stronghold of idiosyncrasy. San Francisco probably rates high on a scale of social diversity, but still the city can be placed on an urban continuum in this regard.

Compared with other large American cities, San Francisco historically has had a high proportion of ethnics and nonconformists, but that is not atypical of a certain type of American urban center. New York, Boston, and other "ports of entry" have been similar to San Francisco in their ethnic diversity, at least as measured by the presence of foreign immigrants. The nonconformist population is more difficult to gauge, but one index is what the U.S. Census now classifies as "nonfamily households." San Francisco is highest in this measure on a comparative list of large American cities, but still is less than Manhattan, and not very much higher than Boston. In its social diversity, San Francisco best represents a compact, densely inhabited central city with a historic role

---

[5]Stephen O. Murray, "The institutional elaboration of a quasi-ethnic community," *International Review of Modern Sociology,* 9 (July-December 1979): 165-177.

as a center of trade, finance, communications, and immigration. The size and range of the city's minority communities is not that unusual in this context, at least not as much as is generally held by the news media and popular opinion. San Francisco in this sense serves as an apt site in which to examine the factors contributing to the emergence of specialized communities in the metropolitan cores of the United States.

CONCEPTUAL BASES

The tendency of both ethnic and nonconformist groups to locate in the American inner city can be understood in terms of subcultural theory, as explained in Chapter 2. Although such subcultures were held to be disorganized and even pathological in classical theories of urbanism, more recent research indicates that ethnic and nonconformist groups manifest an internal order and stability. Sociologist Claude Fischer's conception of subcultural intensification proposes that, rather than breaking down such distinctive social worlds, urbanism actually foments them. The dense, diversified population of the central city provides a demographic "critical mass," which allows "what would otherwise be only a small group of individuals to become a vital, active subculture".[6] But in addition to the demographic qualities of the city, urban spatial structure must also be considered to explain the locational patterns of ethnic and nonconformist subcultures. Such communities form in specific parts of the metropolis around places of residence, work, communication, and other supportive functions. Since all social areas have a certain physical form and spatial organization, resulting from long-term community uses and perceptions, the historical geography of subcultures can be examined in terms of urban morphogenesis.

Geographer James Vance defines the concept of urban morphogenesis as "the creation and transformation of city form".[7] This study extends this concept to the relationship of urban physical form to community formation; the processes through which emergent social groups adapt the existing built environment of the city to new uses therefore may be called *evolutionary community morphogenesis.* The interface between urban community morphogenesis and subcultural identity is a principal theme of this study. Economic models of urban land rent have limited utility in explaining the residential differentiation of the city; sociocultural explanations do better in this regard, but still have tended to downplay the importance of the physical form and spatial

---

[6]Claude S. Fischer, *The Urban Experience* (New York: Harcourt Brace Jovanovich, 1976) p. 37.

[7]James E. Vance, Jr., *This Scene of Man: The Role and Structure of the City in the Geography of Western Civilization* (New York: Harper and Row, 1977) p. 37.

structure of the city in processes of community formation.[8] The initiation and adaptation of city form, so important in the creation of distinctive social areas, must also be considered in explaining the development and distribution of urban subcultures.

The study of urban community morphogenesis involves more than a cursory reference to the "physical setting" as a backdrop for a larger drama, as is all too often the case in urban studies. The morphogenetic approach recognizes that the urban environment is greatly bound up in the processes of community formation, not in a determinist fashion, but still as part of a constant interplay between the human and physical fabrics of the city, a continual dialectic between urban social and spatial structures. These both condition and reflect neighborhood change: physical objects are acted upon by human groups in the city, but the resultant spatial expressions of social forces in turn influence subsequent urban land uses and perceptions. In the end, the physical shaping of communities must be accorded an important place in the study of urban subcultural intensification and succession.

This study has compared the morphogenesis of ethnic and nonconformist communities in terms of historic phases of neighborhood structural change. In Chapter 2 an urban morphogenetic sequence of geographic evolution was proposed for inner-city neighborhoods, taking account of both the frequent downward filtering of aging physical structures, often passed down in time to lower-income minorities, as well as the recent revitalization of some neighborhoods. The differences between ethnic and nonconformist communities become apparent in their respective sequences of subcultural succession. Ethnic neighborhoods experience an initial *migrant penetration* of a few upwardly mobile settlers, followed by a *minority invasion,* in which large numbers of the new group replace the departing population. As the neighborhood undergoes *ethnic consolidation,* the new group comes to predominate in the neighborhood, sometimes reaching high population densities through a crowding of the housing stock. The ethnic subculture in the neighborhood intensifies during these historical stages, after which the area may either repeat a new process of ethnic succession, undergo the gentrification so often associated with initial inroads by nontraditional elements, or simply evolve into a less ethnic but still working-class area.

The nonconformist community life-cycle contrasts sharply with this typical successional sequence in ethnic neighborhoods. Nontraditional community morphogenesis typically starts with a *bohemian influx,* in which a run-down

---

[8]For a review of these economic and sociocultural approaches, refer to La Gory and Pipkin, *Urban Social Space,* pp. 175-182.

neighborhood is "discovered" by such social elements as counter-cultural devotees, homosexuals, artists, and others. These groups constitute the "urban pioneers" who draw attention to a district and inadvertently encourage an incipient neighborhood gentrification. A *middle-class transition* occurs in the wake of speculation in local housing and businesses, as middle-class groups of home-owners and entrepreneurs appear in the neighborhood. The terminal phase involves a *bourgeois consolidation,* when many outside businesses enter the area and rents rise to a level that only a wealthier clientele can afford. Although the neighborhood may not lose its social identity, it certainly becomes more homogeneous in terms of class.

THE HISTORICAL GEOGRAPHY OF SAN FRANCISCO

San Francisco's role as a center of social diversity, a scene of subcultural intensification and succession, can be understood in terms of the city's morphogenesis. During the late nineteenth and early twentieth centuries certain enduring patterns of community location emerged, including sizable ethnic and nonconformist components. Chapter 3 shows the importance of the historical geography of such communities in explaining contemporary patterns: in the relatively short span of time between the Gold Rush and World War II, a highly differentiated cultural mosaic emerged in San Francisco, one that greatly influenced the city's postwar evolution. As waves of immigrant labor flowed into the "instant city," ethnic communities formed in working-class districts, generally located on the older, eastern side of the city; the placement of ethnic groups was greatly correlated with spatial patterns of social stratification. Among the major groups, the Chinese were the most segregated, isolated in Chinatown by both cultural differences and popular prejudices. European immigrant groups were more mobile in social and spatial terms, but they also had areas of concentration.

The Irish-Americans of late nineteenth- and early twentieth-century San Francisco were so numerous that they were found throughout the city, but they tended to cluster most in working-class districts south of Market Street. The Italians also were widespread, but found their ethnic focus in North Beach. Germans were more diverse in religious and linguistic terms, tending to separate more into distinct ethnic subgroupings. While European-origin groups were not strictly segregated, they did find sources of subcultural support in distinctive neighborhoods of the city. Ethnicity was structured largely by social class, so that the lower-status groups were more highly concentrated spatially in working-class neighborhoods.

Unconventional communities also sprang up early in San Francisco. In fact, one of America's first and most famous bohemias arose in the city, centered on cultural radicals of a literary and artistic inclination. Their subcultural identity was comparably

Summary and Conclusions 211

fluid and mobile, but did color the character of the city. The bohemian focal point was the Latin Quarter of North Beach, on the fringe of Chinatown and the Barbary Coast, where the middle-class flight of to the newer sections on the city's western side left areas with low rents and picturesque settings, appealing to the romantic bohemian sensibility. By the early twentieth century, bohemian North Beach was already being discovered by the more conventional members of society.

By World War II, then, certain consistent spatial patterns emerged. The upper classes generally occupied the hills on the city's northern shores and western side, pursued closely by the middle classes. Ethnic quarters were located in working-class districts initially out of functional needs, including low rents and proximity to jobs and social supports; as their residents became more successful and assimilated, they tended to dissipate. Unconventional agglomerations emerged in close proximity to certain ethnic areas, due more to congregation by choice, as attested by their correspondingly fluid and mobile composition.

World War II served as a historic watershed for the city's subcultural makeup, as shown in Chapter 4. Wartime labor shortages and resultant in-migrations ultimately prompted a new alignment of groups. The development of San Francisco's major postwar ethnic groups again resulted largely from initial labor immigration, as for blacks and Hispanics, as well as from more recent political turmoil abroad that has created sizable refugee communities, such as for many Filipinos and Central Americans; once established, social networks reinforce these immigratory patterns. Racial covenants in real estate also were broken after the war, allowing minorities entry into areas of western San Francisco, most notably Asians to the Richmond and Sunset districts and blacks to the Ingleside.

The postwar in-migration of nonconformist elements resulted from the prospects of personal fulfillment in San Francisco's sizable alternative life-style communities. Compared with the functional socioeconomic forces often operating in the movement of ethnic groups, nontraditional elements reacted to a more purely cultural detachment from mainstream American society and attained increasing size, visibility, and group cohesion in postwar San Francisco. Despite their visibility in the news media, the hard-core beats of North Beach numbered only in the hundreds during the late 1950s.[9] In contrast, tens of thousands of hippies were involved in the counter-cultural influx of the

---

[9]Harry T. Moore, "Enter beatniks: The bohème of 1960," addenda to the 1933 edition of Albert Parry's *Garrets and Pretenders: A History of Bohemianism in America* (New York: Dover, 1960), pp. 376-395.

late 1960s.[10] And by the late 1970s, perhaps over 100,000 homosexuals had settled in the city.[11] Within San Francisco, these oppositional communities all emerged in areas of initial low rents, run-down but picturesque settings, and general aesthetic appeal, implying a sense of congregation by choice among adherents of different affinity groups. Each of the major nonconformist communities has shown a tendency to pass through the general sequence of nonconformist subcultural succession, including the phases of bohemian influx, middle-class transition, and bourgeois consolidation.

After periods of penetration, invasion, and consolidation, some ethnic minorities entered into phases of decline. Postwar North Beach, for example, witnessed a decrease in its Italian population, the growth and decline of the beat subculture, and an influx of Chinese and more affluent whites. The precise sequence of subcultural succession in the city's neighborhoods has depended on many factors, including both the availability of areas being abandoned by previous groups and the numbers, socioeconomic status, and culture of the incoming groups. But there are characteristic differences in the morphogenesis of ethnic and nonconformist communities.

THE CASE STUDY OF AN ETHNIC ENCLAVE

In Chapter 5 the evolutionary morphogenesis of a Hispanic *barrio* in the Mission District is used as a case study of ethnic flux. After World War II the still relatively small Latin colony in the Mission began to grow steadily, as older white ethnic groups abandoned the area. It was not such an abrupt racial transformation as with blacks in the Western Addition, but more a gradual ethnic turnover in a long-standing working-class neighborhood. The Spanish-surnamed population of the Mission District rose from 11 percent in 1950 to 23 percent in 1960 and 45 percent in 1970, by which time the Inner Mission was known as *El Barrio*. Although the U.S. Census showed a decline in San Francisco's total Hispanic population during the 1970s, the number of Hispanics counted in the nine census tracts of the Mission District still increased slightly to about 46 percent; the Inner Mission's core area reached about 60 percent Hispanic. Given the presence of many undocumented residents, these figures are probably conservative.

The morphogenesis of the Hispanic *barrio* shows the importance of functional and structural characteristics in initial ethnic community formation. The Pacific maritime

---

[10]These figures are based on several estimates recounted in Sherri Cavan's *Hippies of the Haight* (St. Louis, Mo.: New Critics Press, 1972), pp. 55-56; and Charles Perry, *The Haight-Ashbury: A History* (New York: Random House, 1984), pp. 238, 245.

[11]Manuel Castells and Karen Murphy, "Cultural identity and urban structure: The spatial organization of San Francisco's gay community," *Urban Affairs Review,* 22 (1982): 237-259.

routes, linking San Francisco and Latin America, directed particular immigratory currents to the city; the coffee trade with Central America, for example, brought many Salvadorans and Nicaraguans to San Francisco, a major center for coffee processing on the West Coast. As in the mercantile model of settlement,[12] these long-distance social networks between Central America and San Francisco had their genesis in the socioeconomic relationships of the early twentieth century, long before contemporary politics and refugee resettlement became an important force in intensifying the preexisting immigratory routes.

Although the city's Hispanic community historically had clustered in the Latin Quarter of North Beach, expansion there during the mid-twentieth century was blocked by the large Italian and bohemian communities. The Mission District offered Hispanics cheap and available housing, conveniently situated for employment in the docks, factories, and small workshops south of Market Street. The postwar movement to the Mission District occurred as an extension of this growing *Latino* blue-collar community, much as in the outward movement of European immigrant groups from the South-of-Market area during the late nineteenth and early twentieth centuries. The Hispanic community's growth in the Mission District shows how an ethnic community typically arises initially out of a functional socioeconomic basis, then becomes enduring and culturally autonomous, increasingly conditioning the allocation of urban space. Based on long-standing family traditions and working-class status, in time the ethnic community becomes self-perpetuating, influencing as well as reacting to the urban environment. A purely economic interpretation of ethnic sorting in the city therefore seems inadequate: the relationship of group culture to urban social and spatial structures also needs to be considered.

THE CASE STUDY OF A NONCONFORMIST COMMUNITY

Chapter 6 is an examination of cultural succession in an oppositional area, using the history of the Haight-Ashbury District as a case study. This neighborhood became famous during the counter-cultural influx of the mid-1960s, when thousands of hippies invaded the Haight-Ashbury in what a geographer deemed "one of the most remarkable mass colonizations in modern American urban history".[13] News commentator Harry

---

[12]The mercantile model of settlement, outlined in Chapter 5, originated in a work by James E. Vance, Jr., *The Merchant's World: The Geography of Wholesaling* (Englewood Cliffs, N.J.: Prentice-Hall, 1970).

[13]Peter Hall, "The urban culture and the suburban culture," in Hurst, *I came to the city,* p. 174.

Reasoner called this San Francisco neighborhood "the hippie capital of the world" in a 1967 CBS television documentary.[14]

Estimating the number of hippies in the Haight during this period with any precision is difficult, given their great mobility, the fluid composition of the community, and the lack of official statistics. Probably around 75,000 youthful seekers came to the Haight during 1967, and the resident counter-cultural population reached about 7,000, perhaps a third of the total neighborhood populace. About one-third of the businesses on Haight Street were dedicated to counter-cultural establishments.[15] The "Summer of Love" of 1967 was a meteoric but short-lived phenomenon, however. By the late 1960s the area had degenerated into what David Smith, the Director of the Haight-Ashbury Free Medical Clinic, called a "heroin ghetto," and the neighborhood fell to a socioeconomic nadir around 1970. In recent years the Haight-Ashbury has witnessed a remarkable revitalization, linked in part to a new influx of nontraditional households.

The Haight-Ashbury District is a neighborhood that shows clearly the historic interactions and mutual influences of a variety of nonconformist subcultures: beat, hippie, student, and homosexual. In the early 1960s nascent beatnik, gay, and college-student communities were forming in the district, but these were soon overshadowed by the massive influx of hippies. Perhaps if the "hippie capital" had not emerged in the Haight during the late 1960s, the area would have assumed a different nontraditional character, such as the present-day gay identity of the Castro District. In any case, the revitalized Haight-Ashbury has remained socially somewhat heterogeneous, drawing upon its reputation for social tolerance in the process of urban revitalization. The neighborhood's social identity has become that of a "self-consciously heterogeneous neighborhood"[16], though gentrification and displacement have meant greater class homogeneity and an increasing strain between the neighborhood image and the reality.

The evolution of the Haight-Ashbury District indicates that a nonconformist group succession has emerged in some large American cities, comparable in some ways to the traditional ethnic succession that has long characterized metropolitan areas in the United States. Nonconformists have had a more fleeting presence in the urban fabric, subject to greater changes and fluctuations than ethnic communities, but still a

---

[14]Harry Reasoner, "The hippie temptation," CBS News, 1967.

[15]See Cavan, *Hippies of the Haight,* pp. 55-56; and Perry, *The Haight-Ashbury,* pp. 238, 245.

[16]Christopher Winters, "The social identity of evolving neighborhoods," *Landscape,* 23, No. 1 (1979): 8-14.

persistent oppositional character has come to characterize certain inner-city areas like the Haight. This reflects the more fluid household structures among nonconformist groups. Despite differences in specific cultural forms, the beats, hippies, and gays have all shared an adherence to nontraditional household arrangements, tending to form and rearrange themselves with greater flexibility than would be possible within the more traditional family structure of ethnic communities. Although they do tend to form initially in modest, working-class areas (like ethnic communities), nonconformist communities ultimately enjoy greater freedom from constraints. They may not always be wealthy in objective terms, but nonconformists enjoy the conditional affluence of not having to spend their resources on many traditional pursuits. They are therefore more able to select areas for settlement, based upon a variety of considerations; the nontraditional community has the ability to pick certain elements of the urban landscape that it finds appealing, rather than growing out of a more strictly functional socioeconomic basis for initial location.

The social dynamic of cultural detachment in the Haight-Ashbury, for example, was reflected in both the counter-culture's initial emergence there and the area's subsequent evolution. The Haight was attractive to the hippies because of its quaint architecture and low rents, its proximity both to recreational areas in adjoining parks and to the nearby black Fillmore District, and the local reputation for social tolerance. The counter-culture acted like an ethnic minority in reacting to low rents and sparking a sense of invasion among local residents, but it also laid the basis for future gentrification. The bohemian influx of the 1960s gave way to the middle-class transition of the 1970s, which in turn resulted in the bourgeois consolidation of the 1980s.

The morphological evidence in urban spatial structure—found in the physical forms of businesses, residences, social services, and other gathering spots—suggests that nonconformist communities are also minorities, clustering in special-identity neighborhoods. But they tend to be both more fluid, because of their household structure, and more prone to urban revitalization; as the avant-garde district becomes fashionable, the original bohemians move on. Based essentially upon voluntary association, not long-standing family traditions, the nonconformist community is more mobile in both social and spatial terms. This is reflected in the evolution of the urban landscape: oppositional areas provide evidence of more rapid subcultural intensification and succession.

EVOLUTIONARY COMMUNITY MORPHOGENESIS: SUBCULTURAL IDENTITY AND SPATIAL STRUCTURE

Factors specific to particular groups must be considered to explain the evolution of local areas, but basic subcultural patterns do provide insight into characteristic forms of community location and neighborhood change. Nonconformists are relatively fluid and mobile in their processes of community formation; the smaller and more flexible household arrangements in oppositional areas speed up cultural succession, which is related as much to alternative life-styles as to social class in a strict sense. The very basis of nonconformity, in fact, lies in a conscious group rejection of selected cultural trappings of the American middle class. Ethnic groups, on the other hand, tend to be structured more by familism and social class; functional socioeconomic and structural characteristics of society condition group movements to a greater degree. Patterns of ethnic migration, for example, can often be tied to an initial labor influx, sometimes to political turmoil abroad. While nonconformist communities represent a rejection of certain elements of mainstream culture, the ethnic community is dedicated more to self-preservation. As a community activist in the Mission District put it: "Hispanics are not a counter-culture; we are trying to preserve our culture, not change it."[17]

The spatial configuration of subcultures reflects characteristic patterns of group cohesion and mobility. The similarities between ethnic and nonconformist communities, related to their status as minority subcultures, help to explain their tendencies to cluster in special-identity neighborhoods, often located in close proximity in the central city; the characteristic differences in their rationales for community morphogenesis help to explain the divergences in the periodicity and consequences of their movements. These variables cannot be easily quantified, but still can be interpreted as the basis for certain patterns of community location. Culture is not merely a mental phenomenon, aloof from structural relationships, but is very much bound up in social and spatial structures. Group identities are not primordial, arising mysteriously out of nowhere; they are actively created in particular geographic locales, at particular historic junctures. San Francisco provides vivid morphological evidence of how the evolution of minority subcultures is related both to broad currents of cultural detachment in the United States and to neighborhood change in specific parts of the metropolis.

---

[17]Interview with Dorinda Moreno, March 22, 1984.

Summary and Conclusions

These case studies of ethnic and nonconformist community morphogenesis also say something about the anatomy of culture. At least in complex urban centers, culture is not a totally unified, unitary phenomenon; rather, it is composed of a series of subcultures, specialized social worlds that to different degrees complement and overlap one another, but still display important divergences in their respective social and spatial positions. To the extent that minority groups differ in their culture from that of the dominant society, the morphogenesis of distinctive neighborhoods in the inner city tends to reflect these subcultural identities.

Although economic forces certainly help to explain the broad spatial patterns of social groups in the city, such forces do not determine the precise forms of community in any simplistic sense. These case studies of ethnic and nonconformist communities indicate that sociocultural variables should be accorded some autonomy in urban analyses: studies of urban ground rent and capital movement should not ignore the importance and variability of the human agents involved in these economic processes. Ways of life in the city cannot be reproduced without a functional basis in urban spatial structure and the social relations of production, but urban subcultures do not form in any mechanistic sense as simple by-products of society's material base.

Subcultural identification constitutes an important, if not wholly determinant, force in the evolution of urban social space. Ethnic quarters tend to be more structured by preexisting social class and familism, making for a higher degree of group stability and subcultural continuity in the city; residential proximity in working-class neighborhoods contributes to the persistence of distinctive ethnic ways of life. Typically ethnic neighborhoods pass through historical phases of a migrant penetration, minority invasion, and ethnic consolidation. Nonconformist communities, on the other hand, entail a greater sense of subcultural voluntarism, a conscious group rejection of selected elements of nativist culture, which implies more social and spatial mobility. The nontraditional group succession, then, exhibits a historical sequence involving a bohemian influx, middle-class transition, and bourgeois consolidation. Ethnic communities also evolve in the city, but typically do so more gradually than nonconformist groups, generally on the basis of upward social mobility and outward spatial movement, leaving the working-class ethnic area behind with assimilation into mainstream society.

The dialectic of subcultural identification and spatial structuring should not be overlooked in studies of residential differentiation in the American city. These case studies of San Francisco communities have revealed the city to be composed of interwoven social and physical fabrics: the elements are intertwined in a complex urban pattern. Neighborhood succession is affected by such economic considerations as land rent and capital movement, to be sure, but it also results from the social-geographic patterns of different minority groups. The alternate sequences of change in ethnic and nonconformist communities, as proposed here, show how the forces of class and culture interact in the geographic evolution of inner-city neighborhoods.

References

A. Principal Interviews and Oral Histories

Edward Boyle, long-time owner of a clothing store on Haight Street. Feb. 20, 1980, and August 6, 1986.

Carlos Córdova, instructor of a course on Central Americans in the United States at San Francisco State University. May 24, 1984.

John Keating, retired San Francisco policeman and lifetime resident of the Mission District and Noe Valley. Feb. 24, 1984.

Max Kirkeberg, Professor of Geography at San Francisco State University, Aug. 25, 1983 and July 22, 1986.

Dorinda Moreno, long-time Mission District resident and community activist. March 22, 1984.

Richard Ross, on the staff of a local community center, "409 House," since the 1960s. Feb. 27, 1980.

Ken Thorland, Senior Supervisor of the Refugee Resettlement Program, San Francisco. Oct. 27, 1983.

Charles Wollenberg, Professor of History in the Peralta College District. March 29, 1984.

B. Documentaries

"From the Mission to Marin: The Irish in San Francisco." KPFA radio documentary by Padraigin McGillicuddy, 1983.

"Gay power, gay politics." CBS News special report, 1980.

"The hippie temptation." CBS News report by Harry Reasoner, 1967.

"Marching to a different drummer." CBS News, "60 Minutes" segment by Morley Safer, 1983.

"Mission Street: Four blocks of trouble." KQED public television special report, 1980.

"Saigon U.S.A." KQED public television special report, 1983.

"Thirty minutes on '60 Minutes'." KQED public television special report by Spencer Michels, 1983.

C. Newspaper Articles

Adams, Gerald. "Chinese spice the Italian flavor of North Beach." *San Francisco Examiner,* March 26, 1982, p. 1.

-----. "Dispelling the myths about Chinatown." *San Francisco Sunday Examiner and Chronicle,* Aug. 10, 1980, p. A-9.

-----. "S.F. blamed for Bay Area housing crisis." *San Francisco Examiner,* Nov. 2, 1981.

Alfred, Randy. "On live." *The Sentinel,* San Francisco, March 21, 1980, p. 6.

Beitiks, Edvins. "Uneasy transition for Tenderloin's refugee children." *San Francisco Examiner,* April 10, 1983, pp. B-1, B-4.

Blum, Walter. "Filipinos: A question of identity." *San Francisco Sunday Examiner and Chronicle,* "California Living" Section, March 21, 1982, p. 8.

Braaten, David. "S.F.'s Mission: A place of many voices." *San Francisco Chronicle,* May 1, 1962, pp. 1, 7.

-----. "Signs of a renaissance in the Mission: New buildings rise above dowdy streets." *San Francisco Chronicle,* May 4, 1962, p. 12.

Bronstein, Phil. "Muggings: Gay-Latino confrontations or no?" *San Francisco Examiner,* Nov. 11, 1980, p. B-1.

Butler, Katy, and Gwendolyn Evans. "Gay migration into black neighborhoods." *San Francisco Chronicle,* Sept. 1, 1979, pp. 1, 5.

Caen, Herb. "Everybody's favorite city." *San Francisco Chronicle,* "Sunday Punch" section, June 6, 1982, p. 1.

-----. "Sunday punchdrink." *San Francisco Chronicle,* "Sunday Punch" section, May 1, 1983, p. 1.

Chase, Marilyn. "The Haight-Ashbury turns into a bastion of the middle class." *Wall Street Journal,* July 24, 1978, p. 1.

Clark, Marilyn. "The tragedy of the Fillmore." *San Francisco Bay Guardian,* June 10, 1981, pp. 7-13.

Deniger, Tim. "A tree grows in Haight-Ashbury." *Haight-Ashbury Newspaper,* May 1982, p. 6.

"El Barrio de la Misión: La Puerta de Oro." *La Verdad Hispana,* Dec. 10, 1980, pp. 6-7.

Fosburgh, Lacey. "San Francisco: Unconventional city for the Democratic convention." *New York Times Magazine,* July 1, 1984, pp. 12-38.

Fregoso, Geraldine. "Growing up in the Mission." *San Francisco Sunday Examiner and Chronicle,* "California Living" section, April 21, 1974.

Gaar, Greg. "Baseball in the early Haight." *Haight-Ashbury Newspaper,* November 1981, p. 1.

-----. "Cows in Cole Valley." *Haight-Ashbury Newspaper,* July 1983, p. 4.

-----. "Shoot the Chutes." *Haight-Ashbury Newspaper,* April 1982, p. 4.

"Gentrification in the Mission." A series of articles in *El Tecolote,* July, August, and November 1978.

Glover, Malcolm. "Burgeoning population in S.F., California bucks U.S. trend." *San Francisco Examiner,* April 1, 1983, p. B-6.

"Haight revival." *San Francisco Examiner,* April 28, 1970, p. 36.

Hardy, Charles C. "Faces changing in San Francisco's schools." *San Francisco Examiner,* May 5, 1980, pp. 1, 9.

Harris, Michael. "S.F. is 'singles city'." *San Francisco Chronicle,* Sept. 10, 1982, pp. 1, 5.

"Hippie plea—make it love, not Haight." *San Francisco Examiner,* Feb. 23, 1967, p. 7.

"In the Haight-Ashbury: Violence stalks a street called Terror Terrace." *San Francisco Examiner,* Dec. 15, 1969, p. 4.

Irving, Carl. "The lone precinct that voted to oust Feinstein." *San Francisco Examiner,* May 18, 1983, p. A-2.

Kershner, Vlae. "S.F. Palestinians—the city's grocers." *San Francisco Sunday Examiner and Chronicle,* "Sunday Punch" section, April 8, 1984, pp. 5-6.

Kossen, Sydney. "Dramatic rise forecast in S.F. welfare costs." *San Francisco Examiner,* June 25, 1981, p. A-11.

Lindsey, Robert. "California voters calling halt to uncontrolled city growth." *New York Times,* Nov. 15, 1986, pp. 1, 7.

Ludlow, Lynn, and Mireya Navarro. "Winds of change sweep a polyglot neighborhood." *San Francisco Examiner,* Oct. 19, 1981, p. A-6.

Navarro, Mireya. "Showdown between Latino gangs ends in peace pact." *San Francisco Sunday Examiner and Chronicle,* July 10, 1983, pp. B-1.

"Newcomers boost S.F. population." *San Francisco Examiner,* April 22, 1982, p. B-1.

Nhu, Tran Tuong. "Resettling the Vietnamese." *San Francisco Sunday Examiner and Chronicle,* "California Living" section, Sept. 27, 1981, pp. 4-13.

"Phelan fears his specter: Seeks to offset plague scare with a telegram," *San Francisco Chronicle,* March 27, 1900, p. 1.

"Put a blockade on the Chinese Quarter." *San Francisco Chronicle,* March 7, 1900, p. 1.

"Real estate speculation: What's it doing to the Haight." *Haight-Ashbury Newspaper,* March 1978, pp. 4-5.

Reza, H. G. "Latinos vs. Filipinos: Ethnic feuds at Wilson High." *San Francisco Chronicle,* Jan. 30, 1980, p. 1.

Royko, Mike. "Why S.F. shouldn't get the Demo convention." *San Francisco Examiner,* April 19, 1983, pp. 1, 4.

Saltus, Richard. "Haight clinic still fighting the '60s wars." *San Francisco Examiner,* Oct. 10, 1982, pp. B-1, B-3.

Schreiner, Tim. "The Bay Area exception." *San Francisco Chronicle,* "This World" section, Dec. 14, 1986, p. 15.

"S.F. now ranks 4th in density of population." *San Francisco Examiner,* Nov. 1, 1982, p. A-6.

Shinoff, Paul. "City's gay population peaks in '70s, levels off, surveys reveal." *San Francisco Examiner,* April 29, 1982, p. A-6.

Snider, Burr. "CALVIN: *Nothing* comes between him and his City." *San Francisco Examiner,* Jan. 25, 1987, pp. E-1, E-3, E-4.

Stanley, Peter W. "Exiled in California." *San Francisco Sunday Examiner and Chronicle,* "This World" section, July 19, 1981, pp. 16-19.

Van Winkle, W. A. "The state of the Haight, 1979." *San Francisco Bay Guardian,* May 3, 1979, pp. 13-22.

Waugh, Dexter. "Salvaging the Haight." *San Francisco Examiner,* Jan. 9, 1972.

-----. "Southeast Asians blending in all over the Bay Area." *San Francisco Examiner,* March 30, 1981, pp. B-1, B-10.

Wong, Ken. "Rainbow mural glows again after whitewash backlash." *San Francisco Examiner,* Nov. 16, 1983, pp. A-3.

D. *Directories, Documents, and Reports*

Bob Damron's Address Book. San Francisco listings of gay and lesbian businesses, various years. San Francisco, California.

California Dept. of Savings and Loan Assns. "Public hearing: In the matter of the proposed neighborhood savings and loan association for the approval of the articles of the incorporation." Transcript of tape recording of Exhibit C, San Francisco, Nov. 24, 1976.

Coro Foundation. *The District Handbook: A Coro Foundation Guide to San Francisco's Supervisorial Districts.* 1979

Giles, Sister M. Bernadette. "Topography and history of the Haight-Ashbury District." An extract from *A Changing Parish—A Study of Mobility in St. Agnes Parish, San Francisco, California.* July 1959.

Hubbard, Anita Day. "Cities within the city." *San Francisco Bulletin* (August-September 1924). Transcribed version available at the San Francisco History Room of the Public Library, vol. 2, pp. 105-161.

Joint Mission Coalition Organization/Stanford University Community Development Study. "Summary of trends in housing and population in the Mission Model Neighborhood, 1940-1970." 1972. 51 p.

Liu, John K. C. "San Francisco Chinatown residential hotels." San Francisco: Chinatown Neighborhood Improvement Resource Center, 1980.

Lopez, Carlos U. "Chilenos in California: A study of the 1850, 1852, and 1860 Censuses." San Francisco: R and E Research Associates, 1973.

Mitchell, James. *The Dynamics of Neighborhood Change.* Washington, D.C.: U.S. Dept. of Housing and Urban Development, 1975.

Necesito, Rodolfo. *The Filipino Guide to San Francisco.* San Francisco: Technomedia, 1978.

Polk's San Francisco Directory. Commercial and residential listings from a variety of years.

San Francisco, City and County. *Report of the Citizen's Housing Task Force.* July 29, 1981. 243 p.

San Francisco Dept. of City Planning. *The Downtown Plan.* August 1983. 145 p.

-----. "Haight Street shopping area: A background study." November 1972.

-----. "Housing in the Haight-Ashbury." August 1972. 64 p.

San Francisco Human Rights Commission. "San Francisco ethnic neighborhood problem packet." June 1974.

San Francisco Planning and Urban Research Association (SPUR). "Haight-Ashbury protective rezoning." April 1972. 3 p.

-----. "Thinking about growth," report no. 180. Dec 1981. 7 p.

U.S. Census Bureau. *Social Statistics of Cities,* part 2. Washington, D.C.: Government Printing Office, 1887.

-----. Demographic statistics between 1860 and 1980, drawn from different volumes on population.

U.S. Works Projects Administration (WPA). *1939 Real Property Survey,* San Francisco, 1940. 2 volumes.

Waldhorn, Judith. "Historic preservation in San Francisco's Inner Mission." U.S. Dept. of Housing and Urban Development. Washington, D.C.: U.S. Government Printing Office, 1973. 43 p.

Walsh, James P. *Ethnic Militancy: An Irish Catholic Prototype.* San Francisco: R and E Research Associates, 1972.

E. Articles from Journals and Anthologies

Albright, Thomas. "The elevated underground: The North Beach period." In Robert E. Johnson (ed.), *Rolling Renaissance: San Francisco's Underground Art in Celebration, 1945-1968,* San Francisco, The Center for Religion and the Arts, 1976.

Averbach, Alvin. "San Francisco's South of Market District, 1858-1958: The emergence of a Skid Row." *California Historical Quarterly* 52 (Fall 1973): 196-223

Berry, Brian J. L. "Islands of renewal in seas of decay." In Paul E. Peterson (ed.), *The New Urban Reality,* pp. 76-79. Washington, D.C.: Brookings Institution, 1985.

Berube, Allan. "Coming out under fire." *Mother Jones,* February-March 1983, pp. 23-45.

Buechler, Hans C. "Comments." In Brian M. Du Toit and Helen I. Safa (eds.), *Migration and Urbanization: Models and Adaptive Strategies,* pp. 285-288. The Hague: Mouton, 1975.

Burgess, Ernest W. "The growth of the city: An introduction to a research project." In Robert E. Park, Ernest W. Burgess, and Roderick D. McKenzie (eds.), *The City,* pp. 54-56. University of Chicago Press, 1925; reprinted in 1967.

Canter, Donald. "San Francisco's Western Addition: How Negro removal became black renewal." *City* 4 (October-November 1970): 55-59.

Castells, Manuel, and Karen Murphy. "Cultural identity and urban structure: The spatial organization of San Francisco's gay community." *Urban Affairs Review* 22 (1982): 237-259.

Clay, Phillip L. "The process of black suburbanization." *Urban Affairs Quarterly* 14 (June 1979): 405-424.

Cohen, R. B. "The new international division of labor, multinational corporations and urban hierarchy." In Michael Dear and Allen J. Scott (eds.), *Urbanization and Urban Planning in Capitalist Society,* pp. 287-318. New York: Methuen, 1981.

Conway, Dennis, and Ualthan Bigby. "Residential differentiation among an overlooked black minority: 'New immigrant' West Indians in New York." *Proceedings of the Conference of Latin Americanist Geographers* 9 (1983): 99-109.

Cybriwsky, Roman. "Social aspects of neighborhood change." *Annals of the Association of American Geographers* 9 (1983): 99-109.

Deskins, Donald R., Jr. "Morphogenesis of a Black Ghetto." *Urban Geography* 2 (April-June 1981): 95-114.

De Vise, Pierre. "The expanding singles housing market in Chicago: Implications for reviving city neighborhoods." *Urbanism Past and Present* 9 (Winter 1979—Spring 1980): 30-39.

Firey, Walter. "Symbolism, space, and the upper class." In Michael E. Elliot Hurst (ed.), *I Came to the City: Essays and Comments on the Urban Scene,* pp. 147-150. Boston: Houghton Mifflin, 1975.

Fischer, Claude S. "Toward a subcultural theory of urbanism." *American Journal of Sociology* 80, 6 (1975): 1319-1341.

FitzGerald, Frances. "A reporter at large." *New Yorker,* July 28, 1986, pp. 44-63.

Gale, Dennis E. "Neighborhood resettlement: Washington, D.C." In Shirley Bradway Laska and Daphne Spain (eds.), *Back to the City: Issues in Neighborhood Renovation,* pp. 95-115. Pergamon Press, 1980.

Gleason, Philip. "Confusion compounded: The melting pot in the 1960s and 1970s." *Ethnicity* 6 (1979): 10-20.

Godfrey, Brian J. "Ethnic identities and ethnic enclaves: The morphogenesis of San Francisco's Hispanic *barrio*." *Yearbook of the Conference of Latin Americanist Geographers* 11 (1985): 45-53.

-----. "Inner-city revitalization and cultural succession: The evolution of San Francisco's Haight-Ashbury District." *Yearbook of the Association of Pacific Coast Geographers* 46 (1984): 79-91.

Hall, Peter. "The urban culture and the suburban culture." In Michael E. Elliot Hurst (ed.), *I Came to the City*, pp. 162-177. Boston: Houghton Mifflin, 1975.

Izaki, Yoshiharu. "The residential correspondence between Japanese and other ethnic groups in San Francisco." *Geographical Review of Japan* 54, 3 (1981): 115-126.

Levine, Martin P. "Gay ghetto." In *Gay Men: The Sociology of Male Homosexuality*, pp. 182-205. New York: Harper and Row, 1979.

Loyd, Bonnie, and Lester Rowntree. "Radical feminists and gay men in San Francisco: Social space in dispersed communities." In David A. Lanegran and Risa Palm (eds.), *An Invitation to Geography*, pp. 78-88. New York: McGraw-Hill, 1977.

Midgett, Douglas K. "West Indian ethnicity in Great Britain." In Brian M. Du Toit and Helen I. Safa (eds.), *Migration and Urbanization*, pp. 57-82. The Hague: Mouton, 1975.

Moore, Harry T. "Enter Beatniks: The Bohème of 1960." Addenda to the reprinted 1933 edition of Albert Parry's *Garrets and Pretenders: A History of Bohemianism in America*, pp. 376-395. New York: Dover, 1960.

Murray, Stephen O. "The institutional elaboration of a quasi-ethnic community." *International Review of Modern Sociology* 9 (July-December 1979): 165-177.

Novak, Michael. "The new ethnicity." In David R. Colburn and George E. Pozetta (eds.), *America and the New Ethnicity*, pp. 15-28. Port Washington, N.Y.: Kennikat Press, 1979.

Palm, Risa. "Factorial ecology and the community of outlook." *Annals of the Association of American Geographers* 63 (September 1973): 341-346.

-----. "Reconsidering contemporary neighborhoods." *Landscape* 26, 2 (1982): 17-20.

Redfield, Robert, and Milton B. Singer. "The cultural role of cities." *Economic Development and Cultural Change* 3 (October 1954): 53-73.

Smith, Neil. "Toward a theory of gentrification: A back-to-the-city movement by capital, not people." *American Planning Association Journal,* October 1979.

Sopher, David. "Place and location: Notes on the spatial patterning of culture." In Louis Schneider and Charles M. Bonjean (eds.), *The Idea of Culture in the Social Sciences,* pp. 101-107. Cambridge University Press, 1973.

Vance, James E., Jr. "The American city: Workshop for a national culture." In John S. Adams (ed.), *Contemporary Metropolitan America,* vol. 1, pp. 1-49. Cambridge, Mass.: Ballinger, 1976.

-----. "Man and super-city: The origins and nature of the intricate social geography of the Bay Area." In Michael E. Eliot Hurst (ed.), *I Came to the City: Essays and Comments on the Urban Scene,* pp. 17-38. Boston: Houghton Mifflin, 1975.

Vance, Jean. "The cities by San Francisco Bay." In John S. Adams (ed.), *Contemporary Metropolitan America,* pp. 218-307. Cambridge, Mass.: Ballinger, 1976.

Viviano, Frank. "The new immigrants." *Mother Jones,* January 1983, pp. 26-46.

----- and Alton Chinn. "The Hong Kong connection." *San Francisco Magazine,* February 1982, pp. 54-64.

Ward, David. "The ethnic ghetto in the United States: past and present." *Transactions of the Institute of British Geographers* 7 (1982): 258-275.

Winters, Christopher. "The social identity of evolving neighborhoods." *Landscape* 23, 1 (1979): 8-14.

Wirth, Louis. "Urbanism as a way of life." In Richard Sennett (ed.), *Classic Essays on the Culture of Cities,* pp. 143-164. Englewood Cliffs, N.J.: Prentice-Hall, 1969.

Yu, Connie Young. "A history of San Francisco Chinatown housing." *Amerasia Journal* 8 (Spring-Summer 1981): 93-110.

F. Academic Theses and Dissertations

Bowden, Martyn J. *The Dynamics of City Growth: An Historical Geography of the San Francisco Central District, 1850-1931.* Ph.D. dissertation, Dept. of Geography, University of California, Berkeley, 1967.

González, Hernan Daniel. *La Trayectoria: A Method.* Master's thesis, interdisciplinary, San Francisco State University, 1976.

Lawrence, John A. *Behind the Palaces: The Working Class and the Labor Movement in San Francisco, 1877-1901.* Ph.D. dissertation, Dept. of History, University of California, Berkeley, 1979.

Leyland, R. C. *Puerto Ricans in the San Francisco Bay Area, California: An Historical and Cultural Geography.* Master's thesis, Dept. of Geography, California State University, Hayward, 1980.

Tripp, Michael W. *Russian Routes: Origins and Development of an Ethnic Community in San Francisco.* Master's thesis, Dept. of Geography, San Francisco State University, 1980.

G. Books and Monographs

Altman, Dennis. *The Homosexualization of America, the Americanization of the Homosexual.* New York: St. Martin's Press, 1982.

Anthony, Gene. *The Summer of Love: Haight-Ashbury at its Highest.* Millbrae, Calif.: Celestial Arts, 1980.

Asbury, Herbert. *The Barbary Coast: An Informal History of the San Francisco Underworld.* Garden City: Doubleday, 1933.

Austin, Leonard. *Around the World in San Francisco.* San Francisco: Fearon, 1959.

Becker, Howard S. and Irving Louis Horowitz. *Culture and Civility in San Francisco.* Transaction Books, 1971.

Berry, Brian J. L. *The Human Consequences of Urbanization: Divergent Paths in the Twentieth Century.* New York: St. Martin's Press, 1973.

Burchell, R. A. *The San Francisco Irish, 1848-1880.* Manchester University Press, 1979.

Castells, Manuel. *The City and the Grassroots: A Cross-Cultural Theory of Urban Social Movements.* Berkeley: University of California Press, 1983.

Cavan, Sherri. *Hippies of the Haight.* St. Louis, Mo.: New Critics Press, 1972.

Cherny, Robert W., and William Issel. *San Francisco: Presidio, Port and Metropolis.* San Francisco: Boyd and Fraser, 1981.

Chow, Willard T. *The Re-emergence of and Inner City: The Pivot of Chinese Settlement in the East Bay Region of the San Francisco Bay Area.* San Francisco: R and E Associates, 1977.

Cinel, Dino. *From Italy to San Francisco: The Immigrant Experience.* Stanford University Press, 1982.

Crewdson, John. *The Tarnished Door: The New Immigrants and the Transformation of America.* New York: Times Books, 1983.

Dalton, Roque. *Las Historias Prohibidas del Pulgarcito.* Mexico City: Siglo Veintiuno Editores, 1980.

Daniels, Douglas H. *Pioneer Urbanites: A Social and Cultural History of Black San Francisco.* Philadelphia: Temple University Press, 1980.

Davis, Cary, Carl Haub, and JoAnne Willette. "U.S. Hispanics: Changing the Face of America." *Population Bulletin* 38 (June 1983): 1-44.

Decker, Peter. *Fortunes and Failures: White-Collar Mobility in Nineteenth Century San Francisco.* Cambridge, Mass.: Harvard University Press, 1978.

Decroos, Jean Francis. *The Long Journey: Social Integration and Ethnicity Maintenance among Urban Basques in the San Francisco Bay Region.* Reno, Nev.: Associated University Press, 1983.

Delehanty, Randolph. *San Francisco: Walks and Tours in the Golden Gate City.* New York: Dial Press, 1980.

D'Emilio, John. *Sexual Politics, Sexual Communities: The Making of a Homosexual Minority in the United States, 1940-1970.* University of Chicago Press, 1983.

Dobie, Charles Caldwell. *San Francisco: A Pageant.* New York: D. Appleton-Century Co., 1939.

Doss, Margot Patterson. *San Francisco at Your Feet.* New York: Grove Press, 1974.

Engelhardt, Zephyrin. *San Francisco or Mission Dolores.* Chicago: Franciscan Herald Press, 1924.

Feagin, Joe R. *Racial and Ethnic Relations.* Englewood Cliffs, N.J.: Prentice-Hall, 1978.

Ferlinghetti, Lawrence, and Nancy J. Peters. *Literary San Francisco.* San Francisco: Harper and Row, 1980.

Fischer, Claude S. *To Dwell Among Friends: Personal Networks in Town and City.* University of Chicago Press, 1982.

-----. *The Urban Experience.* New York: Harcourt Brace Jovanovich, 1976.

Fischer, Eric. *Minorities and Minority Problems.* New York: Vantage Press, 1980.

Flamm, Jerry. *Good Life in Hard Times: San Francisco's '20s and '30s.* San Francisco: Chronicle Books, 1978.

Gans, Herbert J. *The Urban Villagers: Group and Class in the Life of Italian-Americans.* New York: Free Press, 1962; reprinted in 1982.

Glazer, Nathan, and Daniel P. Moynihan. *Beyond the Melting Pot,* 2nd ed. Cambridge, Mass.: M.I.T. Press, 1970.

Gumina, Deanna Paoli. *The Italians of San Francisco, 1850-1930.* New York: Center for Migration Studies, 1978.

Handlin, Oscar. *The Uprooted: The Epic Story of the Great Migrations that Made the American People.* New York: Grosset and Dunlap, 1951.

Hannerz, Ulf. *Exploring the City: Inquiries toward an Urban Anthropology.* New York: Columbia University Press, 1980.

Hartman, Chester. *The Transformation of San Francisco.* Rowman and Allanheld, 1984.

-----. *Yerba Buena: Land Grab and Community Resistance in San Francisco.* San Francisco: Glide Publications, 1974.

Hendricks, Glenn. *The Dominican Diaspora: From the Dominican Republic to New York City—Villagers in Transition.* New York: Teachers College Press, 1974.

Herbert, David. *Urban Geography: A Social Perspective.* New York: Praeger, 1972.

Holliday, J. S. *The World Rushed In: The California Gold Rush Experience.* New York: Simon and Schuster, 1981.

Jones, Idwal. *Ark of Empire: San Francisco's Montgomery Block.* Garden City, N.Y.: Doubleday, 1951.

Keller, Suzanne. *The Urban Neighborhood: A Sociological Perspective.* New York: Random House, 1968.

Kitano, Harry H. L. *Japanese Americans: The Evolution of a Subculture.* Englewood Cliffs, N.J.: Prentice-Hall, 1969.

Kornblum, William. *Blue Collar Community.* University of Chicago Press, 1974.

La Gory, Mark, and John Pipkin. *Urban Social Space.* Belmont, Calif.: Wadsworth, 1981.

LeGates, Richard, and Chester Hartman. *Displacement.* Berkeley: California Legal Services Anti-Displacement Project, 1981.

Lewis, Oscar. *Bay Window Bohemia.* Garden City, N.Y.: Doubleday, 1956.

-----. *San Francisco: Mission to Metropolis.* Berkeley: Howell-North Books, 1966.

Lewis, Oscar. *The Children of Sanchez: Autobiography of a Mexican Family.* New York: Random House, 1961.

-----. *La Vida: A Puerto Rican Family in the Culture of Poverty—San Juan and New York*. New York: Random House, 1965.

Lockwood, Charles. *Suddenly San Francisco: The Early Years of an Instant City*. San Francisco: A California Living Book, 1978.

Lotchin, Roger W. *San Francisco, 1846-1856: From Hamlet to City*. New York: Oxford University Press, 1974.

MacGregor, William Laird. *San Francisco in 1876*. Edinburgh: Thomas Laurie, 1876.

Margolin, Malcolm. *The Ohlone Way: Indian Life in the San Francisco-Monterey Bay Area*. Berkeley: Heyday Books, 1978.

Marotta, Toby. *The Politics of Homosexuality*. Boston: Houghton Mifflin, 1981.

Meinig, D. W. (ed.) *The Interpretation of Ordinary Landscapes: Geographical Essays*. Oxford University Press, 1979.

Miller, Richard. *Bohemia: The Prototype Then and Now*. Chicago: Nelson-Hall, 1977.

Narell, Irena. *Our City: The Jews of San Francisco*. San Diego: Howell-North Books, 1981.

Nee, Victor G., and Brett de Bary Nee. *Longtime Californ': A Documentary Study of an American Chinatown*. New York: Pantheon Books, 1972.

Norris, Frank. *Blix*. New York: Doubleday, Page, and Co., 1903.

Osofsky, Gilbert. *Harlem: The Making of a Ghetto*. New York: Harper and Row, 1964.

Parry, Albert. *Garrets and Pretenders: A History of Bohemianism in America*. New York: Dover, 1960.

Perry, Charles. *The Haight-Ashbury: A History*. New York: Random House, 1984.

Perry, Helen S. *The Human Be-In*. New York: Basic Books, 1970.

Piore, Michael J. *Birds of Passage: Migrant Labor and Industrial Societies*. Cambridge University Press, 1979.

Romo, Ricardo. *East Los Angeles: The History of a Barrio*. Austin: University of Texas Press, 1983.

Shepard, Susan. *In the Neighborhoods: A Guide to the Joys and Discoveries of San Francisco's Neighborhoods*. San Francisco: Chronicle Books, 1981.

Shilts, Randy. *The Mayor of Castro Street: The Life and Times of Harvey Milk*. New York: St. Martin's Press, 1982.

Sjoberg, Gideon. *The Preindustrial City, Past and Present*. New York: Free Press, 1960.

Smith, David E., and John Luce. *Love Needs Care: A History of San Francisco's Haight-Ashbury Free Medical Clinic and Its Pioneer Role in Treating Drug-Abuse Problems*. Boston: Little, Brown, 1971.

Starr, Kevin. *Americans and the California Dream, 1850-1915*. Oxford University Press, 1973.

Suttles, Gerald D. *The Social Construction of Communities*. University of Chicago Press, 1968.

-----. *The Social Order of the Slum: Ethnicity and Territory in the Inner City*. University of Chicago Press, 1968.

Valentine Charles A. *Culture and Poverty*. University of Chicago Press, 1968.

Vance, James E., Jr. *Geography and Urban Evolution in the San Francisco Bay Area*. Berkeley: University of California, Institute of Governmental Studies, 1964.

-----. *Location in a System of Global Extent: A Social Model of Settlement*. Geographical Papers, University of Reading, England, 1982.

-----. *The Merchant's World: The Geography of Wholesaling*. Englewood Cliffs, N.J.: Prentice-Hall, 1970.

-----. *This Scene of Man: The Role and Structure of the City in the Geography of Western Civilization*. New York: Harper and Row, 1977.

Ward, David. *Immigrants and Cities*. New York: Oxford University Press, 1971.

Watkins, T. H., and R. R. Olmstead. *Mirror of the Dream: An Illustrated History of San Francisco*. San Francisco: Scrimshaw Press, 1976.

West, Robert C., and John P. Augelli. *Middle America*. Englewood Cliffs, N.J.: Prentice-Hall, 1966.

Wilde, Oscar. *The Picture of Dorian Gray*. Baltimore: Penguin Books, 1982 (first edition 1891).

Wirt, Frederick M. *Power in the City: Decision-Making in San Francisco*. Berkeley: University of California Press, 1974.

Writer's Program of the Works Projects Administration (WPA) in Northern California. *San Francisco: The Bay and Its Cities*. New York: Hastings House, 1940.

References

Wuthnow, Robert. *The Consciousness Reformation.* Berkeley: University of California Press, 1976.

Zorbaugh, Harvey W. *The Gold Coast and the Slum: A Sociological Study of Chicago's Near North Side.* University of Chicago Press, 1929.

Mai 52